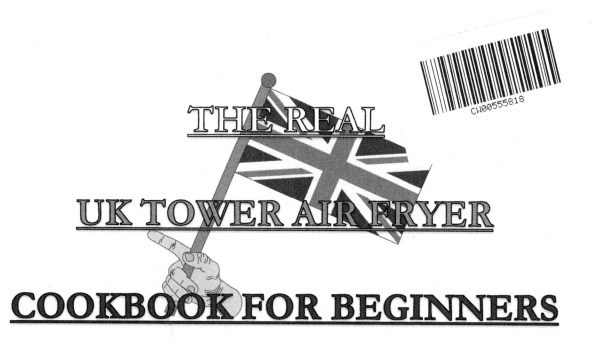

THE REAL

UK TOWER AIR FRYER

COOKBOOK FOR BEGINNERS

1000 Days of Affordable & Easy Recipes

with Measurements & Ingredients for Families & Busy People Living

in the UK

Cathryn J. Goodrich

TABLE OF CONTENT

INTRODUCTION   8

HOW DOES AN AIR FRYER WORK?   8

THE COOKING PROCESS   8

A BEGINNER'S GUIDE   8

AHEAD OF FIRST USE   8
AIR FRYER TRIAL RUN   9
TIPS FOR THE AIR FRYER BASKET   9
HOW TO USE YOUR TOWER AIR FRYER   9

HEALTH BENEFITS OF AIR FRYERS   10

1. LOWER FAT AND CALORIE INTAKE   10
2. IT ENABLES YOU TO KEEP MORE NUTRIENTS IN YOUR FOOD. 10
3. THE USE OF AN AIR FRYER DOESN'T CONFLICT WITH YOUR DIET PLANS.   10
4. SAFER COOKING   10
5. LESS ENERGY CONSUMPTION   10

WHAT CAN YOU COOK IN AN AIR FRYER?   10

HOW TO CLEAN YOUR AIR FRYER   11

CLEANING TIPS FOR YOUR AIR FRYER   11
HOW FREQUENTLY SHOULD YOU CLEAN YOUR AIR FRYER?   11
HOW TO DEEP CLEAN AN AIR FRYER   11

AIR FRYER TIPS AND TRICKS   12

BREAKFAST AND BREAD RECIPE   15

1. CREAMY HASH BROWNS   15
2. OATMEAL CASSEROLE   15
3. BROWN LOAF WITH SEEDS   15
4. HOMEMADE SODA BREAD IN THE AIR FRYER (BREAD SODA) 16
5. GARLIC BREAD IN THE AIR FRYER   16
6. PROSCIUTTO SANDWICH   16
7. CHEESE SANDWICH   17

8. SHRIMP SANDWICHES   17
9. EGGS CASSEROLE   17
10. AIR FRYER-BANANA BREAD   18
11. AIR FRYER GRILLED CHEESE   18
12. QUICK VEGAN AIR FRYER GARLIC BREAD   18
13. RUSTIC BREAKFAST   19
14. TASTY BAKED EGGS   19
15. BREAKFAST EGG BOWLS   19
16. DELICIOUS BREAKFAST SOUFFLÉ   20
17. EGG MUFFINS   20
18. TASTY CINNAMON TOAST   20
19. ASPARAGUS FRITTATA   20
20. HAM BREAKFAST PIE   21
21. SCRAMBLED EGGS   21
22. QUICK EGGS AND TOMATOES   21
23. SMOKED AIR FRIED TOFU BREAKFAST   22
24. DELICIOUS TOFU AND MUSHROOMS   22
25. CHEESY BREAKFAST BREAD   22
26. EGG WHITE OMELET   22
27. ARTICHOKE FRITTATA   23
28. ONION FRITTATA   23
29. LONG BEANS OMELET   23
30. FRENCH BEANS AND EGG BREAKFAST MIX   24
31. CREAMY BREAKFAST TOFU   24
32. GARLIC POTATOES WITH BACON   24
33. HAM ROLLS   24
34. BREAKFAST PEA TORTILLA   25
35. ESPRESSO OATMEAL   25
36. RICE, ALMONDS AND RAISINS PUDDING   25
37. DATES AND MILLET PUDDING   26
38. CHERRIES RISOTTO   26
39. CINNAMON AND CREAM CHEESE OATS   26
40. RED PEPPER FRITTATA   27
41. CREAMY EGGS   27
42. BROCCOLI QUICHE   27
43. MUSHROOM QUICHE   28
44. BLACKBERRY FRENCH TOAST   28
45. TURKEY BURRITO   28
46. POLENTA BITES   29

SNACKS AND APPETIZER RECIPE   30

47. ROASTED BELL PEPPER ROLLS   30
48. AIR FRIED DILL PICKLES   30
49. SALMON PARTY PATTIES   30
50. EGG WHITE CHIPS   31
51. TUNA CAKES   31
52. SAUSAGE BALLS   31
53. CAULIFLOWER BARS   31
54. SHRIMP MUFFINS   32
55. CAJUN SHRIMP APPETIZER   32

56.	CHICKEN DIP	32
57.	CHICKEN ROLLS	33
58.	BUFFALO CAULIFLOWER SNACK	33
59.	FISH NUGGETS	33
60.	STUFFED PEPPERS	34
61.	BANANA SNACK	34
62.	COCONUT CHICKEN BITES	34
63.	SHRIMP AND CHESTNUT ROLLS	35
64.	POTATO SPREAD	35
65.	SALMON MEATBALLS	35
66.	HERBED TOMATOES APPETIZER	36
67.	ZUCCHINI CAKES	36
68.	PUMPKIN MUFFINS	36
69.	CHICKEN BREAST ROLLS	37
70.	ZUCCHINI CHIPS	37
71.	HONEY PARTY WINGS	37
72.	BEEF ROLLS	37
73.	JALAPENO BALLS	38
74.	BANANA CHIPS	38
75.	BREAD STICKS	38
76.	CRISPY RADISH CHIPS	39
77.	SPRING ROLLS	39
78.	BROCCOLI PATTIES	39
79.	EMPANADAS	40
80.	CRAB STICKS	40
81.	CHICKPEAS SNACK	40
82.	SPINACH BALLS	40
83.	CRISPY SHRIMP	41
84.	NACHO COATED PRAWNS	41
85.	ROTI PRATA MINI SAUSAGE ROLLS	41
86.	PUFF PASTRY BANANA ROLLS	42

VEGETABLE RECIPE   **43**

87.	STUFFED POBLANO PEPPERS	43
88.	SESAME MUSTARD GREENS	43
89.	HERBED EGGPLANT AND ZUCCHINI MIX	43
90.	DELICIOUS PORTOBELLO MUSHROOMS	44
91.	CRISPY POTATOES AND PARSLEY	44
92.	BEET, TOMATO, AND GOAT CHEESE MIX	44
93.	SWEET BABY CARROTS DISH	44
94.	RADISH HASH	45
95.	EGGPLANT HASH	45
96.	SPINACH PIE	45
97.	ARTICHOKES AND SPECIAL SAUCE	46
98.	BROCCOLI HASH	46
99.	TOMATO AND BASIL TART	46
100.	FLAVORED AIR FRIED TOMATOES	47
101.	FLAVORED GREEN BEANS	47
102.	SIMPLE STUFFED TOMATOES	47
103.	AIR FRIED ASPARAGUS	48
104.	OKRA AND CORN SALAD	48

105.	BEETS AND BLUE CHEESE SALAD	48
106.	BEET SALAD AND PARSLEY DRESSING	49
107.	BROCCOLI SALAD	49
108.	GREEN BEANS AND PARMESAN	49
109.	SPICY CABBAGE	49
110.	GARLIC TOMATOES	50
111.	SWISS CHARD SALAD	50
112.	BROCCOLI AND TOMATOES AIR FRIED STEW	50
113.	GREEN BEANS AND TOMATOES	51
114.	CHEESY BRUSSELS SPROUTS	51
115.	SPANISH GREENS	51
116.	ITALIAN EGGPLANT STEW	52
117.	BRUSSELS SPROUTS AND BUTTER SAUCE	52
118.	COLLARD GREENS AND TURKEY WINGS	52
119.	AIR FRIED LEEKS	53
120.	INDIAN TURNIPS SALAD	53
121.	INDIAN POTATOES	53
122.	RUTABAGA AND CHERRY TOMATOES MIX	54
123.	ZUCCHINI NOODLES DELIGHT	54
124.	SIMPLE TOMATOES AND BELL PEPPER SAUCE	54
125.	STUFFED BABY PEPPERS	55
126.	BALSAMIC ARTICHOKES	55

FISH AND SEAFOOD RECIPE   **56**

127.	COD FILLETS WITH FENNEL AND GRAPES SALAD	56
128.	AIR-FRYER FISH CAKES	56
129.	AIR-FRIED SALMON WITH HORSERADISH RUB	56
130.	AIR-FRYER SCALLOPS WITH LEMON-HERB SAUCE	57
131.	BUTTERED SHRIMP SKEWERS	57
132.	CAJUN AIR FRYER SALMON	57
133.	AIR FRYER LEMON PEPPER SHRIMP	58
134.	AIR FRYER LOBSTER TAILS WITH LEMON-GARLIC BUTTER	58
135.	AIR FRYER CRAB RANGOON	59
136.	PANKO-CRUSTED AIR FRYER MAHI MAHI	59
137.	AIR-FRIED SHRIMP FAJITAS	60
138.	AIR FRIED SEASONED CRUNCHY COD FILLETS	60
139.	AIR FRYER MAHI MAHI WITH BROWN BUTTER	60
140.	AIR FRYER CATFISH	61
141.	ASIAN SALMON	61
142.	LEMONY SABA FISH	61
143.	COD AND VINAIGRETTE	62
144.	TROUT FILLET AND ORANGE SAUCE	62
145.	THYME AND PARSLEY SALMON	62
146.	CREAMY SALMON	63
147.	SALMON AND ORANGE MARMALADE	63
148.	SALMON AND AVOCADO SALSA	63
149.	TUNA AND CHIMICHURRI SAUCE	64
150.	STUFFED SALMON	64
151.	SWORDFISH AND MANGO SALSA	64
152.	FISH AND COUSCOUS	65

153.	STUFFED CALAMARI	65
154.	SNAPPER FILLETS AND VEGGIES	66
155.	ROASTED COD AND PROSCIUTTO	66
156.	HALIBUT AND SUN-DRIED TOMATOES MIX	66
157.	ORIENTAL FISH	67
158.	BLACK COD AND PLUM SAUCE	67
159.	COD WITH PEARL ONIONS	67
160.	SALMON AND GREEK YOGURT SAUCE	68
161.	TILAPIA AND CHIVES SAUCE	68
162.	DELICIOUS RED SNAPPER	68
163.	AIR FRIED BRANZINO	69
164.	SALMON AND BLACKBERRY GLAZE	69
165.	COCONUT TILAPIA	70
166.	HONEY SEA BASS	70

POULTRY RECIPE 71

167.	CHICKEN AND PARSLEY SAUCE	71
168.	HERBED CHICKEN	71
169.	CREAMY COCONUT CHICKEN	71
170.	HONEY DUCK BREASTS	72
171.	MEXICAN CHICKEN	72
172.	EASY CHICKEN THIGHS AND BABY POTATOES	72
173.	CHICKEN AND CAPERS	72
174.	DUCK AND PLUM SAUCE	73
175.	CHICKEN BREASTS AND TOMATOES SAUCE	73
176.	CHICKEN THIGHS AND APPLE MIX	74
177.	AIR FRIED CHICKEN MIX	74
178.	CHICKEN CACCIATORE	74
179.	LEMON CHICKEN	75
180.	QUICK CREAMY CHICKEN CASSEROLE	75
181.	CHICKEN AND BLACK OLIVES SAUCE	75
182.	PEPPERONI CHICKEN	76
183.	TURKEY, PEAS, AND MUSHROOMS CASSEROLE	76
184.	GREEK CHICKEN	76
185.	CHICKEN AND PEACHES	76
186.	CHICKEN AND RADISH MIX	77
187.	TEA GLAZED CHICKEN	77
188.	CHICKEN BREASTS AND BBQ CHILI SAUCE	78
189.	VEGGIE STUFFED CHICKEN BREASTS	78
190.	CIDER GLAZED CHICKEN	78
191.	CHICKEN AND CHESTNUTS MIX	79
192.	CHICKEN AND SPINACH SALAD	79
193.	DUCK AND VEGGIES	79
194.	CHICKEN AND GARLIC SAUCE	80
195.	CHEESE CRUSTED CHICKEN	80
196.	CHICKEN PARMESAN	80
197.	AIR FRYER LEMON PEPPER WINGS	81
198.	AIR FRYER PINEAPPLE CHICKEN	81
199.	EASY CHILI SPICED AIR FRYER CHICKEN DRUMSTICKS (KETO & PALEO)	82
200.	BROCCOLI CHEDDAR CHICKEN FRITTERS	82
201.	CHICKEN BREAST FILLET WITH BRIE CHEESE AND RAW HAM	83
202.	CRISPY CHICKEN NUGGETS WITH CANARIAN POTATOES	83
203.	SLICED TURKEY	84
204.	CURRY CHICKEN SKEWERS	84
205.	CHICKEN QUESADILLAS	84
206.	CHINESE STUFFED CHICKEN	85

SANDWICHES, PIZZA, AND BURGER RECIPE 86

207.	AMAZING BREAKFAST BURGER	86
208.	AIR FRIED SANDWICH	86
209.	TUNA SANDWICHES	86
210.	CHICKEN SANDWICHES	87
211.	ITALIAN EGGPLANT SANDWICH	87
212.	MEATBALLS SANDWICH	87
213.	TURKEY BURGERS	88
214.	STUFFED MUSHROOMS	88
215.	QUICK LUNCH PIZZAS	88
216.	TUNA AND ZUCCHINI TORTILLAS	89
217.	HOT BACON SANDWICHES	89
218.	CHICKEN PIE	89
219.	HASH BROWN TOASTS	90
220.	TASTY CHEESEBURGERS	90
221.	EASY HOT DOGS	90
222.	AIR FRYER GRILLED CHEESE SANDWICH	91
223.	AIR FRYER HAM AND CHEESE SANDWICH	91
224.	AIR FRYER MONTE CRISTO SANDWICH	91
225.	AIR FRYER PEANUT BUTTER AND JELLY SANDWICH	92
226.	AIR FRYER CLUB SANDWICH	92
227.	AIR FRYER PANINI	93
228.	AIR FRYER GRILLED CHEESE AND TOMATO	93
229.	AIR FRYER VEGGIE SANDWICH	94
230.	AIR FRYER PITA PIZZA	94
231.	AIR FRYER FROZEN TOTINO'S PIZZA	94
232.	AIR FRYER FRENCH BREAD PIZZA	94
233.	AIR FRYER PIZZA BAGELS	95
234.	AIR FRYER NAAN PIZZA	95
235.	EASY AIR FRYER PIZZA ROLL-UPS	96
236.	AIR FRYER TORTILLA PIZZA	96
237.	AIR FRYER PIZZA	96
238.	AIR FRYER BACON WRAPPED HOT DOGS	97
239.	AIR FRYER TURKEY MELT	97
240.	AIR FRYER FROZEN TURKEY BURGERS	98
241.	AIR FRYER SLIDERS	98
242.	AIR FRYER TURKEY AVOCADO BURGERS	99
243.	AIR FRYER BURGERS FROM FROZEN PATTIES	99
244.	AIR FRYER HAM AND CHEESE MELT	100
245.	AIR FRYER AMAZING BURGERS	100
246.	AIR FRYER BREAKFAST SANDWICHES	101

BEEF, PORK, AND LAMB RECIPE   **102**

247.	Garlic and Bell Pepper Beef	102
248.	Chinese Steak and Broccoli	102
249.	Flavored Rib Eye Steak	102
250.	Beef Strips with Snow Peas and Mushrooms	103
251.	Mediterranean Steaks and Scallops	103
252.	Air Fryer Lamb Shanks	103
253.	Indian Pork	104
254.	Lamb Shanks and Carrots	104
255.	Lamb and Creamy Brussels Sprouts	105
256.	Beef Fillets with Garlic Mayo	105
257.	Tasty Lamb Ribs	105
258.	Marinated Pork Chops and Onions	106
259.	Pork with Couscous	106
260.	Fennel Flavored Pork Roast	106
261.	Beef Roast and Wine Sauce	107
262.	Beef Medallions Mix	107
263.	Lemony Lamb Leg	107
264.	Roasted Pork Belly and Apple Sauce	108
265.	Pork Chops and Roasted Peppers	108
266.	Pork Chops and Mushrooms Mix	108
267.	Lamb and Spinach Mix	109
268.	Air Fried Sausage and Mushrooms	109
269.	Sausage and Kale	109
270.	Beef Stuffed Squash	110
271.	Beef Casserole	110
272.	Lamb and Lemon Sauce	110
273.	Lamb and Green Pesto	111
274.	Burgundy Beef Mix	111
275.	Pork Chops and Sage Sauce	112
276.	Creamy Ham and Cauliflower Mix	112
277.	Beef Kabobs	112
278.	Balsamic Beef	113
279.	Pork Chops and Green Beans	113
280.	Ham and Veggie Air Fried Mix	113
281.	Greek Beef Meatballs Salad	113
282.	Short Ribs and Special Sauce	114
283.	Oriental Air Fried Lamb	114
284.	Beef Curry	115
285.	Lamb Roast and Potatoes	115
286.	Beef and Green Onions Marinade	115

SIDE DISHES RECIPE   **117**

287.	Cauliflower Cakes	117
288.	Cheddar Biscuits	117
289.	Green Beans Side Dish	117
290.	Corn with Lime and Cheese	117
291.	Potato Wedges	118
292.	Avocado Fries	118
293.	Sweet Potato Fries	118

294.	Mushroom Cakes	119
295.	Hasselback Potatoes	119
296.	Creamy Roasted Peppers Side Dish	119
297.	Parmesan Mushrooms	120
298.	Eggplant Side Dish	120
299.	Fried Tomatoes	120
300.	Creamy Brussels Sprouts	121
301.	Simple Potato Chips	121
302.	Zucchini Fries	121
303.	Roasted Peppers	122
304.	Rice and Sausage Side Dish	122
305.	Delicious Roasted Carrots	122
306.	Beer Risotto	122
307.	Delicious Air Fried Broccoli	123
308.	Onion Rings Side Dish	123
309.	Tortilla Chips	123
310.	Air Fried Creamy Cabbage	124
311.	Creamy Potatoes	124
312.	Brussels Sprouts and Pomegranate Seeds Side Dish	124
313.	Coconut Cream Potatoes	125
314.	Fried Red Cabbage	125
315.	Flavored Cauliflower Side Dish	125
316.	Cauliflower and Broccoli Delight	126
317.	Cajun Onion Wedges	126
318.	Wild Rice Pilaf	126
319.	Lemony Artichokes	127
320.	Garlic Beet Wedges	127
321.	Artichokes and Tarragon Sauce	127
322.	Veggie Fries	127
323.	Roasted Eggplant	128
324.	Vermouth Mushrooms	128
325.	Creamy Endives	128
326.	Herbed Tomatoes	129

DESSERTS RECIPE   **130**

327.	Tasty Orange Cake	130
328.	Crispy Apple	130
329.	Special Brownies	130
330.	Coffee Cheesecakes	131
331.	Chocolate Cookies	131
332.	Simple Cheesecake	131
333.	Bread Dough and Amaretto Dessert	132
334.	Air Fried Apples	132
335.	Mini Lava Cakes	132
336.	Wrapped Pears	133
337.	Air Fried Bananas	133
338.	Cocoa Cake	133
339.	Strawberry Cobbler	134
340.	Strawberry Pie	134
341.	Cocoa Cookies	134

342.	CASHEW BARS	135
343.	BLUEBERRY SCONES	135
344.	PLUM BARS	135
345.	MACAROONS	136
346.	PEARS AND ESPRESSO CREAM	136
347.	EASY GRANOLA	136
348.	LEMON BARS	137
349.	LENTILS AND DATES BROWNIES	137
350.	BLUEBERRY PUDDING	137
351.	SPONGE CAKE	138
352.	FIGS AND COCONUT BUTTER MIX	138
353.	TASTY ORANGE COOKIES	138
354.	TANGERINE CAKE	139
355.	COCOA AND ALMOND BARS	139
356.	BERRIES MIX	139
357.	PUMPKIN COOKIES	140
358.	BROWN BUTTER COOKIES	140
359.	PEACH PIE	140
360.	SWEET POTATO CHEESECAKE	141
361.	SWEET SQUARES	141
362.	PASSION FRUIT PUDDING	141
363.	CHOCOLATE AND POMEGRANATE BARS	142
364.	BLACK TEA CAKE	142
365.	LIME CHEESECAKE	143
366.	GINGER CHEESECAKE	143

COOKING TIMES   **144**

AIR FRYER CONVERSION CHART   **144**

COST OF COOKING CHART   **145**

CONCLUSION   **146**

INTRODUCTION

The tower air fryer makes it simple to prepare delectable, healthful meals. The appliance employs quick hot air circulation to cook food rather than heated fat and oil that could harm your health. Technique makes the food's exterior crispy and guarantees that the interior is well-cooked.

We can cook a wide variety of foods and nearly anything using the tower air fryer. The tower air fryer can be used to cook a variety of foods, including meat, vegetables, poultry, fruits, fish, and a wide range of desserts. You can make all your meals, from the starters to the main course and dessert. The tower air fryer enables the creation of delectable cakes, sweets, and homemade preserves.

HOW DOES AN AIR FRYER WORK?

The appearance of an air fryer might vary based on its brand, size, and price. However, there are a few constituent parts to anticipate, namely:

- a heating element
- a fan
- a drawer where the food goes
- the controls, typically on the front of the air fryer
- a basket or grate, which elevates and holds the food inside the drawer

By being aware of these components, you can better comprehend how the air fryer operates.

The cooking process

First, it's essential to realize that an air fryer doesn't indeed fry your food. Food is cooked in heated oil when it is fried, by definition. Although frying requires cooking in fat, you can shallow fry in a skillet or deep fry, where the oil surrounds the food.

In principle, an air fryer simulates the idea of a deep fry, where the heat source completely envelops the food and contacts its entire surface area at once (in the case of deep frying, hot oil). Due to this, deep frying produces immediately crispy food: The thing receives intense heat all at once.

Familiar with a convection oven, the air fryer cooks food. You place the food in the cooking drawer after setting the temperature. The fan quickly moves the hot air produced by the heating element throughout the whole food drawer. The hot, moving air contacts all food surfaces as it is lifted inside the basket or grate. You ought to get browned, crispy food with little to no oil.

Comparing air frying to turbocharging roasting is useful. Or, because the hot air surrounds the meal while air frying at lower temperatures, it can rapidly and effectively reheat leftovers. Naturally, frozen food cooks quickly and evenly during defrosting, making frozen food delightful.

You now have the answer to the mystery—an air fryer functions in the same way.

A BEGINNER'S GUIDE

Ahead of First Use

Setting Up

1. You should take off all the stickers and the air fryer's packing before using it for the first time.
2. After that, place it on a solid, heat-resistant surface. Make sure the air fryer is set up far from surfaces and items. This will stop steam from doing any harm.
3. You should remove the basket from the air fryer using the handle to eliminate all the plastic packaging. Utilize the basket release button to separate the inner and outer baskets.

4. Use a non-abrasive sponge or a dishwasher to clean both baskets thoroughly. With a slightly moist towel, clean the basket's interior and outside. The basket can be dried with a dry towel. Put the basket back inside the air fryer after that.

Air fryer trial run

Before utilizing the air fryer for cooking, you should test it at least once. This will assist you in becoming familiar with the various features of your air fryer and ensuring that it is operating correctly. The air fryer can be examined as follows:

1. Connect the air fryer's power plug. A full air fryer basket should be used. Next, give the air fryer some time to warm up. You will see a preheat button on your air fryer if it has multiple functions. Small, pricey air fryers typically use analog control systems. These will need to be manually warmed up to preheat; heat for 5 minutes at 204°C.
2. When the preheating process is finished, the air fryer will beep. Decide on the time and temperature you want. After that, remove the air fryer's basket and give it five minutes to cool. After that, replace the empty basket inside the air fryer. Now check to see if the air fryer is operating correctly.
3. The air fryer will automatically switch off and keep making the "beep beep" sound when the cooking time is up. Then, using the handle, remove the air fryer basket, allowing it to cool for 10 to 30 minutes. If everything goes as planned, your air fryer will be prepared for use.

Tips for The Air Fryer Basket

1. Only remove the air fryer's basket when cooking and cleaning food. Avoid repeatedly removing the basket.
2. The handle's button guard stops the user from unintentionally hitting the release button. To release the basket, slide the button guard forward.
3. When taking out the basket, never hit the basket release button. This is because the basket may fall and create mishaps if the release button is pressed while the basket is being carried.
4. When you're ready, merely press the basket release button. Make sure the surface on which you plan to set it is secure and heat-resistant.
5. The air fryer's handle is affixed to the inside basket rather than the outside basket. As a result, your outer basket will drop when you press the release button on the basket.

How to Use Your Tower Air fryer

1. Before using the air fryer for cooking, it must be preheated. This is so that the food will cook more quickly and have a crispy exterior when the air fryer is preheated. By pushing the preheat button, you can quickly preheat a multi-function device. However, you will need to manually preheat small, inexpensive air fryers. For manual preheating, turn the air fryer on for five minutes at 204°C.
2. Take the air fryer basket out of the air fryer and add the food after the air fryer has finished preheating. However, remember that there shouldn't be too much food in the basket because the food might not be cooked correctly if the basket is overfilled.
3. Put the food-filled air fryer basket inside the air fryer after filling it with food. Next, establish the right temperature and timing for meals. However, you can also adjust the temperature and duration during cooking.
4. Start the air frying by pressing the start button. After you begin cooking, you must watch to ensure the dish is not overdone or burned. To ensure the food is cooked, you can combine the ingredients during the cooking period or turn the food upside down. The air fryer will beep when the cooking period is finished.
5. The air fryer basket should then be removed. But beware of the steam's heat. Serve the food after separating the inside basket from the outer basket. Keep the basket on a flat surface while separating the inside from the outer basket. Before cleaning, the basket must completely cool.

HEALTH BENEFITS OF AIR FRYERS

1.   Lower fat and calorie intake

Let's start with the fundamentals. High-speed fans already installed in an air fryer distribute air evenly while crisping up food with a thin layer of oil. This gadget makes your meals healthier because it doesn't use additional oils, allowing you to live an active lifestyle without having to give up your appetites.

With an air fryer, it's simple to enjoy delectable cuisine without adding extra calories to your diet. According to many studies, using an air fryer to prepare food can dramatically reduce the amount of fat by 50 times, meaning the dish has significantly fewer calories and fat.

2.   It enables you to keep more nutrients in your food.

You'll be happy to learn that air fryers can preserve several nutrients, like Vitamin C and polyphenols, that are typically destroyed during traditional cooking processes. They don't simply offer crispy texture and flavor.

Compared to conventional ovens, air fryers use less heat, allowing food to keep more of its nutritious content and natural flavour. This is particularly crucial for diets high in antioxidants, such as fruits and vegetables. Using this culinary tool will make your food crunchy and flavorful while preserving the nutritional value of a home-cooked meal.

3.   The use of an air fryer doesn't conflict with your diet plans.

When cooking, an air fryer is a healthy method to reduce calories and fat. It uses substantially less oil than conventional ways of cooking, allowing you to enjoy gourmet cuisine without compromising your efforts to lose weight.

Your calorie consumption may be decreased by the meal prepared in an air fryer, aiding in weight loss. It only needs a thin layer or a few drops of oil, so you may satisfy your cravings while keeping the saturated fat level to a minimum.

4.   Safer Cooking

Cooking using an air fryer is faster and safer, which is one of its advantages. This equipment uses less oil and is significantly safer than conventional cooking techniques. It implies that you won't be consuming additional fat, which can raise your risk of heart disease and other health issues.

Additionally, since air frying requires less time than baking or broiling, you may prepare more food in the same amount of time. It is, therefore, a fantastic option for folks who are busy and don't have time to wait for their food to prepare.

5.   Less Energy Consumption

Compared to conventional cooking methods like stovetop or oven cooking, air fryers consume less energy and don't need to be heated up or cooled down. Additionally, it doesn't produce any hazardous smoke or fumes, another risk associated with frying on a stovetop or in an oven.

You'll be pleased to know that Air Fryers are a need for a modern family because they only cost approximately 25 cents per hour of cooking, compared to 40 to 50 cents for a gas or electric oven.

WHAT CAN YOU COOK IN AN AIR FRYER?

The home chef has a wide range of options when using air fryers, from making their hot wings to frying brussels sprouts quickly. Stick to air-frying veggies like carrots, brussels sprouts, or cauliflower steaks, baking or roasting potatoes with no or little oil, or dehydrating fruits to make your apple chips and fruit leathers if you're seeking healthier alternatives.

Health-conscious Carnivores can air fry salmon fillets or chicken breasts that have been spice-rubbed or lightly oiled for more taste. Remember that dry spices will fly everywhere and create a mess. Spices can be kept in their proper place with the aid of a thin oil covering.

Donuts, cookies, potato or vegetable chips, fresh or frozen french fries and sweet potato fries, pizza, and burgers can all be made at home by indulgent home cooks. And if you prefer convenience to anything else, utilising an air fryer instead of a standard oven will help you cook your favourite frozen foods faster and with crispier results.

Foods covered with wet batter or marinades won't be able to be cooked since they will drip and produce a mess. The use of air fryers for roasting whole chickens is debatable among home cooks. Before attempting to air fry a bird that weighs more than three pounds, you might wish to cut it into pieces or spatchcock it. The same is true when cooking burgers and steaks at home; some home cooks claim that it is impossible to produce well-done meat, while others claim that it requires practice.

HOW TO CLEAN YOUR AIR FRYER

Cleaning Tips for Your Air Fryer

Before deep cleaning your air fryer, become familiar with the maintenance dos and don'ts.

- Avoid cleaning the residue and food fragments out of your air fryer with steel wire brushes, abrasive sponges, or metal utensils. This could affect the nonstick coating on the stove surface.
- Keep the water away from your air fryer. The main unit will be harmed since it is an electric appliance.
- Make sure your fryer is unplugged while you are cleaning.
- Try scraping stuck-on food from the crevices with a wooden skewer, toothpick, or even an old toothbrush if you notice a foul stench coming from your air fryer. These hidden crumbs could burn over time, releasing a bad odour and smoking the machine.
- You can also rub the cooking surface and basket with a half-lemon split in half to help with lingering smells. Allow it to sit for around 30 minutes before cleaning.
- Utilize cleaning products that are appropriate to eat. Disinfectants that haven't been cleared for usage around food shouldn't be used.

How Frequently Should You Clean Your Air Fryer?

Following Each Use

After each use, wash the air fryer's basket, tray, and pan with soap and warm water, or put them in the dishwasher. Consult the owner's handbook to ensure these parts can go in the dishwasher. Additionally, you should swiftly clean the interior using a damp cloth and dish soap. After drying, put each component back together.

Following every few uses

Even while it's not required to wash the other important parts regularly, doing so will keep your air fryer in good working order. The outside should occasionally be cleaned with a moist cloth. You should also check the heating coil for any oil or residue. Use a damp cloth to clean the area where you've seen any buildup after the machine has cooled.

How to Deep Clean an Air Fryer

What you'll need is as follows:
- Baking Soda
- Soft-bristle scrub brush
- Clean, dry cloth
- Damp microfiber cloth or non-abrasive sponge
- Dish soap

You can clean your air fryer by doing a few quick things:
1. If you recently used your air fryer, start by unplugging it. Allow it to cool for around 30 mins.

2. Take out the baskets and pans and wash them in hot, soapy water. Give each of these parts at least 10 minutes to soak in hot, soapy water before wiping them down with a non-abrasive sponge if any have food or oil baked on them. Check your manual to see whether any pieces are safe if you want to clean them with a dishwasher.

3. Use a damp microfiber cloth or a non-abrasive sponge dipped in some dish soap to clean the interior. Remove the soap using a clean, moist towel.

4. The heating element should be cleaned with a moist cloth or sponge while the appliance is upside-down.

5. If the primary appliance has any baked-on or hard residue, make a paste with water and baking soda. Work the paste into the residue with a soft-bristled scrub brush before removing it with a clean cloth.

6. Use a moist towel to clean the outside. Take away the soap with a clean, wet cloth.

7. Dry the main unit and any removable parts before reassembling.

AIR FRYER TIPS AND TRICKS

Preheating is not necessary.

It's not mandatory to preheat the air fryer before using it. If you do, the cooking time for your dish might alter. Only preheat if that's what your recipe instructs you to do.

Use little oil

Utilize a modest amount of oil. Food can be crisped up in the air fryer without using oil. Simply drips of extra oil from the food will gather at the machine's base and maybe produce smoke. Simply spritz food with an oily mist to lightly coat it.

There is already a significant amount of oil in the breading of frozen deep-fried items; therefore, no additional oil is needed. Vegetables benefit from mild oiling. Chicken thighs with the skin on don't need any oil.

Use a spray-on oil from a reusable bottle.

Because they create a sticky residue on the air fryer basket and harm the nonstick coating, we don't recommend using nonstick sprays like Pam. Investing in a refillable spray bottle is the best choice. Never use an aerosol spray in the air fryer.

Halfway through, shake the basket.

Shake or flip your meal over at least once while it's cooking for the best results in getting it nice and crispy all over. Some air fryers have a "shake reminder" feature that beeps when it's time to shake the basket. If you don't have a timer, set your own.

Cooking times are approximate.

As with any appliance, none are perfectly calibrated or have the same wattage. There is a chance that you will need to cook anything for longer or for less time than the recipe calls for. Always keep an eye on the food. Expect a 2–5 minute change in cooking time.

Don't stuff the basket too full.

Even if your air fryer has a large basket, not as much food can fit in it as you may believe. Food needs space and airflow in an air fryer to get crispy. If you use the entire bag of frozen fries, the fries won't get as crispy; instead, add half of that quantity. It will also take longer to cook.

Use parchment paper to prevent sticking.

Even while it's not always necessary, when the food is sticky or delicate, you can add parchment paper to keep it from clinging to the basket. I use them when preparing fish so they won't fall apart when I take them out of the basket. Pre-cut parchment paper in square or circular forms with air holes is available to guarantee that the airflow around your meal remains unaffected.

Tin foil is an option.

If you were wondering, you might use tin foil in the air fryer. It can be used to make cleanup easier or stop food from sticking. In the oven, you can wrap liquid dishes like steaming food "en papillote" (covered in foil).

Cooking can also be done in an aluminum pan, which is safe to use in an air fryer. Using disposable foil pans, food like lasagna or a casserole can be heated in the air fryer.

Place the air fryer carefully.

You should take extra care in the vicinity of the air fryer. If you position the machine too close to something that can burn or melt, the heat from the machine may damage the neighboring surfaces.

Avoid laying the air fryer's basket directly on a countertop since it will get very hot when you remove it from the base and could deform or melt.

Before dumping, remove the basket.

The majority of basket-style air fryers are made of two sections. There is also the basket that fits into the cradle or drawer. The urge to take the entire cradle out of the air fryer and empty the contents could be strong, but doing so could result in the oil pouring out of the bottom. Before dumping the contents, always remove the basket.

Other pans can be used inside the air fryer.

Any cake pan or baking sheet used in your oven is safe in the air fryer. Stainless steel, silicone, and oven-safe glass pans are all acceptable. Make sure they don't touch the heating element, though.

Reheat leftovers in the air fryer

Reheat the leftover chicken, ribs, rolls, pizza, and hamburger buns. It works quickly and effectively.

For quick cleanup, immediately soak the basket.

The simplest approach to cleaning the basket is to immerse it in hot, soapy water as soon as it is still warm from use. By transferring the basket immediately to the sink and soaking it, any fatty or sticky food won't have time to dry on and will come off quite quickly.

Use water to prevent smoking.

White smoke should not be released while the air fryer is cooking, but certain models are more likely to do this than others. If your air fryer begins to smoke while cooking fatty meals like pork belly or chicken wings, add a little water to the bottom of the cradle.

Avoid stacking food to ensure uniform browning.

If you want your food to look good, browned, and crispy, don't layer it, especially when cooking pork chops or chicken thighs. It might be necessary to cook in batches, but the finished product will be an excellent food. Some meals don't need to be in a single layer, such as chicken wings or French fries, which you can rotate more readily.

Baking a cake

Anything can be baked in an air fryer. It must fit in the basket, and that is the only criterion. If you have a silicon cake pan that will fit in the air fryer basket, bake your cake in it. How good it tastes and how much faster it cooks than in the oven will wow you.

Prevent cooking light foods

Do not forget to clean the air fryer's interior.

You presumably clean the air fryer's basket after each use. That cannot be avoided. But do you also clean the inside of the air fryer? It might smoke, damage the heating element, or even catch fire if it is caked with lint and grime. You should clean the inside of the air fryer at least once a week or once a month, depending on how often you use it.

Prepare hardboiled eggs

In a strict sense, eggs aren't even boiled when cooked in an air fryer, but the results are still excellent. It takes a little longer than a burner, but you don't have to mess with the water or turn on the flame.

Prepare bread with breadcrumbs, not just flour.

Any breaded dish you prepare in the air fryer will turn out lovely, golden, and crispy. However, to achieve that golden crisp, you must bread the item with breadcrumbs and guarantee that the oil is uniformly distributed throughout when breading chicken in the air fryer with just egg and flour, as you might when deep frying it, the crust will be less flavorful.

Use a meat thermometer to find out the internal temperature of meats.

The only accurate way to tell if meats are fully cooked is to test their interior temperature with a digital thermometer. You can rapidly take the temperature whenever the cooking process is about to be finished to see if something is finished. It is better to rely on the thermometer than the cooking times in the recipe because every air fryer cooks differently.

Hold cheese slices in place with a toothpick.

To prevent it from flying off, attach a slice of cheese with a toothpick to the top of your air-fried hamburgers so they can melt. If not, it could not be there when you check on it again. You may also secure a slice of bread by sticking a toothpick through a slice of bread and one of the holes in the basket.

Disable the beeping

You might be able to stop that beeping depending on the sort of gadget you have. Usually, it requires three seconds of holding down the minus keys. You might need to remove the case to locate and remove the beeping mechanism if that doesn't work.

Moldy egg bites

You may make a huge selection of snacks, muffins, and appetisers using the egg bites mould. An egg bits mould can be used to bake various tasty desserts, even if it comes with your Instant Pot. Make meatballs, meatball bites, cinnamon roll bites, mini cheesecakes, mini pancakes, mini cake balls, mini cornbread muffins, etc.

BREAKFAST AND BREAD RECIPE

1. CREAMY HASH BROWNS

Preparation time: 10 minutes
Cooking time: 20 minutes
Servings: 6

Ingredients:
- 900 g hash browns
- 237 ml whole milk
- 8 bacon slices, chopped
- 255 g cream cheese
- 1 yellow onion, chopped
- 235 g cheddar cheese, shredded
- 6 green onions, chopped
- Salt and black pepper to the taste
- 6 eggs
- Cooking spray

Preparation
1. Preheat your air fryer to 180°C and coat it with cooking spray.
2. Whisk together eggs, milk, cream cheese, cheddar cheese, bacon, onion, salt, and pepper in a mixing bowl.
3. Place hash browns in your air fryer, top with egg mixture, and cook for 20 minutes.
4. Serve on individual plates.
5. Enjoy!

Nutritional information: calories 261, fat 6g, fiber 9g, carbs 8g, protein 12g

2. OATMEAL CASSEROLE

Preparation time: 10 minutes
Cooking time: 20 minutes
Servings: 8

Ingredients:
- 2 cups rolled oats
- 4 ml baking powder
- 67 g brown sugar
- 5 ml cinnamon powder
- 80 g chocolate chips
- 65 g blueberries
- 1 banana, peeled and mashed
- 473 ml milk
- 1 eggs
- 28 g butter
- 5 ml vanilla extract
- Cooking spray

Preparation
1. Stir together sugar, baking powder, cinnamon, chocolate chips, blueberries, and banana in a mixing basin.
2. In a separate dish, whisk together the eggs, vanilla essence, and butter.
3. Preheat your air fryer to 160°C, coat with cooking spray, then layer oats on the bottom.
4. Toss in the cinnamon-egg mixture and simmer for 20 minutes.
5. Stir one more before dividing into bowls and serving for breakfast.
6. Enjoy!

Nutritional information: calories 300, fat 4g, fiber 7g, carbs 12g, protein 10g

3. BROWN LOAF WITH SEEDS

Preparation time 30 minutes,
Cooking time: 18 minutes
Servings: 4

Ingredients
- 100 g whole wheat flour
- 100 g plain flour
- ½ sachet of instant yeast (7 g)
- 50 g sunflower seeds and/or pumpkin seeds
- Small pizza pan or low cake pan, 15 cm diameter

Preparation
1. In a mixing dish, combine both flours, 6 g salt, the yeast, and the seeds. Mix in 150-200 mL lukewarm water while stirring until the dough forms a soft ball.
2. Knead the dough for 5 minutes or until it is smooth and elastic. Form the dough into a ball and set it aside in a bowl. Allow the bowl to rise in a warm area for 30 minutes, covered with plastic wrap.
3. Preheat the air fryer to 200 degrees Celsius. Brush the dough with water on top.

4. Place the cake pan in the fryer basket and place it in the air fryer. Bake the bread for 18 minutes, or until it is golden brown and done. Place the bread on a wire rack to cool.

Nutritional information: calories 92 total carbs 9.6g, net carbs 5.1g, fat 2.5g, protein 5.5g,

4. HOMEMADE SODA BREAD IN THE AIR FRYER (BREAD SODA)

Preparation time: 5 minutes
Cooking time: 20 minutes
Total Time: 25 minutes
servings: 6

Ingredients
- 120 g of all-purpose Flour
- 225 g buttermilk
- 25 g of sugar
- 5 ml baking soda
- 2.5 ml of salt

Preparation
1. In a large mixing basin, combine all of the dry ingredients with a spatula.
2. Add the buttermilk to the dry ingredients, gently combine with a spatula, and shape into a ball with your hands.
3. Divide the dough in half and shape each half into a round loaf.
4. Spray the air fryer basket and set the dough in it; form a cross or score the top of the dough with an X. This allows the dough to bake more quickly and evenly. Simply brush the top of the bread with milk to wash it.
5. Bake the dough for 20 minutes at 148° C, checking for doneness with a toothpick. I rarely turn the bread midway; the scoring allows it to cook evenly without being flipped. Allow to cool before serving after baking. Using the "farts," easily split this bread apart (the cross).

Nutritional information: Calories 193 Total Fat 1.8g Total Carbohydrate 38g Protein 5.6g

5. GARLIC BREAD IN THE AIR FRYER

Preparation time 5 mins
Cooking time 6 mins
Total time 11 mins
Servings 4 slices

Ingredients
- 4 slices bread use gluten-free if desired
- 27 g olive oil or melted butter
- 2 cloves garlic
- 5 ml garlic powder
- 1.25 ml garlic salt
- Crushed Red Pepper Flakes

Preparation
1. Combine the olive oil, garlic, garlic powder, garlic salt, and chilli flakes in a mixing bowl. To blend, stir everything together thoroughly.
2. Brush both sides of the bread with the olive oil mixture.
3. Preheat the air fryer to 160° C. Cook the garlic bread for 6 minutes, without flipping. Enjoy

Nutritional information: Calories: 142kcal Carbohydrates: 15g Protein: 3g Fat: 8g

6. PROSCIUTTO SANDWICH

Preparation time: 10 minutes
Cooking time: 5 minutes
Servings: 1
Ingredients:
- 2 bread slices
- 2 mozzarella slices
- 2 tomato slices
- 2 prosciutto slices
- 2 basil leaves
- 5 ml olive oil
- A pinch of salt and black pepper

Preparation

1. Arrange mozzarella and prosciutto on a bread slice.
2. Season with salt and pepper, place in your air fryer and cook at 204 degrees C for 5 minutes.
3. Drizzle oil over prosciutto, add tomato and basil, cover with the other bread slice, cut sandwich in half and serve.
4. Enjoy!

Nutritional information: calories 172, fat 3g, fiber 7g, carbs 9g, protein 5g

7. CHEESE SANDWICH

Preparation time: 10 minutes
Cooking time: 8 minutes
Servings: 1

Ingredients:

- 2 bread slices
- 10 g butter
- 2 cheddar cheese slices
- A pinch of sweet paprika

Preparation

1. Spread butter over bread slices, top with cheddar cheese, sprinkle with paprika, cut into halves, lay in your air fryer and cook at 187 degrees C for 8 minutes, flipping once, arrange on a platter, and serve.
2. Enjoy!

Nutritional information: calories 130, fat 3g, fiber 5g, carbs 9g, protein 3g

8. SHRIMP SANDWICHES

Preparation time: 10 minutes
Cooking time: 5 minutes
Servings: 4

Ingredients:

- 176 g cheddar, shredded
- 170 g canned tiny shrimp, drained
- 43 g mayonnaise
- 11 g green onions, chopped
- 4 whole wheat bread slices
- 28 g butter, soft

Preparation

1. In a mixing bowl, combine shrimp, cheese, green onion, and mayo.
2. Spread this on half of the bread slices, then top with the remaining bread slices, cut in half diagonally, and spread with butter.
3. Place sandwiches in your air fryer and cook for 5 minutes at 176° C.
4. Serve the shrimp sandwiches for breakfast on plates.
5. Enjoy!

Nutritional information: calories 162, fat 3g, fiber 7g, carbs 12g, protein 4g

9. EGGS CASSEROLE

Preparation time: 10 minutes
Cooking time: 25 minutes
Servings: 6

Ingredients:

- 454 g turkey, ground
- 15 ml olive oil
- 5 ml chili powder
- 12 eggs
- 1 sweet potato, cubed
- 30 g baby spinach
- Salt and black pepper to the taste
- 2 tomatoes, chopped for serving

Preparation

1. Whisk together eggs, salt, pepper, chilli powder, potato, spinach, turkey, and sweet potato in a mixing bowl.
2. Preheat your air fryer to 180°C, then add the oil and heat it up.
3. Spread the egg mixture into your air fryer, cover, and cook for 25 minutes.
4. Serve for breakfast on individual dishes.
5. Enjoy!

Nutritional information; calories 300, fat 5g, fiber 8g, carbs 13g, protein 6g

10. AIR FRYER-BANANA BREAD

Preparation Time: 10 mins
Cooking Time: 20 mins
Total Time: 30 mins
servings: 6

Ingredients
- 180 g of flour
- 118 ml of milk
- 4 g of baking powder
- 5 ml of baking soda
- 2.5 ml g of cinnamon
- 5 ml of salt
- 150 g of sugar
- 118 ml of oil
- 3 overripe bananas

Preparation
1. In a mixer or large mixing basin, combine all of the ingredients.
2. After that, coat your pan with nonstick cooking spray (or use olive oil)
3. Cook for 20-30 minutes in an Air Fryer @ 165°C (air fryer setting). Does the toothpick come out clean from your air fryer? If so, it's finished; otherwise, add a few minutes to your time.
4. Allow to cool before slicing and serving.

Nutritional information: calories184; fat 6g; carbohydrates 29.2g; protein 4g;

11. AIR FRYER GRILLED CHEESE

Preparation Time 5 minutes
Cooking Time 12 minutes
Total Time 17 minutes
Servings: 1

Ingredients
- 2 slices bread
- 5 g butter or cooking spray
- 2 slice cheese
- 1/4 pear thinly sliced

Preparation
1. Preheat the air fryer to 180° C.
2. Butter one side of each slice of bread, making sure to cover the entire bread.
3. Combine the cheese and pear. Fold the cheese slices in between the bread slices, making sure that no cheese sticks out.
4. Cook for 8 minutes in the air fryer before turning and cooking for another 3-4 minutes on the second side.
5. Serve hot.

Nutritional information: Calories: 473kcal
Carbohydrates: 35g Protein: 20g Fat: 28g

12. QUICK VEGAN AIR FRYER

GARLIC BREAD

Preparation time 3 mins
Cooking time 5 mins
Total time 8 mins
Servings 4

Ingredients
- 4 mini flour tortillas
- 56 g vegan butter (or vegan spread)
- 2 large cloves of garlic
- 1.25 ml dried parsley (or fresh, chopped)
- 1 generous pinch of chilli flakes
- 1 pinch salt and pepper

Preparation

1. Peel and crush the garlic, or finely grate it.
2. In a bowl, soften the butter using the back of a spoon.
3. Season with salt and pepper after adding the garlic, herbs, and chilli.
4. Combine thoroughly.
5. Spread the mixture equally over four tiny flour tortillas.
6. Bake for 5 minutes at 180°C in an air fryer. Keep an eye on it, and if you have shelves, you might need to swap them out because the top one cooks faster.
7. Cut into triangles before serving.
8. Enjoy!

Nutritional information: Calories: 88kcal
Carbohydrates: 1g Protein: 0.2g Fat: 9g

13. RUSTIC BREAKFAST

Preparation time: 10 minutes
Cooking time: 13 minutes
Servings: 4

Ingredients:

- 26.3 g baby spinach
- 8 chestnuts mushrooms, halved
- 8 tomatoes, halved
- 1 garlic clove, minced
- 4 chipolatas
- 4 bacon slices, chopped
- Salt and black pepper to the taste
- 4 eggs
- Cooking spray

Preparation

1. Grease a pan with oil and add the tomatoes, garlic, and mushrooms.
2. Finish with bacon and chipolatas, spinach, and cracked eggs.
3. Season with salt and pepper, then set the pan in the air fryer's cooking basket and cook for 13 minutes at 176° C.
4. Serve for breakfast on individual dishes. Enjoy!

Nutritional information: calories 312, fat 6g, fiber 8g, carbs 15g, protein 5g

14. TASTY BAKED EGGS

Preparation time: 10 minutes
Cooking time: 20 minutes
Servings: 4

Ingredients:

- 4 eggs
- 454 g baby spinach, torn
- 200 g ham, chopped
- 60 ml milk
- 15 ml olive oil
- Cooking spray
- Salt and black pepper to the taste

Preparation

1. Heat the oil in a pan over medium heat, add the baby spinach, toss for a couple of minutes, and remove from heat.
2. Cooking spray 4 ramekins and divide baby spinach and ham in each.
3. Crack an egg into each ramekin, split the milk, season with salt and pepper, and bake for 20 minutes in a hot air fryer at 176 degrees C.
4. For breakfast, serve baked eggs.
5. Enjoy!

Nutritional information: calories 321, fat 6g, fiber 8g, carbs 15g, protein 12g

15. BREAKFAST EGG BOWLS

Preparation time: 10 minutes
Cooking time: 20 minutes
Servings: 4

Ingredients:

- 4 dinner rolls, tops cut off and insides scooped out
- 60g heavy cream
- 4 eggs
- 16 g mixed chives and parsley
- Salt and black pepper to the taste
- 22.5 g parmesan, grated

Preparation

1. Place each dinner roll on a baking pan and crack an egg into it.
2. Divide the heavy cream and herbs among the rolls and season with salt and pepper.
3. Sprinkle parmesan on top of your rolls and cook for 20 minutes at 176° C in your air fryer.
4. Serve your bread bowls for breakfast on plates.
5. Enjoy!

Nutritional information: calories 238, fat 4g, fiber 7g, carbs 14g, protein 7g

16. DELICIOUS BREAKFAST SOUFFLÉ

Preparation time: 10 minutes
Cooking time: 8 minutes
Servings: 4

Ingredients:
- 4 eggs, whisked
- 60 g heavy cream
- A pinch of red chili pepper, crushed
- 8 g parsley, chopped
- 8 g chives, chopped
- Salt and black pepper to the taste

Preparation
1. In a mixing bowl, combine the eggs, salt, pepper, heavy cream, red chilli pepper, parsley, and chives; stir well and divide among four soufflé dishes.
2. Arrange dishes in your air fryer and cook soufflés for 8 minutes at 176° C.
3. Serve them immediately.
4. Enjoy!

Nutritional information: calories 300, fat 7g, fiber 9g, carbs 15g, protein 6g

17. EGG MUFFINS

Preparation time: 10 minutes
Cooking time: 15 minutes
Servings: 4

Ingredients:
- 1 egg
- 30 ml olive oil
- 44 ml milk
- 110 g white flour
- 14 g baking powder
- 58 g parmesan, grated
- A splash of Worcestershire sauce

Preparation
1. In a mixing bowl, combine the egg, flour, oil, baking powder, milk, Worcestershire sauce, and parmesan; whisk well and divide among four silicon muffin cups.

2. Place the cups in the cooking basket of your air fryer, cover, and cook at 200°C for 15 minutes.
3. For breakfast, serve warm.
4. Enjoy!

Nutritional information: calories 251, fat 6g, fiber 8g, carbs 9g, protein 3g

18. TASTY CINNAMON TOAST

Preparation time: 10 minutes
Cooking time: 5 minutes
Servings: 6

Ingredients:
- 1 stick butter, soft
- 12 bread slices
- 100 g sugar
- 7.5 ml vanilla extract
- 5 ml cinnamon powder

Preparation
1. In a mixing dish, whisk together soft butter, sugar, vanilla, and cinnamon.
2. Spread this on bread pieces and place them in your air fryer for 5 minutes at 204 degrees C.
3. Divide among plates and serve for breakfast.
4. Enjoy!

Nutritional information: calories 221, fat 4g, fiber 7g, carbs 12g, protein 8g

19. ASPARAGUS FRITTATA

Preparation time: 10 minutes
Cooking time: 5 minutes
Servings: 2

Ingredients:
- 4 eggs, whisked
- 11 g parmesan, grated
- 60 ml milk
- Salt and black pepper to the taste
- 10 asparagus tips, steamed
- Cooking spray

Preparation
1. In a mixing dish, whisk together the eggs, parmesan, milk, salt, and pepper.
2. Preheat your air fryer to 204°C and coat it with cooking spray.
3. Cook for 5 minutes after adding the asparagus and egg mixture.
4. Serve the frittata on plates for breakfast.
5. Enjoy!

Nutritional information: calories 312, fat 5g, fiber 8g, carbs 14g, protein 2g

20. HAM BREAKFAST PIE

Preparation time: 10 minutes
Cooking time: 25 minutes
Servings: 6

Ingredients:
- 453 g crescent rolls dough
- 2 eggs, whisked
- 470 g cheddar cheese, grated
- 15 g parmesan, grated
- 135 g cooked and chopped
- Salt and black pepper to the taste
- Cooking spray

Preparation
1. Heat up your air fryer at 176 degrees C and grease it with cooking spray.
2. In a mixing bowl, whisk together the eggs, cheddar cheese, parmesan, salt, and pepper, then pour over the dough.
3. Spread the ham, then cut the remaining crescent roll dough into strips and put them over the ham. Bake at 148° C for 25 minutes.
4. Serve the pie for breakfast.
5. Enjoy!

Nutritional information: calories 400, fat 27g, fiber 7g, carbs 22g, protein 16g

21. SCRAMBLED EGGS

Preparation time: 10 minutes
Cooking time: 10 minutes
Servings: 2

Ingredients:
- 2 eggs
- 28 g butter
- Salt and black pepper to the taste
- 1 red bell pepper, chopped
- A pinch of sweet paprika

Preparation
1. Whisk eggs with salt, pepper, paprika, and red bell pepper in a mixing bowl.
2. Preheat your air fryer to 60 degrees Celsius, then add the butter and melt it.
3. Cook for 10 minutes after adding the egg mixture.
4. Serve scrambled eggs on plates for breakfast.
5. Enjoy!

Nutritional information: calories 200, fat 4g, fiber 7g, carbs 10g, protein 3g

22. QUICK EGGS AND TOMATOES

Preparation time: 5 minutes
Cooking time: 10 minutes
Servings: 4

Ingredients:
- 4 eggs
- 60 ml milk
- 11 g parmesan, grated
- Salt and black pepper to the taste
- 8 cherry tomatoes, halved
- Cooking spray

Preparation
1. Grease your air fryer with cooking spray and heat it up at 93 degrees C.
2. In a bowl, mix eggs with cheese, milk, salt and pepper and whisk.
3. Add this mix to your air fryer and cook for 6 minutes.
4. Add tomatoes, cook your scrambled eggs for 3 minutes, divide among plates and serve. Enjoy!

Nutritional information: calories 200, fat 4g, fiber 7g, carbs 12g, protein 3g

23. SMOKED AIR FRIED TOFU

BREAKFAST

Preparation time: 10 minutes
Cooking time: 12 minutes
Servings: 2

Ingredients:
- 1 tofu block, pressed and cubed
- Salt and black pepper to the taste
- 6.8 g smoked paprika
- 30 g cornstarch
- Cooking spray

Preparation
1. Grease your air fryer's basket with cooking spray and heat the fryer at 187 degrees C.
2. In a bowl, mix tofu with salt, pepper, smoked paprika and cornstarch and toss well.
3. Add tofu to your air fryer's basket and cook for 12 minutes, shaking the fryer every 4 minutes.
4. Divide into bowls and serve for breakfast.
5. Enjoy!

Nutritional information: calories 172, fat 4g, fiber 7g, carbs 12g, protein 4g

24. DELICIOUS TOFU AND

MUSHROOMS

Preparation time: 10 minutes
Cooking time: 10 minutes
Servings: 2

Ingredients:
- 1 tofu block, pressed and cut into medium pieces
- 119 g panko bread crumbs
- Salt and black pepper to the taste
- 2.5 ml flour
- 1 egg
- 6 g mushrooms, minced

Preparation
1. In a mixing bowl, whisk together the egg, mushrooms, flour, salt, and pepper.

2. Dip tofu in egg mixture, then in panko bread crumbs, then in your air fryer for 10 minutes at 176 degrees Celsius.
3. Serve them immediately for breakfast.
4. Enjoy!

Nutritional information: calories 142, fat 4g, fiber 6g, carbs 8g, protein 3g

25. CHEESY BREAKFAST BREAD

Preparation time: 10 minutes
Cooking time: 8 minutes
Servings: 3

Ingredients:
- 6 bread slices
- 70 g butter, melted
- 3 garlic cloves, minced
- 31 g sun dried tomato pesto
- 225 g mozzarella cheese, grated

Preparation
1. Place the bread slices on a work surface.
2. Spread butter all over, then divide tomato paste, garlic, and shredded cheese on top.
3. Cook the bread slices in a heated air fryer for 8 minutes at 176 degrees C.
4. Serve for breakfast on individual dishes.
5. Enjoy!

Nutritional information: calories 187, fat 5g, fiber 6g, carbs 8g, protein 3g

26. EGG WHITE OMELET

Preparation time: 10 minutes
Cooking time: 15 minutes
Servings: 4

Ingredients:
- 223 g egg whites
- 50 g tomato, chopped
- 30 ml skim milk
- 25 g mushrooms, chopped
- 6 g chives, chopped
- Salt and black pepper to the taste

Preparation

1. In a mixing bowl, combine egg whites, tomato, milk, mushrooms, chives, salt, and pepper, stir well, and pour into the pan of your air fryer.
2. Cook for 15 minutes at 160°C, then cool, slice, divide among plates, and serve.
3. Enjoy!

Nutritional information: calories 100, fat 3g, fiber 6g, carbs 7g, carbs 4g

27. ARTICHOKE FRITTATA

Preparation time: 10 minutes
Cooking time: 15 minutes
Servings: 6

Ingredients:
- 3 canned artichokes hearts, drained and chopped
- 30 ml olive oil
- 2.5 ml oregano, dried
- Salt and black pepper to the taste
- 6 eggs, whisked

Preparation

1. Whisk together the artichokes, oregano, salt, pepper, and eggs in a mixing dish.
2. Cook at 160 degrees C for 15 minutes after adding the oil to the pan of your air fryer.
3. Serve the frittata on plates for breakfast.
4. Enjoy!

Nutritional information: calories 136, fat 6g, fiber 6g, carbs 9g, protein 4g

28. ONION FRITTATA

Preparation time: 10 minutes
Cooking time: 20 minutes
Servings: 6

Ingredients:
- 10 eggs, whisked
- 15 ml olive oil
- 453 g small potatoes, chopped
- 2 yellow onions, chopped
- Salt and black pepper to the taste
- 28 gram cheddar cheese, grated
- 120 g sour cream

Preparation

1. In a large mixing bowl, whisk together the eggs, potatoes, onions, salt, pepper, cheese, and sour cream.
2. Grease the pan of your air fryer with oil, add the egg mixture, and cook for 20 minutes at 160 degrees C.
3. Slice the frittata and divide it among dishes for breakfast.
4. Enjoy!

Nutritional information: calories 231, fat 5g, fiber 7g, carbs 8g, protein 4g

29. LONG BEANS OMELET

Preparation time: 10 minutes
Cooking time: 10 minutes
Servings: 3

Ingredients:
- 3 g soy sauce
- 15 ml olive oil
- 3 eggs, whisked
- A pinch of salt and black pepper
- 4 garlic cloves, minced
- 4 long beans, trimmed and sliced

Preparation

1. Whisk eggs with a bit of salt, black pepper, and soy sauce in a mixing dish.
2. Preheat your air fryer to 160°C, add the oil and garlic, swirl, and brown for 1 minute.
3. Cook for 10 minutes after adding the long beans and egg mixture.
4. Serve the omelette on dishes for breakfast.
5. Enjoy!

Nutritional information: calories 200, fat 3g, fiber 7g, carbs 9g, protein 3g

30. FRENCH BEANS AND EGG BREAKFAST MIX

Preparation time: 10 minutes
Cooking time: 10 minutes
Servings: 3

Ingredients:
- 2 eggs, whisked
- 3 g soy sauce
- 15 ml olive oil
- 4 garlic cloves, minced
- 85 g French beans, trimmed and sliced diagonally
- Salt and white pepper to the taste

Preparation
1. In a mixing bowl, whisk together the eggs, soy sauce, salt, and pepper.
2. Preheat your air fryer to 160°C, then add the oil and heat it up as well.
3. Add garlic and brown for 1 minute.
4. Cook for 10 minutes after adding the French beans and egg mixture.
5. Serve for breakfast on individual dishes.
6. Enjoy!

Nutritional information: calories 182, fat 3g, fiber 6g, carbs 8g, protein 3g

31. CREAMY BREAKFAST TOFU

Preparation time: 15 minutes
Cooking time: 20 minutes
Servings: 4

Ingredients:
- 1 block firm tofu, pressed and cubed
- 5 ml rice vinegar
- 33 g soy sauce
- 10 ml sesame oil
- 10 g potato starch
- 285 g Greek yogurt

Preparation
1. Toss tofu cubes with vinegar, soy sauce, and oil in a mixing basin for 15 minutes.
2. Toss tofu cubes with potato starch, add to air fryer, heat to 187°C, and cook for 20 minutes, shaking halfway.
3. Divide into bowls and serve with Greek yoghurt on the side for breakfast.
4. Enjoy!

Nutritional information: calories 110, fat 4g, fiber 5g, carbs 8g, protein 4g

32. GARLIC POTATOES WITH BACON

Preparation time: 10 minutes
Cooking time: 20 minutes
Servings: 4

Ingredients:
- 4 potatoes, peeled and cut into medium cubes
- 6 garlic cloves, minced
- 4 bacon slices, chopped
- 2 rosemary springs, chopped
- 15 ml olive oil
- Salt and black pepper to the taste
- 2 eggs, whisked

Preparation
1. Whisk together the oil, potatoes, garlic, bacon, rosemary, salt, pepper, and eggs in the pan of your air fryer.
2. Cook potatoes for 20 minutes at 204 degrees C, then divide everything on plates and serve for breakfast.
3. Enjoy!

Nutritional information: calories 211, fat 3g, fiber 5g, carbs 8g, protein 5g

33. HAM ROLLS

Preparation time: 10 minutes
Cooking time: 10 minutes
Servings: 4

Ingredients:
- 1 sheet puff pastry
- 4 handful gruyere cheese, grated
- 60 g mustard
- 8 ham slices, chopped

Preparation
1. On a work area, roll out puff pastry, divide the cheese, ham, and mustard, roll tight, and cut into medium rounds.
2. Place all of the rolls in an air fryer and cook for 10 minutes at 187° C.
3. Serve the rolls on plates for breakfast.
4. Enjoy!

Nutritional information: calories 182, fat 4g, fiber 7g, carbs 9g, protein 8g

34. BREAKFAST PEA TORTILLA

Preparation time: 10 minutes
Cooking time: 7 minutes
Servings: 8

Ingredients:
- 454 g baby peas
- 57 g butter
- 367 g yogurt
- 8 eggs
- 13 g mint, chopped
- Salt and black pepper to the taste

Preparation
1. Heat the butter in a skillet that fits your air fryer over medium heat, then add the peas, stir, and cook for a couple of minutes.
2. Meanwhile, whisk together half of the yoghurt, salt, pepper, eggs, and mint in a mixing bowl.
3. Pour this over the peas, stir, and place in your air fryer for 7 minutes at 176° C.
4. Spread the remaining yoghurt over the tortilla, slice, and serve.
5. Enjoy!

Nutritional information: calories 192, fat 5g, fiber 4g, carbs 8g, protein 7g

35. ESPRESSO OATMEAL

Preparation time: 10 minutes
Cooking time: 17 minutes
Servings: 4

Ingredients:

- 237 ml milk
- 160 g steel cut oats
- 592 ml cups water
- 25 g sugar
- 5 ml espresso powder
- 10 ml vanilla extract

Preparation
1. In a pan that fits your air fryer, mix oats with water, sugar, milk and espresso powder, stir, introduce in your air fryer and cook at 182 degrees C for 17 minutes.
2. Add vanilla extract, stir, leave everything aside for 5 minutes, divide into bowls and serve for breakfast.
3. Enjoy!

Nutritional information: calories 261, fat 7, fiber 6, carbs 39, protein 6

36. RICE , ALMONDS AND RAISINS

PUDDING

Preparation time: 5 minutes
Cooking time: 8 minutes
Servings: 4

Ingredients:
- 202 g brown rice
- 37 g coconut chips
- 237 ml milk
- 473 ml water
- 118 ml maple syrup
- 40 g raisins
- 36 g almonds
- A pinch of cinnamon powder

Preparation
1. Put the rice in a pan that fits your air fryer, add the water, and cook over medium high heat until the rice is soft and Drain.
2. Stir in the milk, coconut chips, almonds, raisins, cinnamon, and maple syrup. Place in the air fryer and cook at 182 degrees C for 8 minutes.
3. Serve rice pudding in individual dishes.
4. Enjoy!

Nutritional information: calories 251, fat 6g, fiber 8g, carbs 39g, protein 12g

37. DATES AND MILLET PUDDING

Preparation time: 10 minutes
Cooking time: 15 minutes
Servings: 4

Ingredients:
- 414 ml milk
- 207 ml water
- 150 g millet
- 4 dates, pitted
- Honey for serving

Preparation
1. Place the millet in a pan that fits your air fryer, add the dates, milk, and water, stir, and cook at 182 degrees C for 15 minutes.
2. Divide across plates, drizzle with honey, and serve for breakfast.
3. Enjoy!

Nutritional information: calories 231, fat 6g, fiber 6g, carbs 18g, protein 6g

38. CHERRIES RISOTTO

Preparation time: 10 minutes
Cooking time: 12 minutes
Servings: 4

Ingredients:
- 301 g Arborio rice
- 7.5 ml cinnamon powder
- 65 g brown sugar
- A pinch of salt
- 28 g butter
- 2 apples, cored and sliced
- 237 ml juice
- 707 ml milk
- 80 g cherries, dried

Preparation
1. Heat up a pan that fit your air fryer with the butter over medium heat, add rice, stir and cook for 4-5 minutes.

2. Add sugar, apples, apple juice, milk, cinnamon and cherries, stir, introduce in your air fryer and cook at 176 degrees C for 8 minutes.
3. Divide into bowls and serve for breakfast.
4. Enjoy!

Nutritional information: calories 162, fat 12g, fiber 6g, carbs 23g, protein 8g

39. CINNAMON AND CREAM CHEESE OATS

Preparation time: 10 minutes
Cooking time: 25 minutes
Servings: 4

Ingredients:
- 160 g steel oats
- 710 ml milk
- 14 g butter
- 119 g raisins
- 5 ml cinnamon powder
- 50 g brown sugar
- 25 g white sugar
- 57 g cream cheese, soft

Preparation
1. Heat up a pan that fits your air fryer with the butter over medium heat, add oats, stir and toast them for 3 minutes.
2. Add milk and raisins, stir, introduce in your air fryer and cook at 182 degrees C for 20 minutes.
3. Meanwhile, in a bowl, mix cinnamon with brown sugar and stir.
4. In a second bowl, mix white sugar with cream cheese and whisk.
5. Divide oats into bowls and top each with cinnamon and cream cheese.
6. Enjoy!

Nutritional information: calories 152, fat 6g, fiber 6g, carbs 25g, protein 7g

40. RED PEPPER FRITTATA

Preparation time: 10mins
Cooking time: 15mins
Servings: 2
Ingredients
- 6 medium British Lion eggs
- 1 large red pepper
- 1 small white onion
- 2 new potatoes
- 1 large handful of Gruyere cheese or mature Cheddar cheese
- Salt and pepper to season

Preparation
1. Preheat the airfryer to 200 degrees Celsius.
2. Boil the fresh potatoes in a pan until they are tender (you should be able to put a knife through them easily).
3. Meanwhile, carefully chop the onion, grate the cheese, and cut the peppers.
4. Whisk the eggs and season with salt and pepper to taste.
5. In a frying pan with a metal handle, heat a tiny amount of oil (very important). Cook the onions and peppers for about five minutes on medium to low heat, or until tender.
6. When the potatoes are soft, drain them and add them to the pan, spacing them equally.
7. Add the eggs right away, followed by the cheese. Allow to cook for a few minutes before placing the pan in the airfryer to finish cooking. This should only take about five minutes, and the top should be golden brown.
8. Remove from the airfryer with care (remember the metal handle) and let aside for a few minutes to allow the frittata to settle before carefully turning it out onto a dish.
9. It can be eaten hot or cold and goes well with a tomato and red onion salad. It's definitely worth a go, and it only takes 25 minutes to prepare.

Nutritional information: calories 189, Carbs 14g, Fat 9.9g, Protein 12g.

41. CREAMY EGGS

Preparation time: 10 minutes
Cooking time: 12 minutes
Servings: 4

Ingredients:
- 9 g butter, soft
- 2 ham slices
- 4 eggs
- 30 g heavy cream
- Salt and black pepper to the taste
- 16.9 g parmesan, grated
- 2 g chives, chopped
- A pinch of smoked paprika

Preparation
1. Grease your air fryer's pan with the butter, line it with the ham and add it to your air fryer's basket.
2. In a bowl, mix 1 egg with heavy cream, salt and pepper, whisk well and add over ham.
3. Crack the rest of the eggs in the pan, sprinkle parmesan and cook your mix for 12 minutes at 160 degrees C.
4. Sprinkle paprika and chives all over, divide among plates and serve for breakfast.
5. Enjoy!

Nutritional information: calories 263, fat 5g, fiber 8g, carbs 12g, protein 5g

42. BROCCOLI QUICHE

Preparation time: 10 minutes
Cooking time: 20 minutes
Servings: 2

Ingredients:
- 1 broccoli head, florets separated and steamed
- 1 tomato, chopped
- 3 carrots, chopped and steamed
- 60 g cheddar cheese, grated
- 2 eggs
- 60 ml milk
- 1.28 g parsley, chopped
- 1 g thyme, chopped
- Salt and black pepper to the taste

Preparation
1. In a mixing dish, whisk together the eggs, milk, parsley, thyme, salt, and pepper.

2. In your air fryer, combine broccoli, carrots, and tomato.
3. Spread the egg mixture on top, then cover and simmer at 176° C for 20 minutes.
4. Serve for breakfast on individual dishes.
5. Enjoy!

Nutritional information: calories 214, fat 4g, fiber 7g, carbs 12g, protein 3g

43. MUSHROOM QUICHE

Preparation time: 10 minutes
Cooking time: 10 minutes
Servings: 4
Ingredients:
- 17 ml flour
- 14 g butter, soft
- 9 inch pie dough
- 2 button mushrooms, chopped
- 37 g ham, chopped
- 3 eggs
- 1 small yellow onion, chopped
- 76 g heavy cream
- A pinch of nutmeg, ground
- Salt and black pepper to the taste
- 2.5 ml thyme, dried
- 56 g Swiss cheese, grated

Preparation
1. Dust a working surface with the flour and roll the pie dough.
2. Press in on the bottom of the pie pan your air fryer has.
3. In a bowl, mix butter with mushrooms, ham, onion, eggs, heavy cream, salt, pepper, thyme and nutmeg and whisk well.
4. Add this over the pie crust, spread, sprinkle Swiss cheese all over and place pie pan in your air fryer.
5. Cook your quiche at 204 degrees C for 10 minutes.
6. Slice and serve for breakfast.
7. Enjoy!

Nutritional information: calories 212, fat 4g, fiber 6g, carbs 7g, protein 7g

44. BLACKBERRY FRENCH TOAST

Preparation time: 10 minutes
Cooking time: 20 minutes
Servings: 6

Ingredients:
- 407 g blackberry jam, warm
- 340 g bread loaf, cubed
- 226 g cream cheese, cubed
- 4 eggs
- 5 ml cinnamon powder
- 450 ml half and half
- 100 g brown sugar
- 5 ml vanilla extract
- Cooking spray

Preparation
1. Grease your air fryer with cooking spray and heat it up at 148 degrees C.
2. Add blueberry jam to the bottom, then half of the bread cubes, cream cheese, and the remaining bread.
3. In a mixing basin, whisk together the eggs, half & half, cinnamon, sugar, and vanilla extract. Pour over the bread mix.
4. Cook for 20 minutes, then divide among plates for breakfast.
5. Enjoy!

Nutritional information: calories 215, fat 6g, fiber 9g, carbs 16g, protein 6g

45. TURKEY BURRITO

Preparation time: 10 minutes
Cooking time: 10 minutes
Servings: 2

Ingredients:
- 4 slices turkey breast already cooked
- ½ red bell pepper, sliced
- 2 eggs
- 1 small avocado, peeled, pitted and sliced
- 36 g salsa
- Salt and black pepper to the taste
- 225 g mozzarella cheese, grated
- Tortillas for serving

Preparation

1. Whisk eggs in a bowl with salt and pepper to taste, then pour them into a pan and place it in the air fryer basket.
2. Cook for 5 minutes at 204°C, then remove pan from fryer and transfer eggs to a plate.
3. Arrange tortillas on a work surface and distribute eggs, turkey meat, bell pepper, cheese, salsa, and avocado among them.
4. Roll your burritos and place them in the air fryer, which has been lined with tin foil.
5. Heat the burritos for 3 minutes at 149 degrees C, then divide them onto plates and serve.
6. Enjoy!

Nutritional information: calories 349, fat 23g, fiber 11g, carbs 20g, protein 21g

46. POLENTA BITES

Preparation time: 10 minutes
Cooking time: 20 minutes
Servings: 4

Ingredients:
For the polenta:
- 14 g butter
- 237 ml cornmeal
- 710 ml water
- Salt and black pepper to the taste

For the polenta bites:
- 30 ml powdered sugar
- Cooking spray

Preparation

1. Cornmeal, water, butter, salt, and pepper should be combined in a skillet and cooked for 10 minutes before being removed from the heat and kept in the refrigerator to cool.
2. 15 ml of polenta should be scooped, formed into a ball, and placed on a work surface.
3. Repeat with the remaining polenta, place all the balls in your air fryer's cooking basket, coat them with cooking spray, cover the pan, and cook for 8 minutes at 193 degrees C.
4. To serve polenta nibbles for breakfast, arrange them on plates and cover with sugar.
5. Enjoy!

Nutritional information: calories 231, fat 7, fiber 8, carbs 12, protein 4

SNACKS AND APPETIZER

RECIPE

47. ROASTED BELL PEPPER ROLLS

Preparation time: 10 minutes
Cooking time: 10 minutes
Servings: 8

Ingredients:
- 1 yellow bell pepper, halved
- 1 orange bell pepper, halved
- Salt and black pepper to the taste
- 113 g feta cheese, crumbled
- 1 green onion, chopped
- 6 g oregano, chopped

Preparation
1. Whisk together the cheese, onion, oregano, salt, and pepper in a mixing bowl.
2. Cook for 10 minutes at 204 degrees C in the air fryer basket, then transfer to a cutting board to cool and peel.
3. Roll each bell pepper half in the cheese mixture, attach with toothpicks, place on a tray, and serve as an appetiser.
4. Enjoy!

Nutritional information: calories 170, fat 1g, fiber 2g, carbs 8g, protein 5g

48. AIR FRIED DILL PICKLES

Preparation time: 10 minutes
Cooking time: 5 minutes
Servings: 4

Ingredients:
- 454 g jarred dill pickles, cut into wedges, and pat dried
- 63 g white flour
- 1 egg
- 59 ml milk
- 5 ml garlic powder
- 2.5 ml sweet paprika
- Cooking spray
- 60 ml ranch sauce

Preparation
1. In a mixing dish, whisk together the milk and the egg.
2. In another basin, mix together the flour, salt, garlic powder, and paprika.
3. Dip pickles in flour, then in egg mixture, and last in flour before placing them in the air fryer.
4. Cook pickle wedges at 204 degrees C for 5 minutes, then transfer to a bowl and serve with ranch sauce on the side.
5. Enjoy!

Nutritional information: calories 109, fat 2g, fiber 2g, carbs 10g, protein 4g

49. SALMON PARTY PATTIES

Preparation time: 10 minutes
Cooking time: 22 minutes
Servings: 4

Ingredients:
- 3 big potatoes, boiled, drained, and mashed
- 1 big salmon fillet, skinless, boneless
- 8 g parsley, chopped
- 7 g dill, chopped
- Salt and black pepper to the taste
- 1 egg
- 15 g bread crumbs
- Cooking spray

Preparation
1. Cook the fish in the air fryer basket for 10 minutes at 182 degrees C.
2. Cool the salmon on a chopping board before flaking it into a bowl.
3. Stir in the mashed potatoes, salt, pepper, dill, parsley, egg, and bread crumbs, and form 8 patties from the mixture.
4. Place the salmon patties in the basket of your air fryer, brush with cooking oil, and cook at 182 degrees C for 12 minutes, flipping halfway. Transfer to a tray and serve as an appetiser.
5. Enjoy!

Nutritional information: calories 231, fat 3, fiber 7, carbs 14, protein 4

50. EGG WHITE CHIPS

Preparation time: 5 minutes
Cooking time: 8 minutes
Servings: 2

Ingredients:
- 7 ml water
- 11 g parmesan, shredded
- 4 eggs whites
- Salt and black pepper to the taste

Preparation
1. Whisk egg whites with salt, pepper, and water in a mixing basin.
2. Spoon this into a muffin tin that fits your air fryer, top with cheese, and cook at 176 degrees Celsius for 8 minutes.
3. Serve the egg white chips as a snack on a plate.
4. Enjoy!

Nutritional information: calories 180, fat 2g, fiber 1g, carbs 12g, protein 7g

51. TUNA CAKES

Preparation time: 10 minutes
Cooking time: 10 minutes
Servings: 12

Ingredients:
- 425 g canned tuna, drain and flaked
- 3 eggs
- 2.5 ml dill, dried
- 2.5 ml parsley, dried
- 26 g red onion, chopped
- 5 ml garlic powder
- Salt and black pepper to the taste
- Cooking spray

Preparation
1. In a mixing basin, combine tuna, salt, pepper, dill, parsley, onion, garlic powder, and eggs; whisk well and shape into medium cakes.

2. Place tuna cakes in the basket of your air fryer, spray with cooking oil and cook at 176 °C for 10 minutes, flipping halfway.
3. Serve as an appetiser by arranging them on a dish.
4. Enjoy!

Nutritional information: calories 140, fat 2g, fiber 1g, carbs 8g, protein 6g

52. SAUSAGE BALLS

Preparation time: 10 minutes
Cooking time: 15 minutes
Servings: 9
Ingredients:
- 113 g sausage meat, ground
- Salt and black pepper to the taste
- 4 g sage
- 5 ml garlic, minced
- 1 small onion, chopped
- 7 g breadcrumbs

Preparation
1. In a mixing dish, combine sausage, salt, pepper, sage, garlic, onion, and breadcrumbs; toss well and shape into small balls.
2. Put them in air fryer basket, cook at 182 degrees Celsius for 15 minutes, then divide into dishes and serve as a snack.
3. Enjoy!

Nutritional information: calories 130g, fat 7g, fiber 1g, carbs 13g, protein 4g

53. CAULIFLOWER BARS

Preparation time: 10 minutes
Cooking time: 25 minutes
Servings: 12

Ingredients:
- 1 big cauliflower head, florets separated
- 112 g mozzarella, shredded
- 60 ml egg whites
- 1.25 ml Italian seasoning
- Salt and black pepper to the taste

Preparation

1. In a food processor, pulse cauliflower florets until perfectly chopped. Spread on a lined baking sheet that fits your air fryer, place in the fryer, and cook at 182 degrees Celsius for 10 minutes.
2. Transfer cauliflower to a mixing bowl, season with salt, pepper, cheese, egg whites, and Italian seasoning, and combine well. Spread this into a rectangular pan that fits your air fryer, press well, and cook at 182 degrees C for 15 minutes more.
3. Cut the bars into 12 pieces, place them on a tray, and serve as a snack.
4. Enjoy!

Nutritional information: calories 50, fat 1g, fiber 2g, carbs 3g, protein 3g

54. SHRIMP MUFFINS

Preparation time: 10 minutes
Cooking time: 26 minutes
Servings: 6

Ingredients:
- 1 spaghetti squash, peeled and halved
- 28 g mayonnaise
- 28 g mozzarella, shredded
- 227 g shrimp, peeled, cooked, and chopped
- 126 g cups panko
- 5 ml parsley flakes
- 1 garlic clove, minced
- Salt and black pepper to the taste
- Cooking spray

Preparation

1. Place squash halves in your air fryer and cook at 176°C for 16 minutes, then set aside to cool and scrape flesh into a basin.
2. Stir in the salt, pepper, parsley flakes, panko, shrimp, mayo, and mozzarella.
3. Cooking sprays a muffin pan that fits your air fryer and distributes the squash and shrimp mixture into each cup.
4. Place them in your air fryer and cook for 10 minutes at 360 degrees F.
5. Serve the muffins as a snack on a tray.
6. Enjoy!

Nutritional information: calories 60g, fat 2g, fiber 0.4g, carbs 4g, protein 4g

55. CAJUN SHRIMP APPETIZER

Preparation time: 10 minutes
Cooking time: 5 minutes
Servings: 2

Ingredients:
- 20 tiger shrimp, peeled and deveined
- Salt and black pepper to the taste
- 2.5 ml old bay seasoning
- 15 ml olive oil
- 1.25 ml smoked paprika

Preparation

1. Toss shrimp in a bowl with oil, salt, pepper, old bay spice, and paprika to coat.
2. Cook the shrimp in the air fryer basket for 5 minutes at 198 degrees C.
3. Serve as an appetiser by arranging them on a dish.
4. Enjoy!

Nutritional information: calories 162, fat 6g, fiber 4g, carbs 8g, protein 14g

56. CHICKEN DIP

Preparation time: 10 minutes
Cooking time: 25 minutes
Servings: 10

Ingredients:
- 43 g butter, melted
- 245 g yogurt
- 340 g cream cheese
- 360 g chicken meat, cooked and shredded
- 10 ml curry powder
- 4 scallions, chopped
- 170 g Monterey jack cheese, grated
- 53 g cup raisins
- 60 g cilantro, chopped
- 46 g almonds, sliced
- Salt and black pepper to the taste
- 136 g chutney

Preparation
1. In a mixing dish, combine cream cheese and yoghurt and whisk with an electric mixer.
2. Stir in the curry powder, scallions, chicken meat, raisins, cheese, cilantro, salt, and pepper.
3. Spread this onto a baking dish that fits your air fryer, top with almonds, bake at 149 degrees C for 25 minutes, split into bowls, top with chutney, and serve as an appetiser.
4. Enjoy!

Nutritional information: calories 240, fat 10g, fiber 2g, carbs 24g, protein 12g

57. CHICKEN ROLLS

Preparation time: 2 hours and 10 minutes
Cooking time: 10 minutes
Servings: 12

Ingredients:
- 113 g blue cheese, crumbled
- 280 g chicken, cooked and chopped
- Salt and black pepper to the taste
- 2 green onions, chopped
- 2 celery stalks, finely chopped
- 118 ml tomato sauce
- 12 egg roll wrappers
- Cooking spray

Preparation
1. In a mixing dish, combine the chicken meat, blue cheese, salt, pepper, green onions, celery, and tomato sauce; swirl well and chill for 2 hours.
2. Place egg wrappers on a work surface, divide the chicken mixture among them, then roll and seal the edges.
3. Place the rolls in the basket of your air fryer, drizzle with cooking oil, and cook at 176 degrees C for 10 minutes, flipping halfway.
4. Enjoy!

Nutritional information: calories 220, fat 7g, fiber 2g, carbs 14g, protein 10g

58. BUFFALO CAULIFLOWER SNACK

Preparation time: 10 minutes
Cooking time: 15 minutes
Servings: 4

Ingredients:
- 64 g cauliflower florets
- 64 g panko bread crumbs
- 57 g butter, melted
- 60 ml buffalo sauce
- Mayonnaise for serving

Preparation
1. Whisk together buffalo sauce and butter in a mixing basin.
2. Dip cauliflower florets in this mixture, then coat them with panko bread crumbs.
3. Put them in your air fryer basket, then cook for 15 minutes at 176° C.
4. Serve on a dish with mayonnaise on the side.
5. Enjoy!

Nutritional information: calories 241, fat 4g, fiber 7g, carbs 8g, protein 4g

59. FISH NUGGETS

Preparation time: 10 minutes
Cooking time: 12 minutes
Servings: 4

Ingredients:
- 794 g fish fillets, skinless and cut into medium pieces
- Salt and black pepper to the taste
- 40 g flour
- 1 egg, whisked
- 74 ml water
- 85 g panko bread crumbs
- 15 ml garlic powder
- 6.8 g smoked paprika
- 58 g homemade mayonnaise
- Lemon juice from ½ lemon
- 1 g dill, dried
- Cooking spray

Preparation
1. Mix flour and water in a mixing bowl.
2. Whisk in the egg, salt, and pepper.
3. In a separate bowl, combine panko, garlic powder, and paprika and toss well.
4. Dip fish in flour and egg mixture, then in panko mixture, place in the air fryer basket, spray with oil and cook at 204 degrees C for 12 minutes.
5. Meanwhile, whisk together the mayonnaise, dill, and lemon juice in a mixing dish.
6. Serve the fish nuggets on a dish with dill mayo on the side.
7. Enjoy!

Nutritional information: calories 332, fat 12g, fiber 6g, carbs 17g, protein 15g

60. STUFFED PEPPERS

Preparation time: 10 minutes
Cooking time: 8 minutes
Servings: 8

Ingredients:
- 8 small bell peppers, tops cut off and seeds removed
- 15 ml olive oil
- Salt and black pepper to the taste
- 100 g goat cheese, cut into 8 pieces

Preparation
1. Toss the cheese with the oil, salt, and pepper in a mixing bowl.
2. Stuff each pepper with goat cheese, place in an air fryer basket and cook for 8 minutes at 204 degrees C. Arrange on a dish and serve as an appetiser.
3. Enjoy!

Nutritional information: calories 120, fat 1g, fiber 1g, carbs 12g, protein 8g

61. BANANA SNACK

Preparation time: 10 minutes
Cooking time: 5 minutes
Servings: 8
Ingredients:

- 16 baking cups crust
- 60 g peanut butter
- 120 g chocolate chips
- 1 banana, peeled and sliced into 16 pieces
- 15 ml vegetable oil

Preparation
1. Put chocolate chips in a small pot, heat up over low heat, stir until it melts and take off the heat.
2. In a bowl, mix peanut butter with coconut oil and whisk well.
3. Spoon 3 g chocolate mix in a cup, add 1 banana slice, and top with 5 g butter mix
4. Repeat with the rest of the cups, place them all into a dish that fits your air fryer, cook at 160 degrees C for 5 minutes, transfer to a freezer, and keep there until you serve them as a snack.
5. Enjoy!

Nutritional information: calories 70, fat 4g, fiber 1g, carbs 10g, protein 1g

62. COCONUT CHICKEN BITES

Preparation time: 10 minutes
Cooking time: 13 minutes
Servings: 4

Ingredients:
- 10 ml garlic powder
- 2 eggs
- Salt and black pepper to the taste
- 75 g panko bread crumbs
- 72 g coconut, shredded
- Cooking spray
- 8 chicken tenders

Preparation
1. Whisk eggs with salt, pepper, and garlic powder in a mixing basin.
2. In a separate bowl, combine the coconut and panko and whisk thoroughly.
3. Dip chicken tenders in egg mixture, then in coconut mixture.
4. Spray the chicken bites with cooking spray, set them in the air fryer basket, and cook for 10 minutes at 176 degrees C.

5. Serve as an appetiser by arranging them on a dish.
6. Enjoy!

Nutritional information: calories 252, fat 4g, fiber 2g, carbs 14g, protein 24g

63. SHRIMP AND CHESTNUT ROLLS

Preparation time: 10 minutes
Cooking time: 15 minutes
Servings: 4

Ingredients:
- 226 g already cooked shrimp, chopped
- 236 ml water chestnuts, chopped
- 226 g shiitake mushrooms, chopped
- 180 g cabbage, chopped
- 30 ml olive oil
- 1 garlic clove, minced
- 2 g ginger, grated
- 3 scallions, chopped
- Salt and black pepper to the taste
- 15 ml water
- 1 egg yolk
- 6 spring roll wrappers

Preparation
1. Heat the oil in a skillet over medium-high heat, then add the cabbage, shrimp, chestnuts, mushrooms, garlic, ginger, scallions, salt, & pepper and cook for 2 minutes.
2. In a mixing bowl, whisk together the egg and the water.
3. Arrange the roll wrappers on a work surface, divide the shrimp and veggie mixture among them, seal the edges with egg wash, set them all in the basket of your air fryer, cook at 182 degrees C for 15 minutes, remove to a platter, and serve as an appetiser.
4. Enjoy!

Nutritional information: calories 140, fat 3g, fiber 1g, carbs 12g, protein 3g

64. POTATO SPREAD

Preparation time: 10 minutes
Cooking time: 10 minutes

Servings: 10

Ingredients:
- 540 g canned garbanzo beans, drained
- 133 g sweet potatoes, peeled and chopped
- 60 ml tahini
- 30 ml lemon juice
- 15 ml olive oil
- 5 garlic cloves, minced
- 2.5 ml cumin, ground
- 30 ml water
- A pinch of salt and white pepper

Preparation
1. Put the potatoes in your air fryer, basket cook at 182 degrees Celsius for 15 minutes, then cool, peel, and puree in a food processor. basket,
2. Pulse in the sesame paste, garlic, beans, lemon juice, cumin, water, and oil.
3. Add salt & pepper to taste, pulse one more, divide into dishes, and serve.
4. Enjoy!

Nutritional information: calories 200, fat 3g, fiber 10g, carbs 20g, protein 11g

65. SALMON MEATBALLS

Preparation time: 10 minutes
Cooking time: 12 minutes
Servings: 4

Ingredients:
- 5 g cilantro, minced
- 454 g salmon, skinless and chopped
- 1 small yellow onion, chopped
- 1 egg white
- Salt and black pepper to the taste
- 2 garlic cloves, minced
- 2.5 ml paprika
- 26 g panko
- 2.5 ml oregano, ground
- Cooking spray

Preparation
1. In a food processor, combine salmon, onion, cilantro, egg white, garlic cloves, salt, pepper, paprika, and oregano, and pulse to combine.

2. Blend in the panko and form meatballs with your palms from this mixture.
3. Place them in your basket of your air fryer, spray with cooking spray, and cook at 160° C for 12 minutes, shaking the fryer halfway through.
4. Arrange the meatballs on a dish as an appetiser.
5. Enjoy!

Nutritional information: calories 289, fat 12g, fiber 3g, carbs 22g, protein 23g

66. HERBED TOMATOES APPETIZER

Preparation time: 10 minutes
Cooking time: 20 minutes
Servings: 2

Ingredients:
- 2 tomatoes, halved
- Cooking spray
- Salt and black pepper to the taste
- 5 ml g parsley, dried
- 5 ml g basil, dried
- 5 ml oregano, dried
- 5 ml rosemary, dried

Preparation
1. Cooking oil should be sprayed on tomato halves before seasoning with salt, pepper, parsley, basil, oregano, and rosemary.
2. Place them in air fryer basket and cook for 20 minutes at 160° C.
3. Serve as an appetiser by arranging them on a dish.
4. Enjoy!

Nutritional information: calories 100, fat 1g, fiber 1g, carbs 4g, protein 1g

67. ZUCCHINI CAKES

Preparation time: 10 minutes
Cooking time: 12 minutes
Servings: 12

Ingredients:
- Cooking spray
- 70 g dill, chopped

- 1 egg
- 65 g whole wheat flour
- Salt and black pepper to the taste
- 1 yellow onion, chopped
- 2 garlic cloves, minced
- 3 zucchinis, grated

Preparation
1. In a mixing bowl, combine zucchini, garlic, onion, flour, salt, pepper, egg, and dill; whisk well. Form small patties from this mixture, spray with cooking spray and cook at 187 degrees C for 6 minutes on each side.
2. Serve them immediately as a snack.
3. Enjoy!

Nutritional information: calories 60, fat 1g, fiber 2g, carbs 6g, protein 2g

68. PUMPKIN MUFFINS

Preparation time: 10 minutes
Cooking time: 15 minutes
Servings: 18

Ingredients:
- 57 g butter
- 169 g pumpkin puree
- 20 g flaxseed meal
- 34 g flour
- 100 g sugar
- 2.5 ml nutmeg, ground
- 5 ml cinnamon powder
- 2.5 ml baking soda
- 1 egg
- 2.5 ml baking powder

Preparation
1. In a mixing bowl, combine the butter, pumpkin puree, and egg.
2. Stir in the flaxseed meal, flour, sugar, baking soda, baking powder, nutmeg, and cinnamon.
3. Fill a muffin tin that fits your fryer with this. Bake for 15 minutes at 176 degrees Celsius in the fryer.
4. As a snack, serve muffins cold.
5. Enjoy!

Nutritional information: calories 50, fat 3g, fiber 1g, carbs 2g, protein 2g

69. CHICKEN BREAST ROLLS

Preparation time: 10 minutes
Cooking time: 22 minutes
Servings: 4

Ingredients:
- 60 g baby spinach
- 4 chicken breasts, boneless and skinless
- 116 g sun-dried tomatoes, chopped
- Salt and black pepper to the taste
- 22.5 g Italian seasoning
- 4 mozzarella slices
- A drizzle of olive oil

Preparation
1. Flatten the chicken breasts with a meat tenderizer, then divide the tomatoes, mozzarella, and spinach among them, season with salt, pepper, & Italian seasoning, and roll and seal.
2. Place them in air fryer basket, spray with oil, and cook at 190 degrees C for 17 minutes, flipping once.
3. Serve the chicken rolls as an appetiser on a plate.
4. Enjoy!

Nutritional information: calories 300, fat 1g, fiber 4g, carbs 7g, protein 10g

70. ZUCCHINI CHIPS

Preparation time: 10 minutes
Cooking time: 1 hour
Servings: 6

Ingredients:
- 3 zucchinis, thinly sliced
- Salt and black pepper to the taste
- 30 ml olive oil
- 30 ml balsamic vinegar

Preparation
1. Whisk together the oil, vinegar, salt, & pepper in a mixing bowl.
2. Add zucchini slices, stir to coat well, and place in air fryer for 1 hour at 93 degrees C.
3. As a snack, serve zucchini chips chilled.

4. Enjoy!

Nutritional information: calories 40, fat 3g, fiber 7g, carbs 3g, protein 7g

71. HONEY PARTY WINGS

Preparation time: 1 hour
Cooking time: 12 minutes
Servings: 8

Ingredients:
- 16 chicken wings, halved
- 30 ml soy sauce
- 30 ml honey
- Salt and black pepper to the taste
- 30 ml lime juice

Preparation
1. In a mixing basin, combine chicken wings, soy sauce, honey, salt, pepper, and lime juice; toss well and chill for 1 hour.
2. Cook the chicken wings in an air fryer at 182 degrees Celsius for 12 minutes, flipping halfway through.
3. Serve as an appetiser by arranging them on a dish.
4. Enjoy!

Nutritional information: calories 211, fat 4g, fiber 7g, carbs 14g, protein 3g

72. BEEF ROLLS

Preparation time: 10 minutes
Cooking time: 14 minutes
Servings: 4

Ingredients:
- 900 g beef steak, opened and flattened with a meat tenderizer
- Salt and black pepper to the taste
- 36 g baby spinach
- 85 g red bell pepper, roasted and chopped
- 6 slices provolone cheese
- 45 ml pesto

Preparation

1. Place a flattened beef steak on a cutting board, spread pesto all over, stack cheese in a single layer, and season with salt & pepper to taste.
2. Roll your steak, secure using toothpicks, season with salt and pepper again, place in an air fryer basket, and cook at 204° C for 14 minutes, turning halfway.
3. Allow to cool before cutting into 2-inch smaller rolls, arranging on a tray, and serving as an appetiser.
4. Enjoy!

Nutritional information: calories 230, fat 1g, fiber 3g, carbs 12g, protein 10g

73. JALAPENO BALLS

Preparation time: 10 minutes
Cooking time: 4 minutes
Servings: 3

Ingredients:

- 3 bacon slices, cooked and crumbled
- 85 g cream cheese
- 1.25 ml onion powder
- Salt and black pepper to the taste
- 1 jalapeno pepper, chopped
- 2.5 ml parsley, dried
- 1.25 ml garlic powder

Preparation

1. In a mixing dish, combine cream cheese, jalapeño pepper, onion and garlic powder, parsley, bacon salt, and pepper.
2. Form tiny balls from this mixture set them in the basket of your air fryer, and cook for 4 minutes at 176 degrees C. Arrange on a tray and serve as an appetiser.
3. Enjoy!

Nutritional information: calories 172, fat 4g, fiber 1g, carbs 12g, protein 5g

74. BANANA CHIPS

Preparation time: 10 minutes
Cooking time: 15 minutes
Servings: 4

Ingredients:

- 4 bananas, peeled and sliced
- A pinch of salt
- 2.5 ml turmeric powder
- 2.5 ml chaat masala
- 5 ml olive oil

Preparation

1. Toss banana slices with salt, turmeric, chaat masala, and oil in a mixing dish for 10 minutes.
2. Cook the banana slices in your prepared air fryer at 182 degrees C for 15 minutes, flipping once.
3. As a snack, serve.
4. Enjoy!

Nutritional information: calories 121, fat 1g, fiber 2g, carbs 3g, protein 3g

75. BREAD STICKS

Preparation time: 10 minutes
Cooking time: 10 minutes
Servings: 2

Ingredients:

- 4 bread slices, each cut into 4 sticks
- 2 eggs
- 60 ml milk
- 5 ml cinnamon powder
- 15 ml honey
- 50 g brown sugar
- A pinch of nutmeg

Preparation

1. In a mixing bowl, whisk together the eggs, milk, brown sugar, cinnamon, nutmeg, and honey.
2. Dip bread sticks in this mixture, then place them in the basket of your air fryer and cook for 10 minutes at 182 degrees C.
3. As a snack, divide bread sticks into bowls.
4. Enjoy!

Nutritional information: calories 140, fat 1g, fiber 4g, carbs 8g, protein 4g

76. CRISPY RADISH CHIPS

Preparation time: 10 minutes
Cooking time: 10 minutes
Servings: 4

Ingredients:

- Cooking spray
- 15 radishes, sliced
- Salt and black pepper to the taste
- 3 g chives, chopped

Preparation

1. Arrange radish slices in the basket of your air fryer, spray with cooking oil, season with salt and black pepper to taste, cook at 176° C for 10 minutes, flipping halfway, transfer to dishes, and serve with chives sprinkled on top.
2. Enjoy!

Nutritional information: calories 80, fat 1g, fiber 1g, carbs 1g, protein 1g

77. SPRING ROLLS

Preparation time: 10 minutes
Cooking time: 25 minutes
Servings: 8

Ingredients:

- 2 cups green cabbage, shredded
- 2 yellow onions, chopped
- 1 carrot, grated
- ½ chili pepper, minced
- 6 g ginger, grated
- 3 garlic cloves, minced
- 5 ml sugar
- Salt and black pepper to the taste
- 5 ml soy sauce
- 30 ml olive oil
- 10 spring roll sheets
- 9 g corn flour
- 30 ml water

Preparation

1. Heat the oil in a skillet over medium-heat, then add the cabbage, onions, carrots, chilli pepper, ginger, garlic, sugar, salt, pepper, and soy sauce, stirring well. Cook for about 2-3 mins, then remove from heat and cool.
2. Divide the cabbage mix among the spring roll sheets and roll them up.
3. Mix corn flour and water in a basin, then seal spring rolls with this mixture.
4. Place spring rolls in the basket of your air fryer and cook for 10 minutes at 182 degrees C.
5. Cook for another 10 mins on the other side.
6. Serve as an appetiser, arranged on a dish.
7. Enjoy!

Nutritional information: calories 214, fat 4g, fiber 4g, carbs 12g, protein 4g

78. BROCCOLI PATTIES

Preparation time: 10 minutes
Cooking time: 10 minutes
Servings: 12

Ingredients:

- 4 cups broccoli florets
- 144 g almond flour
- 5 ml paprika
- Salt and black pepper to the taste
- 2 eggs
- 57 g olive oil
- 470 g cheddar cheese, grated
- 5 ml garlic powder
- 2.5 ml apple cider vinegar
- 2.5 ml baking soda

Preparation

1. In a food processor, combine broccoli florets, salt, and pepper, and pulse until smooth. Transfer to a bowl.
2. Stir in the almond flour, salt, pepper, paprika, garlic powder, baking soda, cheese, oil, eggs, and vinegar. Form 12 patties from this mixture.
3. Cook for 10 minutes at 176 degrees Celsius in a preheated air fryer basket.
4. Serve the patties as an appetiser on a plate.
5. Enjoy!

Nutritional information: calories 203, fat 12g, fiber 2g, carbs 14g, protein 2g

79. EMPANADAS

Preparation time: 10 minutes
Cooking time: 25 minutes
Servings: 4

Ingredients:
- 1 package of empanada shells
- 15 ml olive oil
- 454 g beef meat, ground
- 1 yellow onion, chopped
- Salt and black pepper to the taste
- 2 garlic cloves, minced
- 2.5 ml cumin, ground
- 56 g tomato salsa
- 1 egg yolk whisked with 15 ml water
- 1 green bell pepper, chopped

Preparation
1. Heat the oil in a pan over medium-high heat, then add the beef and brown on all sides.
2. Cook for 15 minutes after adding the onion, garlic, salt, pepper, bell pepper, and tomato salsa.
3. Fill empanada shells with cooked meat, brush with egg wash, and seal.
4. Place them in the steamer basket of your air fryer and cook for 10 minutes at 176° C.
5. Serve as an appetiser, arranged on a dish.
6. Enjoy!

Nutritional information: calories 274, fat 17g, fiber 14g, carbs 20g, protein 7g

80. CRAB STICKS

Preparation time: 10 minutes
Cooking time: 12 minutes
Servings: 4

Ingredients:
- 10 crabsticks, halved
- 10 ml sesame oil
- 10 ml Cajun seasoning

Preparation
1. Toss crab sticks in a bowl with sesame oil and Cajun spice, then transfer to an air fryer basket and cook at 176° C for 12 minutes.
2. Serve as an appetiser, arranged on a dish.
3. Enjoy!

Nutritional information: calories 110, fat 0g, fiber 1g, carbs 4g, protein 2g

81. CHICKPEAS SNACK

Preparation time: 10 minutes
Cooking time: 10 minutes
Servings: 4

Ingredients:
- 425 g canned chickpeas, drained
- 2.5 ml g cumin, ground
- 15 ml olive oil
- 5 ml smoked paprika
- Salt and black pepper to the taste

Preparation
1. Toss chickpeas in a basin with oil, cumin, paprika, salt, and pepper to coat, then pour into a fryer basket and cook at 198 degrees C for 10 minutes.
2. Serve as a snack in individual bowls.
3. Enjoy!

Nutritional information: calories 140, fat 1g, fiber 6g, carbs 20g, protein 6g

82. SPINACH BALLS

Preparation time: 10 minutes
Cooking time: 7 minutes
Servings: 30

Ingredients:
- 57 g butter, melted
- 2 eggs
- 250 g flour
- 454 g spinach
- 50 g feta cheese, crumbled
- 1.25 ml g nutmeg, ground
- 30 g parmesan, grated
- Salt and black pepper to the taste
- 15 ml onion powder
- 15 g whipping cream
- 5 ml garlic powder

Preparation
1. Blend spinach, butter, eggs, flour, feta cheese, parmesan, nutmeg, whipped cream, salt, pepper, onion, and garlic pepper in a blender until smooth. Place in the freezer for 10 minutes.
2. Form 30 spinach balls, lay them in the basket of your air fryer, and cook for 7 minutes at 149 degrees C.
3. Serve as an appetiser during a party.
4. Enjoy!

Nutritional information: calories 60, fat 5g, fiber 1g, carbs 1g, protein 2g

83. CRISPY SHRIMP

Preparation time: 10 minutes
Cooking time: 5 minutes
Servings: 4

Ingredients:
- 12 big shrimp, deveined and peeled
- 2 egg whites
- 100 g shredded
- 84 g panko bread crumbs
- 250 g white flour
- Salt and black pepper to the taste

Preparation
1. Stir together panko and coconut in a mixing basin.
2. In a second bowl, combine the flour, salt, and pepper, and in a third, whisk the egg whites.
3. Dip shrimp in flour, egg white mixture, and coconut, then place in an air fryer basket and cook at 176°C for 10 minutes, flipping halfway.
4. Serve as an appetiser, arranged on a dish.
5. Enjoy!

Nutritional information: calories 140, fat 4g, fiber 0g, carbs 3, protein 4g

84. NACHO COATED PRAWNS

Preparation: 30 minutes
Cooking time: 8 minutes
Servings: 3-4

Ingredients:
- 255 of nacho chips
- 1 egg, whisked
- 18 medium-sized prawns

Preparation
1. Remove the prawns' shells and veins, then thoroughly wash and dry them.
2. In a basin, grind the chips until the bits resemble breadcrumbs.
3. Dip each prawn in the egg, then in the chip crumbs.
4. Preheat the air fryer to 180 degrees Celsius.
5. Cook the prawns in the air fryer for 8 minutes. Serve with salsa or sour cream on the side.

Nutritional information: Calories 42 Total Fat 0.9g Total Carbohydrate 3.4g Dietary Fiber 0.2g Protein 4.7g

85. ROTI PRATA MINI SAUSAGE

ROLLS

Preparation: 5 minutes
Cooking time: 15 minutes
Servings: 4

Ingredients:
- 1 packet of Roti prata
- 10 mini beef sausage

Preparation
1. Prata should be cut into triangles. Roll each sausage in a prata triangle until completely covered.
2. Preheat air fryer to 180 degrees Celsius and lay the rolls in the fryer basket. Bake for 15 mins, or until the rolls are crisp, rotating halfway through.

Nutritional information: Carbs. 24 g. Dietary Fiber. 2.6 g. Sugar. 0 g. Fat. 15.4 g. Protein 6.7g

86. PUFF PASTRY BANANA ROLLS

Preparation: 10 minutes
Cooking time: 10 minutes
Servings: 3

Ingredients:
- 2 puff pastry sheets
- 3 medium-sized bananas, peeled

Preparation
1. Make thin strips out of the pastry sheets. To make a cord, twine two strips together. Make as many cords as you require.
2. Wind the cords around the bananas until the entire banana is covered in pastry.
3. Preheat your air fryer to 180°C and cook the wrapped bananas for 10 minutes, or until golden.

Nutritional information: Carbs. 55 g; Dietary Fiber. 9 g; Sugar. 23 g; Fat. 7 g; Saturated. 3 g. Protein 27 g

VEGETABLE RECIPE

87. STUFFED POBLANO PEPPERS

Preparation time: 10 minutes
Cooking time: 15 minutes
Servings: 4

Ingredients:

- 6 g garlic, minced
- 1 white onion, chopped
- 10 poblano peppers, tops cut off and deseeded
- 15 ml olive oil
- 227 g mushrooms, chopped
- Salt and black pepper to the taste
- 9 g cilantro, chopped

Preparation

1. Heat the oil in a saucepan on medium-high heat, add the onion and mushrooms and cook for 5 minutes, stirring occasionally.
2. Cook for 2 mins after adding the garlic, cilantro, salt, and black pepper.
3. Divide this mixture among the poblanos, place them in the air fryer, and cook for 15 minutes at 176° C.
4. Serve on individual plates.
5. Enjoy!

Nutritional information: calories 150, fat 3g, fiber 2g, carbs 7g, protein 10g

88. SESAME MUSTARD GREENS

Preparation time: 10 minutes
Cooking time: 11 minutes
Servings: 4

Ingredients:

- 2 garlic cloves, minced
- 454 g mustard greens, torn
- 15 ml olive oil
- 26 g yellow onion, sliced
- Salt and black pepper to the taste
- 45 ml veggie stock
- 5 ml dark sesame oil

Preparation

1. Heat the oil in a skillet that fits your air fryer over medium heat, then add the onions, swirl, and brown them for 5 minutes.
2. Stir in the garlic, stock, greens, salt, and pepper, then place in the air fryer and cook at 176°C for 6 minutes.
3. Toss with sesame oil to coat, then divide among plates and serve.
4. Enjoy!

Nutritional information: calories 120, fat 3g, fiber 1g, carbs 3g, protein 7g

89. HERBED EGGPLANT AND ZUCCHINI MIX

Preparation time: 10 minutes
Cooking time: 8 minutes
Servings: 4

Ingredients:

- 1 eggplant, roughly cubed
- 3 zucchinis, roughly cubed
- 30 ml lemon juice
- Salt and black pepper to the taste
- 5 ml thyme, dried
- 5 ml oregano, dried
- 40 g olive oil

Preparation

1. Put eggplant in an air fryer-safe dish, add zucchinis, lemon juice, salt, pepper, thyme, oregano, and olive oil, toss, and cook at 182 degrees C for 8 minutes.
2. Serve immediately on individual plates.
3. Enjoy!

Nutritional information: calories 152, fat 5g, fiber 7g, carbs 19g, protein 5g

90. DELICIOUS PORTOBELLO MUSHROOMS

Preparation time: 10 minutes
Cooking time: 12 minutes
Servings: 4

Ingredients:
- 10 basil leaves
- 36 g baby spinach
- 3 garlic cloves, chopped
- 92 g almonds, roughly chopped
- 4 g parsley
- 60 ml olive oil
- 8 cherry tomatoes, halved
- Salt and black pepper to the taste
- 4 Portobello mushrooms, stems removed and chopped

Preparation
1. In a food processor, mix basil, spinach, garlic, almonds, parsley, oil, salt, black pepper to taste, and mushroom stems.
2. Stuff each mushroom with this mixture and cook for 12 minutes at 176° C in an air fryer.
3. Serve the mushrooms on plates.
4. Enjoy!

Nutritional information: calories 145, fat 3g, fiber 2g, carbs 6g, protein 17g

91. CRISPY POTATOES AND PARSLEY

Preparation time: 10 minutes
Cooking time: 10 minutes
Servings: 4

Ingredients:
- 454 g gold potatoes, cut into wedges
- Salt and black pepper to the taste
- 30 ml olive
- Juice from ½ lemon
- 15 g parsley leaves, chopped

Preparation
1. Rub potatoes with salt, pepper, lemon juice, and olive oil before placing them in the air fryer and cooking for 10 minutes at 176 degrees C.
2. Divide among plates, sprinkle with parsley and serve.
3. Enjoy!

Nutritional information: calories 152, fat 3g, fiber 7g, carbs 17g, protein 4g

92. BEET, TOMATO, AND GOAT CHEESE MIX

Preparation time: 30 minutes
Cooking time: 14 minutes
Servings: 8

Ingredients:
- 8 small beets, trimmed, peeled, and halved
- 1 red onion, sliced
- 113 g goat cheese, crumbled
- 15 ml balsamic vinegar
- Salt and black pepper to the taste
- 25 g sugar
- 1 pint mixed cherry tomatoes, halved
- 57 g pecans
- 30 ml olive oil

Preparation
1. Season the beets in the air fryer with salt and pepper, cook at 176 degrees Celsius for 14 minutes, and transfer to a salad bowl.
2. Toss in the onion, cherry tomatoes, and pecans.
3. In a separate dish, whisk together the vinegar, sugar, and oil until the sugar dissolves, then add to the salad.
4. Toss in the goat cheese and serve.
5. Enjoy!

Nutritional information: calories 124, fat 7g, fiber 5g, carbs 12g, protein 6g

93. SWEET BABY CARROTS DISH

Preparation time: 10 minutes
Cooking time: 10 minutes
Servings: 4

Ingredients:
- 100 g baby carrots
- A pinch of salt and black pepper
- 13 g brown sugar
- 7.5 g butter, melted

Preparation
1. Toss baby carrots with butter, salt, pepper, and sugar on a plate that fits your air fryer, then place in your air fryer and cook at 176 degrees C for 10 minutes.
2. Serve on individual plates.
3. Enjoy!

Nutritional information: calories 100, fat 2g, fiber 3g, carbs 7g, protein 4g

94. RADISH HASH

Preparation time: 10 minutes
Cooking time: 7 minutes
Servings: 4

Ingredients:
- 5 ml onion powder
- 454 g radishes, sliced
- 5 ml garlic powder
- Salt and black pepper to the taste
- 4 eggs
- 30 g parmesan, grated

Preparation
1. In a mixing bowl, combine radishes, salt, pepper, onion and garlic powder, eggs, and parmesan.
2. Cook the radishes in an air fryer pan for 7 minutes at 176 degrees Celsius.
3. Serve the hash on individual plates.
4. Enjoy!

Nutritional information: calories 80, fat 5g, fiber 2g, carbs 5g, protein 7g

95. EGGPLANT HASH

Preparation time: 20 minutes
Cooking time: 10 minutes
Servings: 4

Ingredients:
- 1 eggplant, roughly chopped
- 118 ml olive oil
- 227 g cherry tomatoes, halved
- 5 ml Tabasco sauce
- 5 g basil, chopped
- 8 g mint, chopped
- Salt and black pepper to the taste

Preparation
1. Heat half of the oil in a pan that fits your air fryer over medium-high heat; add eggplant pieces, cook for 3 minutes, flip, cook for 3 minutes more, and move to a bowl.
2. Heat the remaining oil in the same pan over medium-high heat, add the tomatoes, swirl, and cook for 1-2 minutes.
3. Return the eggplant pieces to the pan, season with salt, black pepper, basil, mint, and Tabasco sauce, and cook at 160° C for 6 minutes.
4. Serve on individual plates.
5. Enjoy!

Nutritional information: calories 120, fat 1g, fiber 4, carbs 8g, protein 15g

96. SPINACH PIE

Preparation time: 10 minutes
Cooking time: 15 minutes
Servings: 4

Ingredients:
- 198 g flour
- 28 g butter
- 198 g spinach
- 15 ml olive oil
- 2 eggs
- 30 ml milk
- 85 g cottage cheese
- Salt and black pepper to the taste
- 1 yellow onion, chopped

Preparation
1. Mix flour, butter, 1 egg, milk, salt, and pepper in a food processor until well combined. Transfer to a bowl, knead, cover, and set aside for 10 minutes.

2. Heat the oil in your pan over medium-high heat, add the onion and spinach, swirl, and cook for 2 minutes.
3. Withdraw from heat and whisk in salt, pepper, the remaining egg, and cottage cheese.
4. Divide dough into 4 pieces, roll each piece, place on the bottom of a ramekin, top with spinach filling, place ramekins in an air fryer basket, and cook for 15 minutes at 182 degrees C.
5. Serve hot, and enjoy!

Nutritional information: calories 250, fat 12g, fiber 2g, carbs 23g, protein 12g

97. ARTICHOKES AND SPECIAL SAUCE

Preparation time: 10 minutes
Cooking time: 6 minutes
Servings: 2

Ingredients:
- 2 artichokes, trimmed
- A drizzle of olive oil
- 2 garlic cloves, minced
- 15 ml lemon juice

For the sauce:
- 60 ml coconut oil
- 60 ml extra virgin olive oil
- 3 anchovy fillets
- 3 garlic cloves

Preparation
1. Toss artichokes with oil, 2 garlic cloves, and lemon juice in a bowl, then place in an air fryer and cook at 176 degrees C for 6 minutes. Divide among plates.
2. Blend coconut oil, anchovies, 3 garlic cloves, and olive oil in a food processor until smooth. Drizzle over artichokes and serve.
3. Enjoy!

Nutritional information: calories 261, fat 4g, fiber 7g, carbs 20g, protein 12g

98. BROCCOLI HASH

Preparation time: 30 minutes
Cooking time: 8 minutes
Servings: 2

Ingredients:
- 284 g mushrooms, halved
- 1 broccoli head, florets separated
- 1 garlic clove, minced
- 15 ml balsamic vinegar
- 1 yellow onion, chopped
- 15 ml olive oil
- Salt and black pepper
- 5 ml basil, dried
- 1 avocado, peeled and pitted
- A pinch of red pepper flakes

Preparation:
1. Combine mushrooms, broccoli, onion, garlic, and avocado in a mixing bowl.
2. In a another bowl, whisk together the vinegar, oil, salt, pepper, and basil.
3. Pour this over the vegetables, mix to coat, and set aside for 30 minutes. Transfer to the air fryer basket then cook for 8 minutes at 176 degrees C.
4. Divide among plates and serve with pepper flakes on top.
5. Enjoy!

Nutritional information: calories 182, fat 3g, fiber 3g, carbs 5,g protein 8g

99. TOMATO AND BASIL TART

Preparation time: 10 minutes
Cooking time: 14 minutes
Servings: 2

Ingredients:
- 1 bunch basil, chopped
- 4 eggs
- 1 garlic clove, minced
- Salt and black pepper to the taste
- 114 g cherry tomatoes, halved
- 60 g cheddar cheese, grated

Preparation

1. Whisk together the eggs, salt, black pepper, cheese, and basil in a mixing dish.
2. Pour this into a baking dish that fits your air fryer, lay tomatoes on top, and place in the fryer for 14 minutes at 160 degrees C.
3. Serve immediately after slicing.
4. Enjoy!

Nutritional information: calories 140, fat 1g, fiber 1g, carbs 2g, protein 10g

100.   FLAVORED AIR FRIED TOMATOES

Preparation time: 10 minutes
Cooking time: 15
Servings: 8

Ingredients:

- 1 jalapeno pepper, chopped
- 4 garlic cloves, minced
- 907 g cherry tomatoes, halved
- Salt and black pepper to the taste
- 60 ml olive oil
- 2.5 ml oregano, dried
- 1.25 ml basil, chopped
- 45 g parmesan, grated

Preparation

1. In a mixing basin, combine tomatoes, garlic, and jalapeno, season with salt, pepper, and oregano, and drizzle with oil, tossing to cover. Place in your air fryer then cook at 193 degrees Celsius for 15 minutes.
2. Toss tomatoes with basil and parmesan in a bowl and serve.
3. Enjoy!

Nutritional information: calories 140, fat 2g, fiber 2g, carbs 6g, protein 8g

101.   FLAVORED GREEN BEANS

Preparation time: 10 minutes
Cooking time: 15 minutes
Servings: 4

Ingredients:

- 454 g red potatoes, cut into wedges
- 454 g green beans
- 2 garlic cloves, minced
- 30 ml olive oil
- Salt and black pepper to the taste
- 5 ml oregano, dried

Preparation

1. Combine potatoes, green beans, garlic, oil, salt, pepper, and oregano in a pan that fits your air fryer, stir, and cook at 193 degrees C for 15 minutes.
2. Serve on individual plates.
3. Enjoy!

Nutritional information: calories 211, fat 6g, fiber 7g, carbs 8g, protein 5g

102.   SIMPLE STUFFED TOMATOES

Preparation time: 10 minutes
Cooking time: 15 minutes
Servings: 4

Ingredients:

- 4 tomatoes, tops cut off and pulp scooped and chopped
- Salt and black pepper to the taste
- 1 yellow onion, chopped
- 14 g butter
- 15 g celery, chopped
- 50 g mushrooms, chopped
- 7 g bread crumbs
- 162 g cottage cheese
- 1.25 ml caraway seeds
- 4 g parsley, chopped

Preparation

1. Melt the butter in your pan over medium heat, add the onion and celery, mix, and cook for 3 minutes.
2. Cook for 1 minute more after adding tomato pulp and mushrooms.

3. Cook for 4 minutes further after adding salt, pepper, crumbled bread, cheese, caraway seeds, and parsley, stirring constantly.
4. Stuff tomatoes with this mixture and cook for 8 minutes at 176° C in an air fryer.
5. Serve the stuffed tomatoes on plates.
6. Enjoy!

Nutritional information: calories 143, fat 4g, fiber 6g, carbs 4g, protein 4g

103. AIR FRIED ASPARAGUS

Preparation time: 10 minutes
Cooking time: 15 minutes
Servings: 4

Ingredients:
- 454 g fresh asparagus, trimmed
- 60 ml olive oil
- Salt and black pepper to the taste
- 5 ml lemon zest
- 4 garlic cloves, minced
- 2.5 ml oregano, dried
- 1.25 ml red pepper flakes
- 113 g feta cheese, crumbled
- 8 g parsley, finely chopped
- Juice from 1 lemon

Preparation
1. Mix the oil, lemon zest, garlic, pepper flakes, and oregano in a mixing bowl.
2. Toss in the asparagus, cheese, salt, and pepper, then put in your air fryer basket and cook for 8 minutes at 176 degrees C. Arrange asparagus on plates, drizzle with lemon juice, and top with parsley.
3. Enjoy!

Nutritional information: calories 162, fat 13g, fiber 5g, carbs 12g, protein 8g

104. OKRA AND CORN SALAD

Preparation time: 10 minutes
Cooking time: 12 minutes
Servings: 6

Ingredients:

- 454 g okra, trimmed
- 6 scallions, chopped
- 3 green bell peppers, chopped
- Salt and black pepper to the taste
- 30 ml olive oil
- 5 g sugar
- 794 g canned tomatoes, chopped
- 128 g con

Preparation
1. Heat the oil in a skillet that fits your air fryer over medium-high heat, then add the scallions and bell peppers, stir, and cook for 5 minutes.
2. Stir in the okra, salt, pepper, sugar, tomatoes, and corn before placing it in the air fryer and cooking at 182 degrees C for 7 minutes.
3. Serve the okra mixture on plates while still heated.
4. Enjoy!

Nutritional information: calories 152, fat 4g, fiber 3g, carbs 18g, protein 4g

105. BEETS AND BLUE

CHEESE SALAD

Preparation time: 10 minutes
Cooking time: 14 minutes
Servings: 6

Ingredients:
- 6 beets, peeled and quartered
- Salt and black pepper to the taste
- 56 g blue cheese, crumbled
- 15 ml olive oil

Preparation
1. Cook the beets in your air fryer for 14 minutes at 176 degrees Celsius before transferring them to a bowl.
2. Toss in the blue cheese, salt, pepper, and oil before serving.
3. Enjoy!

Nutritional information: calories 100, fat 4g, fiber 4g, carbs 10g, protein 5g

106. BEET SALAD AND PARSLEY DRESSING

Preparation time: 10 minutes
Cooking time: 14 minutes
Servings: 4

Ingredients:
- 4 beets
- 30 ml balsamic vinegar
- A bunch of parsley, chopped
- Salt and black pepper to the taste
- 15 ml extra virgin olive oil
- 1 garlic clove, chopped
- 15 g capers

Preparation
1. Cook the beets in your air fryer for 14 minutes at 182 degrees C.
2. Meanwhile, combine parsley, garlic, salt, pepper, olive oil, and capers in a mixing bowl and well combine.
3. Transfer the beets to a chopping board to cool before peeling and slicing them into a salad bowl.
4. Pour in the vinegar, then drizzle with the parsley dressing and serve.
5. Enjoy!

Nutritional information: calories 70, fat 2g, fiber 1g, carbs 6g, protein 4g

107. BROCCOLI SALAD

Preparation time: 10 minutes
Cooking time: 8 minutes
Servings: 4

Ingredients:
- 1 broccoli head, florets separated
- 15 ml peanut oil
- 6 garlic cloves, minced
- 15 ml Chinese rice wine vinegar
- Salt and black pepper to the taste

Preparation
1. Toss broccoli with salt, pepper, and half of the oil in a bowl, then put in an air fryer and cook at 176 degrees C for 8 minutes, shaking halfway through.
2. Transfer the broccoli to a salad dish, stir with the remaining peanut oil, garlic, and rice vinegar, and serve.
3. Enjoy!

Nutritional information: calories 121, fat 3g, fiber 4g, carbs 4g, protein 4g

108. GREEN BEANS AND PARMESAN

Preparation time: 10 minutes
Cooking time: 8 minutes
Servings: 4

Ingredients:
- 340 g green beans
- 6 g garlic, minced
- 30 ml olive oil
- Salt and black pepper to the taste
- 1 egg, whisked
- 30 g parmesan, grated

Preparation
1. Mix the oil, salt, pepper, garlic, and egg in a bowl.
2. Toss in the green beans and sprinkle with parmesan cheese.
3. Cook the green beans in the air fryer for 8 minutes at 198 degrees C.
4. Place green beans on plates and serve immediately.
5. Enjoy!

Nutritional information: calories 120, fat 8g, fiber 2g, carbs 7g, protein 4g

109. SPICY CABBAGE

Preparation time: 10 minutes
Cooking time: 8 minutes
Servings: 4

Ingredients:
- 1 cabbage, cut into 8 wedges

- 15 ml sesame seed oil
- 1 carrot, grated
- 60 ml apple cider vinegar
- 60 ml apple juice
- 2.5 ml cayenne pepper
- 5 ml g red pepper flakes, crushed

Preparation
1. Combine cabbage, oil, carrot, vinegar, apple juice, cayenne pepper, and pepper flakes in a pan that fits your air fryer, stir, and cook at 176 degrees C for 8 minutes.
2. Serve the cabbage mixture on plates.
3. Enjoy!

Nutritional information: calories 100, fat 4g, fiber 2g, carbs 11g, protein 7g

110. GARLIC TOMATOES

Preparation time: 10 minutes
Cooking time: 15 minutes
Servings: 4

Ingredients:
- 4 garlic cloves, crushed
- 454 mixed cherry tomatoes
- 3 thyme springs, chopped
- Salt and black pepper to the taste
- 60 ml olive oil

Preparation
1. Toss tomatoes with salt, black pepper, garlic, olive oil, and thyme in a bowl, then place in an air fryer and cook at 182 degrees C for 15 minutes.
2. Serve the tomato mixture on plates.
3. Enjoy!

Nutritional information: calories 100, fat 0g, fiber 1g, carbs 1g, protein 6g

111. SWISS CHARD SALAD

Preparation time: 10 minutes
Cooking time: 13 minutes
Servings: 4

Ingredients:

- 1 bunch Swiss chard, torn
- 30 ml olive oil
- 1 small yellow onion, chopped
- A pinch of red pepper flakes
- 35 g pine nuts, toasted
- 40 g raisins
- 15 ml balsamic vinegar
- Salt and black pepper to the taste

Preparation
1. Heat the oil in a skillet that fits your air fryer over medium heat, then add the chard and onions, stir, and cook for 5 minutes.
2. Add salt, pepper, pepper flakes, raisins, pine nuts, and vinegar, whisk, and place in your air fryer for 8 minutes at 176 degrees C.
3. Serve on individual plates.
4. Enjoy!

Nutritional information: calories 120, fat 2g, fiber 1g, carbs 8g, protein 8g

112. BROCCOLI AND

TOMATOES AIR FRIED STEW

Preparation time: 10 minutes
Cooking time: 20 minutes
Servings: 4

Ingredients:
- 1 broccoli head, florets separated
- 10 ml coriander seeds
- 15 ml olive oil
- 1 yellow onion, chopped
- Salt and black pepper to the taste
- A pinch of red pepper, crushed
- 1 small ginger piece, chopped
- 1 garlic clove, minced
- 794 g canned tomatoes, pureed

Preparation
1. Heat the oil in a skillet that fits your air fryer over medium heat, then add the onions, salt, pepper, and red pepper, stir, and cook for 7 minutes.
2. Stir in the ginger, garlic, coriander seeds, tomatoes, and broccoli, then place in the air

fryer and cook at 182 degrees Celsius for 12
minutes.
3. Serve in individual bowls.
4. Enjoy!

Nutritional information: calories 150, fat 4, fiber 2, carbs 7, protein 12

113. GREEN BEANS AND TOMATOES

Preparation time: 10 minutes
Cooking time: 15 minutes
Servings: 4

Ingredients:
- 1-pint cherry tomatoes
- 454 g green beans
- 30 ml olive oil
- Salt and black pepper to the taste

Preparation
1. Toss cherry tomatoes with green beans in a bowl with olive oil, salt, and pepper, then move to an air fryer and cook at 204 degrees C for 15 minutes.
2. Serve immediately on individual plates.
3. Enjoy!

Nutritional information: calories 162, fat 6, fiber 5, carbs 8, protein 9

114. CHEESY BRUSSELS SPROUTS

Preparation time: 10 minutes
Cooking time: 8 minutes
Servings: 4

Ingredients:
- 454 g Brussels sprouts, washed
- Juice of 1 lemon
- Salt and black pepper to the taste
- 28 g butter
- 44 g parmesan, grated

Preparation
1. Place Brussels sprouts in an air fryer and cook at 176°C for 8 minutes before transferring them to a dish.
2. Heat the butter in your pan over medium heat, then add the lemon juice, salt, and pepper, mix well, and pour over the Brussels sprouts.
3. Toss in the parmesan until it melts, then serve.
4. Enjoy!

Nutritional information: calories 152, fat 6g, fiber 6g, carbs 8g, protein 12g

115. SPANISH GREENS

Preparation time: 10 minutes
Cooking time: 8 minutes
Servings: 4
Ingredients:
- 1 apple, cored and chopped
- 1 yellow onion, sliced
- 45 ml olive oil
- 40 g raisins
- 6 garlic cloves, chopped
- 35 g pine nuts, toasted
- 60 ml balsamic vinegar
- 100 g mixed spinach and chard
- Salt and black pepper to the taste
- A pinch of nutmeg

Preparation
1. Heat the oil in a pan that fits your air fryer over medium-high heat, add the onion, swirl, and cook for 3 minutes.
2. Stir in the apple, garlic, raisins, vinegar, mixed spinach and chard, nutmeg, salt, and pepper, and simmer at 176 degrees C for 5 minutes.
3. Divide among plates, cover with pine nuts and serve.
4. Enjoy!

Nutritional information: calories 120, fat 1g, fiber 2g, carbs 3g, protein 6g

116.   ITALIAN EGGPLANT STEW

Preparation time: 10 minutes
Cooking time: 15 minutes
Servings: 4

Ingredients:
- 1 red onion, chopped
- 2 garlic cloves, chopped
- 1 bunch parsley, chopped
- Salt and black pepper to the taste
- 5 ml oregano, dried
- 2 eggplants, cut into medium chunks
- 30 ml olive oil
- 15 g capers, chopped
- 1 handful of green olives, pitted and sliced
- 5 tomatoes, chopped
- 45 ml herb vinegar

Preparation
1. Heat the oil in a pan that fits your air fryer over medium heat, then add the eggplant, oregano, salt, and pepper and cook for 5 minutes.
2. Stir in the garlic, onion, parsley, capers, olives, vinegar, and tomatoes. Place in your air fryer then cook at 182 degrees C for 15 minutes.
3. Serve in individual bowls.
4. Enjoy!

Nutritional information: calories 170, fat 13g, fiber 3g, carbs 5g, protein 7g

117.   BRUSSELS SPROUTS AND
BUTTER SAUCE

Preparation time: 4 minutes
Cooking time: 10 minutes
Servings: 4

Ingredients:
- 454 g Brussels sprouts, trimmed
- Salt and black pepper to the taste
- ½ cup bacon, cooked and chopped
- 15 g mustard
- 15 g butter
- 2 g dill, finely chopped

Preparation
1. Cook Brussels sprouts in your air fryer for 10 minutes at 176 degrees Celsius.
2. Heat the butter in your pan over medium-high heat, add the bacon, mustard, and dill and mix thoroughly.
3. Serve Brussels sprouts on plates with butter sauce drizzled all over.
4. Enjoy!

Nutritional information: calories 162, fat 8g, fiber 8g, carbs 14g, protein 5g

118.   COLLARD GREENS AND
TURKEY WINGS

Preparation time: 10 minutes
Cooking time: 20 minutes
Servings: 6

Ingredients:
- 1 sweet onion, chopped
- 2 smoked turkey wings
- 30 ml olive oil
- 3 garlic cloves, minced
- 1134 g collard greens, chopped
- Salt and black pepper to the taste
- 30 ml apple cider vinegar
- 13 g brown sugar
- 2.5 ml crushed red pepper

Preparation
1. Heat the oil in a pan that fits your air fryer over medium-high heat, add the onions, swirl, and cook for 2 minutes.
2. Add garlic, greens, vinegar, salt, pepper, crushed red pepper, sugar, and smoked turkey to an air fryer and cook for 15 mins at 176 degrees C.
3. Serve the greens and turkey on separate plates.
4. Enjoy!

Nutritional information: calories 262, fat 4g, fiber 8g, carbs 12g, protein 4g

119.   AIR FRIED LEEKS

Preparation time: 10 minutes
Cooking time: 7 minutes
Servings: 4

Ingredients:
- 4 leeks, washed, and halved
- 14 g butter, melted
- 15 ml lemon juice
- Salt and black pepper to the taste

Preparation
1. Rub leeks with thawed butter, season with salt and pepper, and cook for 7 minutes at 176° C in an air fryer.
2. Arrange on a dish, drizzle with lemon juice, and serve.
3. Enjoy!

Nutritional information: calories 100, fat 4g, fiber 2g, carbs 6g, protein 2g

120.   INDIAN TURNIPS SALAD

Preparation time: 10 minutes
Cooking time: 12 minutes
Servings: 4

Ingredients:
- 567 g turnips, peeled and chopped
- 5 ml garlic, minced
- 5 ml ginger, grated
- 2 yellow onions, chopped
- 2 tomatoes, chopped
- 5 ml cumin, ground
- 5 ml coriander, ground
- 2 green chilies, chopped
- 2.5 ml turmeric powder
- 28 g butter
- Salt and black pepper to the taste
- A handful of coriander leaves, chopped

Preparation
1. Melt the butter in a skillet that fits your air fryer, add the green chilies, garlic, and ginger, stir, and cook for 1 minute.

2. Stir in the onions, salt, pepper, tomatoes, turmeric, cumin, ground coriander, and turnips, then place in the air fryer and cook at 176°C for 10 minutes.
3. Divide among plates, top with fresh coriander, and serve.
4. Enjoy!

Nutritional information: calories 100, fat 3g, fiber 6g, carbs 12g, protein 4g

121.   INDIAN POTATOES

Preparation time: 10 minutes
Cooking time: 12 minutes
Servings: 4

Ingredients:
- 15 ml coriander seeds
- 15 ml cumin seeds
- Salt and black pepper to the taste
- 2.5 ml turmeric powder
- 2.5 ml red chili powder
- 5 ml pomegranate powder
- 20 g pickled mango, chopped
- 10 ml fenugreek, dried
- 5 potatoes, boiled, peeled, and cubed
- 30 ml olive oil

Preparation
1. Heat the oil in a pan that fits your air fryer over medium heat, add the coriander and cumin seeds, mix, and cook for 2 minutes.
2. Toss in salt, pepper, turmeric, chili powder, pomegranate powder, mango, fenugreek, and potatoes—Cook at 182 degrees C for 10 minutes.
3. Serve immediately on plates.
4. Enjoy!

Nutritional information: calories 251, fat 7g, fiber 4g, carbs 12g, protein 7g

122. RUTABAGA AND CHERRY TOMATOES MIX

Preparation time: 10 minutes
Cooking time: 15 minutes
Servings: 4

Ingredients:
- 10 g shallot, chopped
- 1 garlic clove, minced
- 94 g cashews, soaked for a couple of hours and drained
- 21 g nutritional yeast
- 118 ml veggie stock
- Salt and black pepper to the taste
- 30 ml lemon juice
- For the pasta:
- 150 g cherry tomatoes, halved
- 75 g olive oil
- 2.5 ml garlic powder
- 2 rutabagas, peeled and cut into thick noodles

Preparation
1. Place the tomatoes and rutabaga noodles in an air fryer-safe pan, sprinkle with oil, season with salt, black pepper, and garlic powder, toss to coat, and cook for 15 minutes at 176 degrees C.
2. Meanwhile, in your food processor, combine garlic, shallots, cashews, vegetable stock, nutritional yeast, lemon juice, and a sprinkling of sea salt and black pepper to taste.
3. Divide the rutabaga pasta among the plates, top with the tomatoes, and drizzle with the sauce before serving.
4. Enjoy!

Nutritional information: calories 160, fat 2g, fiber 5g, carbs 10g, protein 8g

123. ZUCCHINI NOODLES DELIGHT

Preparation time: 10 minutes
Cooking time: 20 minutes
Servings: 6

Ingredients:
- 30 ml olive oil
- 3 zucchinis, cut with a spiralizer
- 454 g mushrooms, sliced
- 14 g sun-dried tomatoes, chopped
- 3 g garlic, minced
- 114 g cherry tomatoes, halved
- 450 g tomatoes sauce
- 60 g spinach, torn
- Salt and black pepper to the taste
- Handful basil, chopped

Preparation
1. Place the zucchini noodles in a bowl, season with salt and black pepper, and set aside for 10 minutes.
2. Heat the oil in a pan that fits your air fryer over medium-high heat, add the garlic, swirl, and cook for 1 minute.
3. Stir in the mushrooms, sun-dried tomatoes, cherry tomatoes, spinach, cayenne pepper sauce, and zucchini noodles before putting them in your air fryer and cooking at 160° C for 10 minutes.
4. Serve on plates with a sprinkling of basil on top.
5. Enjoy!

Nutritional information: calories 120, fat 1g, fiber 1g, carbs 2g, protein 9g

124. SIMPLE TOMATOES AND BELL PEPPER SAUCE

Preparation time: 10 minutes
Cooking time: 15 minutes
Servings: 4

Ingredients:
- 2 red bell peppers, chopped
- 2 garlic cloves, minced
- 454 g cherry tomatoes, halved
- 5 ml rosemary, dried
- 3 bay leaves
- 30 ml olive oil
- 15 ml balsamic vinegar
- Salt and black pepper to the taste

Preparation

1. Toss tomatoes with garlic, salt, black pepper, rosemary, bay leaves, half of the oil, and half of the vinegar in a dish, toss to coat and place in an air fryer for 15 minutes at 160 degrees C.
2. Meanwhile, in a food processor, combine bell peppers, a pinch of sea salt, black pepper, the remaining oil, and the remaining vinegar, and blend thoroughly.
3. Serve the roasted tomatoes on plates with the bell pepper sauce drizzled over them.
4. Enjoy!

Nutritional information: calories 123, fat 1g, fiber 1g, carbs 8g, protein 10g

125.   STUFFED BABY PEPPERS

Preparation time: 10 minutes
Cooking time: 6 minutes
Servings: 4

Ingredients:

- 12 baby bell peppers, cut into halves lengthwise
- 1.25 ml red pepper flakes, crushed
- 454 g shrimp, cooked, peeled, and deveined
- 90 g jarred basil pesto
- Salt and black pepper to the taste
- 15 ml lemon juice
- 15ml olive oil
- Handful parsley, chopped

Preparation

1. Mix shrimp with pepper flakes, pesto, salt, black pepper, lemon juice, oil, and parsley in a bowl, then stuff bell pepper halves with this mixture.
2. Cook for 6 mins at 160 degrees Celsius in an air fryer. Arrange peppers on plates and serve.
3. Enjoy!

Nutritional information: calories 130, fat 2g, fiber 1g, carbs 3g, protein 15g

126.   BALSAMIC ARTICHOKES

Preparation time: 10 minutes
Cooking time: 7 minutes
Servings: 4

Ingredients:

- 4 big artichokes, trimmed
- Salt and black pepper to the taste
- 30 ml lemon juice
- 60 ml extra virgin olive oil
- 10 ml balsamic vinegar
- 5 ml oregano, dried
- 2 garlic cloves, minced

Preparation

1. Salt and pepper the artichokes, then rub them with half the oil and half the lemon juice before placing them in your air fryer to cook for seven minutes at 182 degrees C.
2. In the meantime, thoroughly combine the remaining lemon juice, vinegar, remaining oil, salt, pepper, garlic, and oregano in a bowl.
3. Place the artichokes in a serving tray, top with the balsamic vinaigrette, and serve.
4. Enjoy!

Nutritional information: calories 200, fat 3g, fiber 6g, carbs 12g, protein 4g

FISH AND SEAFOOD

RECIPE

127.　COD FILLETS WITH

FENNEL AND GRAPES SALAD

Preparation time: 10 minutes
Cooking time: 15 minutes
Servings: 2

Ingredients:
- 2 black cod fillets, boneless
- 15 ml olive oil
- Salt and black pepper to the taste
- 1 fennel bulb, thinly sliced
- 150 g grapes, halved
- 54 g pecans

Preparation
1. Drizzle half of the oil over the fish fillets, season with salt and pepper, rub well, place fillets in the basket of your air fryer, and cook for 10 minutes at 204 degrees C before transferring to a dish.
2. Toss pecans with grapes, fennel, the rest of the oil, salt, and pepper in a bowl, then transfer to a pan that fits your air fryer and cook at 204°C for 5 minutes.
3. Serve the cod with the fennel and grapes mixture on the side.
4. Enjoy!

Nutritional information: calories 300, fat 4g, fiber 2g, carbs 32g, protein 22g

128.　AIR-FRYER FISH CAKES

Preparation Time: 10 mins
Total Time: 20 mins
Servings: 2

Ingredients
- Nonstick cooking spray
- 284 g finely chopped white fish (such as grouper, catfish, or cod)
- 54 g whole-wheat panko breadcrumbs

- 11 g finely chopped fresh cilantro
- 20 ml Thai sweet chili sauce
- 28 g canola mayonnaise
- 1 large egg
- 1.25 ml salt
- 2.5 ml ground pepper
- 2 lime wedges

Preparation
1. Spray cooking spray on the air fryer's basket.
2. In a medium bowl, stir together the fish, panko, cilantro, chilli sauce, mayonnaise, egg, salt, and pepper. Create four 3-inch-diameter cakes out of the mixture.
3. Place the cakes in the prepared basket after spraying them with cooking spray. Cook the cakes for 9 to 10 minutes at 204°C or until they are browned, and the internal temperature reaches 60°C. Wedges of lime are optional.

Nutritional information: Calories 399 Fat 16g Carbs 28g Protein 35g

129.　AIR-FRIED SALMON WITH

HORSERADISH RUB

Preparation Time: 10 mins
Total Time: 30 mins
Servings: 2
Ingredients
- Nonstick cooking spray
- 10 g finely grated horseradish
- 4 g finely chopped flat-leaf parsley
- 9 g capers, finely chopped
- 15 ml extra-virgin olive oil
- 1 (340 g) skinless salmon fillet (about 1 inch thick)
- 1.25 salt
- 2.5 ml ground pepper

Preparation
1. Spray cooking spray to the air fryer's basket.
2. In a small bowl, mix the horseradish, parsley, capers, and oil. Put some salt and pepper on

the salmon. Over the fish, spoon the horseradish mixture. Spray some frying oil on.

3. Salmon should be placed in the ready-made basket. Cook for around 15 minutes at 190°C or until the internal temperature reaches 54°C. Before serving, allow it to rest for five minutes.

Nutritional information: Calories 305 Fat 15g Carbs 7g Protein 35g

130.   AIR-FRYER SCALLOPS

WITH LEMON-HERB SAUCE

Preparation Time: 10 mins
Total Time: 20 mins
Servings: 2

Ingredients
- 8 large (28 g.) sea scallops, cleaned and patted very dry
- 1.25 ml g ground pepper
- 1.25 ml salt
- cooking spray
- 60 ml extra-virgin olive oil
- 8 g very finely chopped flat-leaf parsley
- 5 g capers, very finely chopped
- 2 g finely grated lemon zest
- 2.5 ml finely chopped garlic
- lemon wedges, optional

Preparation
1. Add salt and pepper to the scallops. Spray cooking spray to the air fryer's basket. Put the scallops in the basket and sprinkle cooking spray on them. In the fryer, put the basket. The scallops should be prepared at 204°C for 6 minutes or until they reach an internal temperature of 48°C.
2. In a small bowl, mix the oil, parsley, capers, lemon zest, and garlic. On top of the scallops, drizzle. If desired, garnish with lemon slices.

Nutritional information: Calories 348 Fat 30gCarbs 5g Protein 14g

131.   BUTTERED SHRIMP

SKEWERS

Preparation time: 10 minutes
Cooking time: 6 minutes
Servings: 2

Ingredients:
- 8 shrimps, peeled and deveined
- 4 garlic cloves, minced
- Salt and black pepper to the taste
- 8 green bell pepper slices
- 2 g rosemary, chopped
- 14 g butter, melted

Preparation
1. Shrimp, garlic, butter, salt, pepper, rosemary, and bell pepper slices should all be combined in a basin. Toss to combine, then put aside for 10 mins.
2. Put two shrimp and two slices of bell pepper on a skewer, then do the same with the remaining shrimp and peppers.
3. They should all be put in the basket of your air fryer and cooked for 6 minutes at 182 degrees C.
4. Distribute among plates, then serve immediately.
5. Enjoy!

Nutritional information: calories 140, fat 1g, fiber 12g, carbs 15g, protein 7g

132.   CAJUN AIR FRYER

SALMON

Prep Time: 10 mins
Cook Time: 10 mins
Total Time: 20 mins

Ingredients
- 2 (170 g) skin-on salmon fillets
- cooking spray
- 12 g Cajun seasoning
- 4 g brown sugar

Preparation
1. Set the air fryer's temperature to 200 C.

2. Salmon fillets should be rinsed, and paper towel dried. Fillets are sprayed with cooking spray. In a small basin, mix the brown sugar and Cajun seasoning. Toss some on a plate. Incorporate the seasoning mixture into the fillets' flesh sides.

3. Place the salmon fillets skin-side down in the basket of the air fryer after spraying with cooking spray. Salmon is once more lightly sprayed with cooking spray.

4. For 8 minutes, cook. Take out of the air fryer, then wait two minutes before serving.

Nutritional information: calories 327 total fat 19g total carbohydrate 4g total sugars 2g protein 34g

133. AIR FRYER LEMON PEPPER SHRIMP

Prep Time: 5 mins
Cook Time: 10 mins
Total Time: 15 mins

Ingredients
- 15 ml olive oil
- 1 lemon, juiced
- 5 g lemon pepper
- 1.25 ml g paprika
- 1.25 ml g garlic powder
- 340 g uncooked medium shrimp, peeled and deveined
- 1 lemon, sliced

Preparation
1. In accordance with the recommendations of the manufacturer, heat an air fryer to 200 degrees C.

2. In a bowl, mix the oil, paprika, garlic powder, lemon juice, and lemon pepper. Add the shrimp and coat well.

3. Cook shrimp in the preheated air fryer for 6 to 8 minutes, or until the meat is opaque and the shrimp are brilliant pink on the outside. Add lemon wedges to the dish.

Nutritional information: calories 215 total fat 9g total carbohydrate 13g dietary fiber 6g protein 29g

134. AIR FRYER LOBSTER TAILS WITH LEMON-GARLIC BUTTER

Prep Time: 10 mins
Cook Time: 10 mins
Total Time: 20 mins

Ingredients
- 2 (113 g) lobster tails
- 57 g butter
- 5 ml lemon zest
- 1 clove of garlic, grated
- salt and ground black pepper to taste
- 5 ml chopped fresh parsley
- 2 wedges lemon

Preparation
1. Heat air fryer up to 195 degrees Celsius.

2. By using kitchen shears to cut through the centres of the meat and hard top shells lengthwise, you may butterfly lobster tails. Cut up to the bases of the shells but not past them. Disperse the tail parts. Lobster meat facing up should be placed in the air fryer basket with the tails.

3. In a small pan over medium heat, melt the butter. Add lemon zest and garlic; cook for 30 seconds or until garlic is aromatic.

4. To prevent contamination from raw lobster, transfer 28 g of the butter mixture to a small bowl and brush it onto the lobster tails. Discard any leftover butter. Use salt and pepper to season lobster.

5. Cook in preheated air fryer for 5 to 7 minutes or until the lobster meat is opaque.

6. Over the lobster meat, pour the saucepan's reserved butter. Serve with lemon wedges and parsley on top.

Nutritional information: calories 313 total fat 26g total carbohydrate 3g dietary fiber 1g protein 18g

135.   AIR FRYER CRAB RANGOON

Prep Time: 15 mins
Cook Time: 20 mins
Total Time: 35 mins
Ingredients
- 1 (227 g) package cream cheese, softened
- 113 g lump crab meat
- 12 g chopped scallions
- 5 ml soy sauce
- 5 ml Worcestershire sauce
- 1 serving nonstick cooking spray
- 24 wonton wrappers
- 30 ml Asian sweet chili sauce for dipping

Preparation
1. In a bowl, whisk together the cream cheese, crab meat, scallions, soy sauce, and Worcestershire sauce.
2. Set the temperature of an air fryer to 175 °C. Cooking spray should be used on the air fryer's basket. Warm water should be put in a small bowl.
3. 12 wonton wrappers should be placed on a tidy work surface. Each wonton wrapper should have 5 g of the cream cheese mixture placed in the centre of it. Each wonton wrapper's sides should be moistened by dipping your index finger into some warm water. To create dumplings, crimp the wrapping corners upward until they converge in the centre.
4. Spray the tops of the dumplings with cooking spray before placing them in the prepared basket.
5. Cook dumplings for 8 to 10 minutes, or until desired crispness is achieved. Transfer to a platter covered with paper towels.
6. Assemble the remaining dumplings using the remaining wrappers and filling while the first batch is cooking.
7. Serve with dipping sweet chilli sauce.

Nutritional information: calories 127 total fat 7g total carbohydrate 11g total sugars 1g protein 5g

136.   PANKO-CRUSTED AIR FRYER MAHI MAHI

Prep Time: 5 mins
Cook Time: 15 mins
Total Time: 20 mins

Ingredients
- 4 (113 g) mahi mahi fillets
- 30 ml grapeseed oil
- 238 g panko bread crumbs
- 5 ml everything bagel seasoning
- 1.25 ml garlic salt
- 2.5 ml ground turmeric
- 2.5 ml ground black pepper
- nonstick cooking spray
- 5 ml chopped fresh parsley
- 1 medium lemon, cut into 4 wedges

Preparation
1. For five minutes, heat the air fryer to 200 degrees Celsius.
2. Mahi Mahi fillets should be placed on a tray and covered with grapeseed oil in the meantime.
3. In a shallow dish, combine panko, bagel seasoning, garlic salt, turmeric, and pepper. Place the fillets in the air fryer basket in a single layer after coating each with the panko mixture. Use nonstick spray to coat.
4. Cook in a preheated air fryer for 12 - 15 mins, flipping halfway through, or until fish flakes easily with a fork.
5. From the air fryer, remove. Lemon wedges and parsley are used as a garnish. Serve right away.

Nutritional information: calories 304 total fat 9g total carbohydrate 41g dietary fiber 1g protein 27g

137.   AIR-FRIED SHRIMP
FAJITAS

Prep Time: 15 mins
Cook Time: 10 mins
Total Time: 25 mins

Ingredients
- 227 g large shrimp, peeled and deveined
- 1 small onion, cut into thin strips
- 1 small green bell pepper, cut into slim strips
- 1 small red bell pepper, cut into thin strips
- cooking spray
- 8 g family-style fajita seasoning or to taste
- 10 ml lime juice
- 4 flour tortillas, warmed

Preparation
1. For three minutes, heat the air fryer to 200 degrees Celsius.
2. In a bowl, mix the shrimp, onion, and bell peppers. Spray with oil spray sparingly. Mix up the shrimp mixture and fajita seasoning. Transfer to an air fryer basket.
3. For eight minutes, air fry. Give the shrimp mixture a squeeze of lime juice. As soon as possible, serve with warm tortillas.

Nutritional information: calories 580 total fat 13g total carbohydrate 84g dietary fiber 7g total sugars 7g protein 32g

138.   AIR FRIED SEASONED
CRUNCHY COD FILLETS

Prep Time: 10 mins
Cook Time: 12 mins
Total Time: 22 mins

Ingredients
- avocado oil cooking spray
- 33 g unseasoned panko bread crumbs
- 53 g stone-ground yellow cornmeal
- 6 g seasoning mix
- 5 ml paprika
- 2.5 ml salt, or to taste

- 118 ml buttermilk
- 3 (142 g) cod fillets
- 8 g all-purpose flour

Preparation
1. In the bottom of a basket-style air fryer, make a 3-inch wide foil sling that extends across the bottom and up the sides. Make a few holes in the foil sling's bottom that correspond to the holes in the basket. Use avocado oil to spritz on the sling. Skip this step if using a shelf-style air fryer.
2. Preheat the air fryer's temperature to 200 C.
3. In a small basin, mix the panko crumbs, yellow cornmeal, seasoning mix, paprika, and salt. Add buttermilk to a different bowl.
4. With paper towels, pat dries the cod fillets, then lightly sprinkle both sides with flour. Each flour-coated fillet should be dipped into buttermilk before being coated with the crumb mixture. Place each fillet on the foil sling, if using, or on the rack of a shelf-style air fryer, and pat all sides with the crumb mixture. Spray avocado oil on each fish fillet.
5. Cook in air fryer for 10 to 12 mins, or until the salmon flakes easily. Cod fillets should be taken out of the air fryer using the sling and served right away.

Nutritional information: calories 224 total fat 2g total carbohydrate 23g dietary fiber 1g total sugars 2g protein 30g

139.   AIR FRYER MAHI MAHI
WITH BROWN BUTTER

Prep Time: 5 mins
Cook Time: 15 mins
Total Time: 20 mins

Ingredients
- 4 (170 g) mahi mahi fillets
- salt and ground black pepper to taste
- cooking spray
- 151 g butter

Preparation
1. Preheat the air fryer to 175 degrees Celsius.

2. Mahi Mahi fillets are seasoned with salt and pepper, and then both sides are sprayed with cooking spray. Make sure to leave room between each fillet when you place it in the air fryer basket.
3. Fish should be cooked in the preheated air fryer for 12 minutes or until it flakes easily with a fork and turns golden.
4. In the meantime, melt the butter in a small skillet over medium heat; simmer the butter for 3 - 5 minutes, or until it foams and acquires a rich brown colour. Get rid of the heat.
5. Fish fillets should be placed on a platter with brown butter drizzled over them.

Nutritional information: calories 416 total fat 32g saturated fat 20g protein 32g

140.   AIR FRYER CATFISH

Preparation time: 10 minutes
Cooking time: 20 minutes
Servings: 4

Ingredients:
- 4 catfish fillets
- Salt and black pepper to the taste
- A pinch of sweet paprika
- 4 g parsley, chopped
- 15 ml lemon juice
- 15 ml olive oil

Preparation
1. Catfish fillets should be well-seasoned with salt, pepper, and paprika. They should then be placed in the basket of your air fryer and cooked for 20 minutes at 204 degrees C, turning the fish over after 10 minutes.
2. Fish should be divided among plates, then should be covered in lemon juice and parsley, and served.
3. Enjoy!

Nutritional information: calories 253, fat 6g, fiber 12g, carbs 26g, protein 22g

141.   ASIAN SALMON

Preparation time: 1 hour
Cooking time: 15 minutes
Servings: 2

Ingredients:
- 2 medium salmon fillets
- 89 ml light soy sauce
- 15 ml mirin
- 5 ml water
- 89 ml honey

Preparation
1. In a basin, whisk together soy sauce, honey, water, and mirin. Add salmon, rub well, and chill for 1 hour.
2. Cook the fish in air fryer for 15 minutes at 182 degrees Celsius, flipping after 7 minutes.
3. Meanwhile, boil up the soy marinade in a pan over medium heat, mix well, cook for 2 minutes, and remove from heat.
4. Serve the salmon on plates with the marinade drizzled all over it.
5. Enjoy!

Nutritional information: calories 300, fat 12g, fiber 8g, carbs 13g, protein 24g

142.   LEMONY SABA FISH

Preparation time: 10 minutes
Cooking time: 8 minutes
Servings: 1
Ingredients:
- 4 Saba fish fillet, boneless
- Salt and black pepper to the taste
- 3 red chili pepper, chopped
- 30 ml lemon juice
- 30 ml olive oil
- 17 g garlic, minced

Preparation
1. Place the fish fillets in a basin and season with salt and pepper.
2. Toss with the lemon juice, oil, chile, and garlic, then place in the air fryer and cook for 8 minutes, flipping halfway.
3. Divide among plates and top with fries.

4. Enjoy!

Nutritional information: calories 300, fat 4g, fiber 8g, carbs 15g, protein 15g

143. COD AND VINAIGRETTE

Preparation time: 10 minutes
Cooking time: 15 minutes
Servings: 4

Ingredients:
- 4 cod fillets, skinless and boneless
- 12 cherry tomatoes, halved
- 8 black olives, pitted and roughly chopped
- 30 ml lemon juice
- Salt and black pepper to the taste
- 30 ml olive oil
- Cooking spray
- 1 bunch basil, chopped

Preparation
1. Season cod to taste with salt & pepper, place in air fryer basket, and cook at 182 degrees C for 10 minutes, flipping after 5 minutes.
2. Meanwhile, heat the oil in a skillet over medium heat, then add the tomatoes, olives, and lemon juice, mix, bring to a simmer, add the basil, salt, and pepper, toss well, and remove from heat.
3. Serve the fish on plates with the vinaigrette poured on top.
4. Enjoy!

Nutritional information: calories 300, fat 5g, fiber 8g, carbs 12g, protein 8g

144. TROUT FILLET AND ORANGE SAUCE

Preparation time: 10 minutes
Cooking time: 10 minutes
Servings: 4

Ingredients:
- 4 trout fillets, skinless and boneless
- 4 spring onions, chopped
- 15 ml olive oil
- 8 g ginger, minced
- Salt and black pepper to the taste
- Juice and zest from 1 orange

Preparation
1. Season trout fillets with salt and pepper, massage with olive oil, place in a pan that fits your air fryer, stir with ginger, green onions, orange zest, and juice cook at 182 degrees C for 10 minutes.
2. Serve the fish and sauce immediately on plates.
3. Enjoy!

Nutritional information: calories 239, fat 10g, fiber 7g, carbs 18g, protein 23g

145. THYME AND PARSLEY SALMON

Preparation time: 10 minutes
Cooking time: 15 minutes
Servings: 4

Ingredients:
- 4 salmon fillets, boneless
- Juice from 1 lemon
- 1 yellow onion, chopped
- 3 tomatoes, sliced
- 4 thyme springs
- 4 parsley springs
- 45 ml extra virgin olive oil
- Salt and black pepper to the taste

Preparation
1. Drizzle 15 mL oil in a pan that fits your air fryer, add a layer of tomatoes, salt, and pepper, drizzle 1 tablespoon oil, add fish, season with salt and pepper, drizzle the rest of the oil, add thyme and parsley springs, onions, lemon juice, salt and pepper, place in your air fryer's basket and cook at 182 °C for 12 minutes, shaking once.
2. Divide everything onto plates and serve immediately.
3. Enjoy!

Nutritional information: calories 242, fat 9g, fiber 12g, carbs 20g, protein 31g

146. CREAMY SALMON

Preparation time: 10 minutes
Cooking time: 10 minutes
Servings: 4
Ingredients:

- 4 salmon fillets, boneless
- 15 ml olive oil
- Salt and black pepper to the taste
- 78 g cheddar cheese, grated
- 2 g teaspoon mustard
- 90 g coconut cream

Preparation

1. Season the salmon with salt & pepper, then rub it in the oil.
2. In a mixing bowl, combine the coconut cream, cheddar, mustard, salt, and pepper.
3. Transfer fish to an air fryer-compatible pan, top with the coconut cream mixture, and cook at 160° C for 10 minutes.
4. Serve on individual plates.
5. Enjoy!

Nutritional information: calories 200, fat 6g, fiber 14g, carbs 17g, protein 20g

147. SALMON AND ORANGE MARMALADE

Preparation time: 10 minutes
Cooking time: 15 minutes
Servings: 4
Ingredients:

- 454 g wild salmon, skinless, boneless, and cubed
- 2 lemons, sliced
- 60 ml balsamic vinegar
- 60 ml orange juice
- 106 g orange marmalade
- A pinch of salt and black pepper

Preparation

1. Heat the vinegar in a pot over medium heat, then add the marmalade and orange juice, stir, bring to a simmer, cook for 1 minute, then remove from heat.
2. Thread salmon cubes and lemon slices onto skewers, season with salt and black pepper, brush with half of the orange marmalade mixture, set in air fryer basket, and cook for 3 minutes on each side at 182 degrees C.
3. Brush the remaining vinegar mixture over the skewers, divide among plates, and serve immediately with a side salad.
4. Enjoy!

Nutritional information: calories 240, fat 9g, fiber 12g, carbs 14g, protein 10g

148. SALMON AND AVOCADO SALSA

Preparation time: 30 minutes
Cooking time: 10 minutes
Servings: 4

Ingredients:

- 4 salmon fillets
- 15 ml olive oil
- Salt and black pepper to the taste
- 5 ml cumin, ground
- 5 ml sweet paprika
- 2.5 ml chili powder
- 5 ml garlic powder

For the salsa:

- 1 small red onion, chopped
- 1 avocado, pitted, peeled, and chopped
- 8 g cilantro, chopped
- Juice from 2 limes
- Salt and black pepper to the taste

Preparation

1. Mix salt, pepper, chilli powder, onion powder, paprika, and cumin in a dish, stir, rub salmon with this mixture, drizzle with oil, rub again, and cook at 176 degrees C for 5 minutes on each side.

2. Meanwhile, combine avocado, red onion, salt, pepper, cilantro, and lime juice in a mixing bowl.
3. Serve the fillets on plates with the avocado salsa.
4. Enjoy!

Nutritional information: calories 300, fat 14g, fiber 4g, carbs 18g, protein 16g

149.   TUNA AND CHIMICHURRI

SAUCE

Preparation time: 10 minutes
Cooking time: 8 minutes
Servings: 4

Ingredients:
- 30 g cilantro, chopped
- 79 ml olive oil+ 15 ml
- 1 small red onion, chopped
- 45 ml balsamic vinegar
- 8 g parsley, chopped
- 3 g basil, chopped
- 1 jalapeno pepper, chopped
- 454 sushi tuna steak
- Salt and black pepper to the taste
- 5 ml red pepper flakes
- 5 ml thyme, chopped
- 3 garlic cloves, minced
- 2 avocados, pitted, peeled, and sliced
- 170 g baby arugula

Preparation
1. In a mixing bowl, whisk together 79 mL oil, jalapeño, vinegar, onion, cilantro, basil, garlic, parsley, pepper flakes, thyme, salt, and pepper.
2. Season tuna with salt and pepper, massage with the remaining oil and cook at 182 degrees C for 3 minutes on each side.
3. Toss the arugula with half of the chimichurri mixture to coat.
4. Split arugula among dishes, then slice tuna and divide among plates, finishing with the remaining chimichurri and serving.
5. Enjoy!

Nutritional information: calories 276, fat 3g, fiber 1g, carbs 14g, protein 20g

150.   STUFFED SALMON

Preparation time: 10 minutes
Cooking time: 20 minutes
Servings: 2

Ingredients:
- 2 salmon fillets, skinless and boneless
- 15 ml olive oil
- 142 g tiger shrimp, peeled, deveined, and chopped
- 6 mushrooms, chopped
- 3 green onions, chopped
- 60 g spinach, torn
- 30 g macadamia nuts, toasted and chopped
- Salt and black pepper to the taste

Preparation
1. Heat 1/2 of the oil in a pan over medium-high heat, then add the mushrooms, onions, salt, and pepper and cook for 4 minutes.
2. Stir in the macadamia nuts, spinach, and shrimp, cook for 3 minutes, and remove from heat.
3. In each salmon fillet, make a lengthwise incision, season with salt and pepper, divide spinach and shrimp mixture into incisions, and rub with the remaining olive oil.
4. Cook for 10 minutes, flipping halfway, in your air fryer basket at 182 degrees C.
5. Serve the packed fish on plates.
6. Enjoy!

Nutritional information: calories 290, fat 15g, fiber 3g, carbs 12g, protein 31g

151.   SWORDFISH AND MANGO

SALSA

Preparation time: 10 minutes
Cooking time: 6 minutes
Servings: 2

Ingredients:

- 2 medium swordfish steaks
- Salt and black pepper to the taste
- 30 ml avocado oil
- 4 g cilantro, chopped
- 1 mango, chopped
- 1 avocado, pitted, peeled, and chopped
- A pinch of cumin
- A pinch of onion powder
- A pinch of garlic powder
- 1 orange, peeled and sliced
- 8 ml balsamic vinegar

Preparation

1. Season the fish steaks with salt, pepper, garlic powder, onion powder, and cumin, then coat with half of the oil and set in the air fryer at 182 °C for 6 minutes, flipping halfway.
2. Meanwhile, in a mixing bowl, combine the avocado, mango, cilantro, balsamic vinegar, salt, pepper, and the remaining oil.
3. Serve the fish on plates with mango salsa and orange slices on the side.
4. Enjoy!

Nutritional information: calories 200, fat 7g, fiber 2g, carbs 14g, protein 14g

152.   FISH AND COUSCOUS

Preparation time: 10 minutes
Cooking time: 15 minutes
Servings: 4

Ingredients:
- 2 red onions, chopped
- Cooking spray
- 2 small fennel bulbs, cored and sliced
- 18 g almonds, toasted and sliced
- Salt and black pepper to the taste
- 1133 g sea bass, gutted
- 10 g fennel seeds
- 124 g whole wheat couscous, cooked

Preparation

1. Season fish with salt & pepper, coat with cooking spray and cook at 176 degrees C for 10 minutes.
2. Meanwhile, coat a pan with cooking spray and heat it over medium heat.

3. Stir in the fennel seeds and roast them for 1 minute.
4. Stir in the onion, salt, pepper, fennel bulbs, almonds, and couscous, and simmer for 2-3 minutes before dividing among plates.
5. Serve immediately after adding the fish to the couscous mixture.
6. Enjoy!

Nutritional information: calories 354, fat 7, fiber 10, carbs 20, protein 30

153.   STUFFED CALAMARI

Preparation time: 10 minutes
Cooking time: 25 minutes
Servings: 4
Ingredients:
- 4 big calamari, tentacles separated and chopped, and tubes reserved
- 8 g parsley, chopped
- 142 g kale, chopped
- 2 garlic cloves, minced
- 1 red bell pepper, chopped
- 15 ml olive oil
- 57 g canned tomato puree
- 1 yellow onion, chopped
- Salt and black pepper to the taste

Preparation

1. Heat oil in a pan over medium heat, then add the onion and garlic, constantly stirring for 2 minutes.
2. Stir in the bell pepper, tomato puree, calamari tentacles, kale, salt, and pepper, and simmer for 10 minutes before turning off the heat. Cook for 3 minutes, stirring occasionally.
3. Stuff calamari tubes with this mixture, secure with toothpicks and cook for 20 minutes at 182 degrees C in an air fryer.
4. Serve calamari on plates with parsley sprinkled on top.
5. Enjoy!

Nutritional information: calories 322, fat 10g, fiber 14g, carbs 14g, protein 22g

154.   SNAPPER FILLETS AND VEGGIES

Preparation time: 10 minutes
Cooking time: 14 minutes
Servings: 2

Ingredients:

- 2 red snapper fillets, boneless
- 15 ml olive oil
- 74 g red bell pepper, chopped
- 74 g green bell pepper, chopped
- 45 g leeks, chopped
- Salt and black pepper to the taste
- 5 ml tarragon, dried
- A splash of white wine

Preparation

1. Mix fish fillets with salt, pepper, oil, green bell pepper, red bell pepper, leeks, tarragon, and wine in a heatproof dish that fits your air fryer, toss well, and place in a warmed air fryer at 176 degrees C for 14 minutes, flipping midway.
2. Serve the fish and vegetables on heated plates.
3. Enjoy!

Nutritional information: calories 300, fat 12g, fiber 8g, carbs 29g, protein 12g

155.   ROASTED COD AND PROSCIUTTO

Preparation time: 10 minutes
Cooking time: 10 minutes
Servings: 4

Ingredients:

- 4 g parsley, chopped
- 4 medium cod filets
- 57 g butter, melted
- 2 garlic cloves, minced
- 30 ml lemon juice
- 3 tablespoons prosciutto, chopped
- 5 g Dijon mustard
- 1 shallot, chopped
- Salt and black pepper to the taste

Preparation

1. Whisk together mustard, butter, garlic, parsley, shallot, lemon juice, prosciutto, salt, and pepper in a mixing bowl.
2. Season the fish with salt & pepper, then cover with the prosciutto mixture and cook for 10 minutes at 198° C in your air fryer.
3. Serve on individual plates.
4. Enjoy!

Nutritional information: calories 200, fat 4g, fiber 7g, carbs 12g, protein 6g

156.   HALIBUT AND SUN-DRIED TOMATOES MIX

Preparation time: 10 minutes
Cooking time: 10 minutes
Servings: 2

Ingredients:

- 2 medium halibut fillets
- 2 garlic cloves, minced
- 10 ml olive oil
- Salt and black pepper to the taste
- 6 sun-dried tomatoes, chopped
- 2 small red onions, sliced
- 1 fennel bulb, sliced
- 9 black olives, pitted and sliced
- 4 rosemary springs, chopped
- 5 ml red pepper flakes, crushed

Preparation

1. Season the fish with salt & pepper, then massage it with garlic and oil in a heat-resistant dish that fits your air fryer.
2. Add onion slices, sun-dried tomatoes, fennel, olives, rosemary, and pepper flakes to your air fryer and cook for 10 minutes at 193 degrees C.
3. Serve the fish and vegetables on separate plates.
4. Enjoy!

Nutritional information: calories 300, fat 12g, fiber 9g, carbs 18g, protein 30g

157.   ORIENTAL FISH

Preparation time: 10 minutes
Cooking time: 12 minutes
Servings: 4

Ingredients:
- 907 g red snapper fillets, boneless
- Salt and black pepper to the taste
- 3 garlic cloves, minced
- 1 yellow onion, chopped
- 15 g tamarind paste
- 15 ml oriental sesame oil
- 6 g ginger, grated
- 30 ml water
- 2.5 ml cumin, ground
- 15 ml lemon juice
- 5 g mint, chopped

Preparation
1. In a food processor, combine garlic, onion, salt, pepper, tamarind paste, sesame oil, ginger, water, and cumin; pulse well and brush this mixture over the fish.
2. Cook for 12 minutes, flipping halfway, in a hot air fryer set to 160 degrees Celsius.
3. Place the fish on plates, pour with lemon juice, garnish with mint, and serve immediately.
4. Enjoy!

Nutritional information: calories 241, fat 8, fiber 16, carbs 17, protein 12

158.   BLACK COD AND PLUM

SAUCE

Preparation time: 10 minutes
Cooking time: 15 minutes
Servings: 2

Ingredients:
- 1 egg white
- ½ cup red quinoa, already cooked
- 5 g whole wheat flour
- 20 ml lemon juice
- 2.5 ml smoked paprika
- 5 ml olive oil

- 2 medium black cod fillets, skinless and boneless
- 1 red plum, pitted and chopped
- 13 ml raw honey
- 1.25 ml black peppercorns, crushed
- 10 ml parsley
- 60 ml water

Preparation
1. In a mixing dish, whisk together 1 teaspoon lemon juice, egg white, flour, and 1.25 ml paprika.
2. In a mixing bowl, combine quinoa and 1/3 of the egg white mixture.
3. Toss the fish in the basin with the remaining egg white mixture.
4. Coat the fish in the quinoa mixture and set aside for 10 minutes.
5. Heat 5 mL oil in a skillet over medium heat, then add the peppercorns, honey, and plum, stir, bring to a simmer, and cook for 1 minute.
6. Stir in the remaining lemon juice, paprika, and water, and continue to cook for 5 minutes.
7. Stir in the parsley, then remove the sauce from the heat and set it aside for now.
8. Cook the fish in air fryer for 10 minutes at 193 degrees Celsius.
9. Arrange the fish on plates, sprinkle with plum sauce, and serve.
10. Enjoy!

Nutritional information: calories 324, fat 14g, fiber 22g, carbs 27g, protein 22g

159.   COD WITH PEARL

ONIONS

Preparation time: 10 minutes
Cooking time: 15 minutes
Servings: 2

Ingredients:
- 397 g pearl onions
- 2 medium cod fillets
- 2 g parsley, dried
- 5 ml thyme, dried
- Black pepper to the taste
- 227 g mushrooms, sliced

Preparation

1. Put the fish in a heatproof dish that fits your air fryer, stir with the onions, parsley, mushrooms, thyme, and black pepper, and cook at 176 degrees C for 15 minutes.
2. Serve everything on individual plates.
3. Enjoy!

Nutritional information: calories 270, fat 14g, fiber 8g, carbs 14g, protein 22g

160. SALMON AND GREEK YOGURT SAUCE

Preparation time: 10 minutes
Cooking time: 20 minutes
Servings: 2

Ingredients:
- 2 medium salmon fillets
- 1 g basil, chopped
- 6 lemon slices
- Sea salt and black pepper to the taste
- 237 ml Greek yogurt
- 5 g curry powder
- A pinch of cayenne pepper
- 1 garlic clove, minced
- 1 g cilantro, chopped
- 0.5 g mint, chopped

Preparation

1. Lay each salmon fillet on a piece of parchment paper, do three splits in each, and stuff with basil.
2. Season with salt & pepper, top each fillet with 3 lemon slices, fold parchment, seal edges, and bake for 20 minutes in the air fryer at 204 degrees C.
3. Meanwhile, whisk together yoghurt, cayenne pepper, salt to taste, garlic, curry, mint, and cilantro in a mixing dish.
4. Transfer the fish to a plate, top with the yoghurt sauce you just made, and serve immediately!
5. Enjoy!

Nutritional information: calories 242, fat 1g, fiber 2g, carbs 3, protein 3g

161. TILAPIA AND CHIVES SAUCE

Preparation time: 10 minutes
Cooking time: 8 minutes
Servings: 4

Ingredients:
- 4 medium tilapia fillets
- Cooking spray
- Salt and black pepper to the taste
- 10 ml honey
- 60 ml Greek yogurt
- Juice from 1 lemon
- 6 g chives, chopped

Preparation

1. Season fish with salt & pepper, coat with cooking spray, and place in a prepared air fryer at 176°C for 8 minutes flipping midway through.
2. Meanwhile, whisk together the yoghurt, honey, salt, pepper, chives, and lemon juice in a large mixing dish.
3. Serve the air fryer fish on plates with the yoghurt sauce drizzled all over.
4. Enjoy!

Nutritional information: calories 261, fat 8g, fiber 18g, carbs 24g, protein 21g

162. DELICIOUS RED SNAPPER

Preparation time: 30 minutes
Cooking time: 15 minutes
Servings: 4

Ingredients:
- 1 big red snapper cleaned and scored
- Salt and black pepper to the taste
- 3 garlic cloves, minced
- 1 jalapeno, chopped
- 113 g okra, chopped
- 14 g butter

- 30 ml olive oil
- 1 red bell pepper, chopped
- 30 ml white wine
- 8 g parsley, chopped

Preparation
1. Mix the jalapeño, wine, and garlic in a bowl, then rub it all over the snapper.
2. Set aside for 30 minutes after seasoning the fish with salt and pepper.
3. Meanwhile, melt 1 tablespoon butter in a pan over medium heat, add the bell pepper and okra, stir, and cook for 5 minutes.
4. Stuff the red snapper's belly with this mixture, along with parsley and olive oil.
5. Cook for 15 minutes at 204 degrees C in a preheated air fryer, flipping halfway through.
6. Serve on individual plates.
7. Enjoy!

Nutritional information: calories 261, fat 7g, fiber 18g, carbs 28g, protein 18g

163. AIR FRIED BRANZINO

Preparation time: 10 minutes
Cooking time: 10 minutes
Servings: 4

Ingredients:
- Zest from 1 lemon, grated
- Zest from 1 orange, grated
- Juice from ½ lemon
- Juice from ½ orange
- Salt and black pepper to the taste
- 4 medium branzino fillets, boneless
- 31 g parsley, chopped
- 30 ml olive oil
- A pinch of red pepper flakes, crushed

Preparation
1. Toss fish fillets with lemon zest, orange zest, lemon juice, orange juice, salt, pepper, oil, and pepper flakes in a big mixing basin, then place in a hot air fryer at 176 degrees C and bake for 10 minutes, flipping once.
2. Serve the fish immediately on plates sprinkled with parsley.
3. Enjoy!

Nutritional information: calories 261, fat 8g, fiber 12g, carbs 21g, protein 12g

164. SALMON AND BLACKBERRY GLAZE

Preparation time: 10 minutes
Cooking time: 33 minutes
Servings: 4
Ingredients:
- 237 g water
- 1-inch ginger piece, grated
- Juice from ½ lemon
- 340 g blackberries
- 15 ml olive oil
- 50 g sugar
- 4 medium salmon fillets, skinless
- Salt and black pepper to the taste

Preparation
1. Heat the water in a pot over medium-high heat, then add the ginger, lemon juice, and blackberries, stir, bring to a boil, cook for 4-5 minutes, remove from heat, pour into a bowl, return to the pan, and combine with the sugar.
2. Stir this mixture, then bring it to a simmer over medium-low heat for 20 minutes.
3. Allow the blackberry sauce to cool before brushing it on the salmon, seasoning it with salt and pepper, drizzling olive oil all over, and thoroughly rubbing it in.
4. Cook for 10 minutes, flipping fish fillets once, in a prepared air fryer set to 176 degrees Celsius.
5. Divide among dishes and top with some of the remaining blackberry sauce.
6. Enjoy!

Nutritional information: calories 312, fat 4g, fiber 9g, carbs 19g, protein 14g

165.   COCONUT TILAPIA

Preparation time: 10 minutes
Cooking time: 10 minutes
Servings: 4

Ingredients:
- 4 medium tilapia fillets
- Salt and black pepper to the taste
- 118 ml coconut milk
- 2 g ginger, grated
- 17 g cilantro, chopped
- 2 garlic cloves, chopped
- 1 g garam masala
- Cooking spray
- ½ jalapeno, chopped

Preparation
1. Combine coconut milk, salt, pepper, cilantro, ginger, garlic, jalapeño, and garam masala in a food processor and pulse until smooth.
2. Cook at 204 degrees C for 10 minutes after spraying the fish with cooking spray and spreading the coconut mixture all over it.
3. Serve immediately on plates.
4. Enjoy!

Nutritional information: calories 200, fat 5g, fiber 6g, carbs 25g, protein 26g

166.   HONEY SEA BASS

Preparation time: 10 minutes
Cooking time: 10 minutes
Servings: 2

Ingredients:
- 2 sea bass fillets
- Zest from ½ orange, grated
- Juice from ½ orange
- A pinch of salt and black pepper
- 30 g mustard
- 10 ml honey
- 30 ml olive oil
- 227 g canned lentils, drained
- A small bunch of dill, chopped
- 57 g watercress
- A small bunch of parsley, chopped

Preparation
1. Season fish fillets with salt & pepper, add orange zest and juice, rub with 1 tablespoon oil, honey, and mustard, rub, put in air fryer, and cook for 10 minutes, flipping halfway, at 176 degrees C.
2. Meanwhile, cook the lentils in a small pot over medium heat, then add the remaining oil, watercress, dill, and parsley, stir well, and divide among plates.
3. Serve immediately with the fish fillets.
4. Enjoy!

Nutritional information: calories 212, fat 8g, fiber 12g, carbs 9g, protein 17g

POULTRY RECIPE

167.   CHICKEN AND PARSLEY

SAUCE

Preparation time: 30 minutes
Cooking time: 25 minutes
Servings: 6

Ingredients:
- 25 g parsley, chopped
- 5 ml oregano, dried
- 118 ml olive oil
- 60 ml red wine
- 4 garlic cloves
- A pinch of salt
- A drizzle of maple syrup
- 12 chicken thighs

Preparation
1. In a food processor, mix parsley, oregano, garlic, salt, oil, wine, and maple syrup and pulse until well combined.
2. Toss the chicken with the parsley sauce in a mixing bowl and chill for 30 minutes.
3. Drain the chicken and place it in the basket of your air fryer. Cook at 193°C for 25 minutes, flipping once.
4. Serve the chicken on plates with the parsley sauce drizzled all over it.
5. Enjoy!

Nutritional information: calories 354, fat 10g, fiber 12g, carbs 22g, protein 17g

168.   HERBED CHICKEN

Preparation time: 30 minutes
Cooking time: 40 minutes
Servings: 4

Ingredients:
- 1 whole chicken
- Salt and black pepper to the taste
- 5 ml garlic powder
- 5 ml onion powder
- 2.5 ml g thyme, dried
- 5 ml rosemary, dried
- 15 ml lemon juice
- 30 ml olive oil

Preparation
1. Season the chicken with salt & pepper, then rub it with thyme, rosemary, garlic powder, onion powder, lemon juice, and olive oil. Set aside for 30 minutes.
2. Cook the chicken in air fryer for 20 mins on each side at 182 degrees Celsius.
3. Allow the chicken to cool before carving and serving.
4. Enjoy!

Nutritional information: calories 390, fat 10g, fiber 5g, carbs 22g, protein 20g

169.   CREAMY COCONUT

CHICKEN

Preparation time: 2 hours Cooking time: 25 minutes
Servings: 4

Ingredients:
- 4 big chicken legs
- 15 g turmeric powder
- 12 g ginger, grated
- Salt and black pepper to the taste
- 60 ml coconut cream

Preparation
1. In a mixing dish, whisk together the cream, turmeric, ginger, salt, and pepper. Add the chicken pieces, toss well, and set aside for 2 hours.
2. Transfer the chicken to a prepared air fryer and cook for 25 minutes at 187°C and serve with a side salad.
3. Enjoy!

Nutritional information: calories 300, fat 4g, fiber 12g, carbs 22g, protein 20g

170. HONEY DUCK BREASTS

Preparation time: 10 minutes
Cooking time: 22 minutes
Servings: 2

Ingredients:
- 1 smoked duck breast, halved
- 5 ml honey
- 5 g tomato paste
- 15 g mustard
- 3 ml apple vinegar

Preparation
1. In a mixing bowl, whisk together honey, tomato paste, mustard, and vinegar. Add duck breast pieces, toss to coat well, and cook at 187 C degrees for 15 minutes.
2. Remove the duck breast from air fryer, combine it with the honey mixture, return to air fryer, and cook at 187 degrees C for 6 minutes more.
3. Serve with a side salad on individual plates.
4. Enjoy!

Nutritional information: calories 274, fat 11, fiber 13, carbs 22, protein 13

171. MEXICAN CHICKEN

Preparation time: 10 minutes
Cooking time: 20 minutes
Servings: 4

Ingredients:
- 454 g salsa verde
- 15 ml olive oil
- Salt and black pepper to the taste
- 454 g chicken breast, boneless and skinless
- 113 g Monterey Jack cheese, grated
- 60 ml cilantro, chopped
- 5 ml garlic powder

Preparation
1. Pour salsa verde into an air fryer-safe baking dish, season chicken with salt, pepper, and garlic powder, drizzle with olive oil, and arrange it on top of the salsa verde.

2. Cook for 20 minutes at 193 degrees Celsius in your air fryer.
3. Cook for 2 mins more after adding the cheese.
4. Serve immediately on plates.
5. Enjoy!

Nutritional information: calories 340, fat 18g, fiber 14g, carbs 32g, protein 18g

172. EASY CHICKEN THIGHS AND BABY POTATOES

Preparation time: 10 minutes
Cooking time: 30 minutes
Servings: 4

Ingredients:
- 8 chicken thighs
- 30 ml olive oil
- 454 g baby potatoes, halved
- 10 ml oregano, dried
- 10 ml rosemary, dried
- 2.5 ml sweet paprika
- Salt and black pepper to the taste
- 2 garlic cloves, minced
- 1 red onion, chopped
- 10 ml thyme, chopped

Preparation
1. Combine chicken thighs, potatoes, salt, pepper, thyme, paprika, onion, rosemary, garlic, oregano, and oil in a mixing bowl.
2. Toss to coat, then spread everything in a heat-proof dish that fits your air fryer and cooks for 30 minutes, shaking midway.
3. Serve on individual plates.
4. Enjoy!

Nutritional information: calories 364, fat 14g, fiber 13g, carbs 21g, protein 34g

173. CHICKEN AND CAPERS

Preparation time: 10 minutes
Cooking time: 20 minutes
Servings: 2

Ingredients:
- 4 chicken thighs
- 23 g capers
- 4 garlic cloves, minced
- 45 g butter, melted
- Salt and black pepper to the taste
- 50 g chicken stock
- 1 lemon, sliced
- 4 green onions, chopped

Preparation
1. Brush the chicken with butter, season with salt and pepper to taste, and place it in an air fryer-compatible baking dish.
2. Add capers, garlic, chicken stock, and lemon slices, toss to coat, and place in your air fryer at 187 °C for 20 minutes, shaking halfway through.
3. Sprinkle with green onions, divide between plates, and serve.
4. Enjoy!

Nutritional information: calories 200, fat 9g, fiber 10g, carbs 17g, protein 7g

174.   DUCK AND PLUM SAUCE

Preparation time: 10 minutes
Cooking time: 32 minutes
Servings: 2

Ingredients:
- 2 duck breasts
- 14 g butter, melted
- 1-star anise
- 15 ml olive oil
- 1 shallot, chopped
- 255 g red plumps, stoned, cut into small wedges
- 25 g sugar
- 30 ml red wine
- 200 ml beef stock

Preparation
1. Heat olive oil in the pan over medium heat, add the shallot, swirl, and cook for 5 minutes.
2. Stir in the sugar and plums until the sugar melts.

3. Stir in the stock and wine, cook for 15 minutes, then remove from heat and keep warm for now.
4. 4. Score duck breasts, season with salt and pepper, rub with melted butter, transfer to a heat-proof dish that fits your air fryer, add star anise and plum sauce, place in air fryer, and cook for 12 mins at 182 degrees C.
5. Serve everything on individual plates.
6. Enjoy!

Nutritional information: calories 400, fat 25g, fiber 12g, carbs 29g, protein 44g

175.   CHICKEN BREASTS AND TOMATOES SAUCE

Preparation time: 10 minutes
Cooking time: 20 minutes
Servings: 4

Ingredients:
- 1 red onion, chopped
- 4 chicken breasts, skinless and boneless
- 60 ml balsamic vinegar
- 397 g canned tomatoes, chopped
- Salt and black pepper to the taste
- 23 g parmesan, grated
- 1.25 ml garlic powder
- Cooking spray

Preparation
1. Spray a baking dish that fits the air fryer with cooking oil, add chicken, season with salt, pepper, balsamic vinegar, garlic powder, tomatoes, and cheese, toss, and place in your air fryer for 20 minutes at 204 degrees C.
2. Serve immediately on plates.
3. Enjoy!

Nutritional information: calories 250, fat 12, fiber 12, carbs 19, protein 28

176. CHICKEN THIGHS AND APPLE MIX

Preparation time: 12 hours
Cooking time: 30 minutes
Servings: 4

Ingredients:
- 8 chicken thighs, bone-in & skin on
- Salt and black pepper to the taste
- 15 ml apple cider vinegar
- 10 g onion, chopped
- 6 g ginger, grated
- 5 ml thyme, dried
- 3 apples, cored and cut into quarters
- 177 g apple juice
- 118 g maple syrup

Preparation
1. Toss chicken with salt, pepper, vinegar, onion, ginger, thyme, apple juice, and maple syrup in a mixing basin, cover, and chill for 12 hours.
2. Transfer this entire mixture to a baking dish that fits your air fryer, add apple chunks, and cook at 176 degrees C for 30 minutes.
3. Serve heated, divided among plates.
4. Enjoy!

Nutritional information: calories 314, fat 8g, fiber 11g, carbs 34g, protein 22g

177. AIR FRIED CHICKEN MIX

Preparation time: 10 minutes
Cooking time: 20 minutes
Servings: 8

Ingredients:
- 1360 g chicken breasts, skinless and boneless
- 1 yellow onion, chopped
- 1 garlic clove, minced
- Salt and black pepper to the taste
- 10 white mushrooms, halved
- 15 ml olive oil
- 1 red bell pepper, chopped
- 1 green bell pepper
- 7 g mozzarella cheese, shredded
- Cooking spray

Preparation
1. Season chicken with salt & pepper, rub with garlic, spray with cooking spray, and cook at 198 degrees C for 12 mins.
2. Meanwhile, heat the oil in pan over medium heat, add the onion, swirl, and cook for 2 minutes.
3. Cook for 8 minutes after adding the mushrooms, garlic, and bell peppers.
4. Divide the chicken among the dishes, serve with the mushroom mixture on the side, and top with the cheese while the chicken is still hot.
5. Enjoy!

Nutritional information: calories 305, fat 12g, fiber 11g, carbs 26g, protein 32g

178. CHICKEN CACCIATORE

Preparation time: 10 minutes
Cooking time: 20 minutes
Servings: 4

Ingredients:
- Salt and black pepper to the taste
- 8 chicken drumsticks, bone-in
- 1 bay leaf
- 5 ml garlic powder
- 1 yellow onion, chopped
- 794 g canned tomatoes and juice, crushed
- 5 ml oregano, dried
- 90 g black olives, pitted and sliced

Preparation
1. Toss chicken with salt, pepper, garlic powder, bay leaf, onion, tomatoes and juice, oregano, and olives in a heat resistance dish that fits your air fryer, and cook at 185 degrees C for 20 minutes.
2. Serve on individual plates.
3. Enjoy!

Nutritional information: calories 300, fat 12g, fiber 8g, carbs 20g, protein 24g

179.   LEMON CHICKEN

Preparation time: 10 minutes
Cooking time: 30 minutes
Servings: 6

Ingredients:

- 1 whole chicken, cut into medium pieces
- 15 ml olive oil
- Salt and black pepper to the taste
- Juice from 2 lemons
- Zest from 2 lemons, grated

Preparation

1. Season chicken with salt & pepper, rub with oil and lemon zest, drizzle with lemon juice, and cook at 176° C for 30 minutes, rotating chicken pieces halfway through.
2. Serve with a side salad on individual plates.
3. Enjoy!

Nutritional information: calories 334, fat 24g, fiber 12g, carbs 26g, protein 20g

180.   QUICK CREAMY CHICKEN CASSEROLE

Preparation time: 10 minutes
Cooking time: 12 minutes
Servings: 4

Ingredients:

- 284 g spinach, chopped
- 57 g butter
- 27 g flour
- 375 ml milk
- 45 g parmesan, grated
- 118 ml heavy cream
- Salt and black pepper to the taste
- 280 g chicken breasts, skinless, boneless, and cubed
- 60 g bread crumbs

Preparation

1. Melt the butter in a pan over medium heat, then add the flour and whisk well.
2. Stir in the milk, heavy cream, and parmesan, then simmer for another 1-2 minutes before turning off the heat.
3. Spread chicken and spinach in a pan that fits your air fryer.
4. Toss in the salt and pepper.
5. Spread the cream mixture on top, then place in the air fryer for 12 minutes at 176 degrees Celsius.
6. Serve the chicken and spinach mixture on plates.
7. Enjoy!

Nutritional information: calories 321, fat 9g, fiber 12g, carbs 22g, protein 17g

181.   CHICKEN AND BLACK OLIVES SAUCE

Preparation time: 10 minutes
Cooking time: 8 minutes
Servings: 2

Ingredients:

- 1 chicken breast cut into 4 pieces
- 30 ml olive oil
- 3 garlic cloves, minced

For the sauce:

- 180 g black olives, pitted
- Salt and black pepper to the taste
- 30 ml olive oil
- 15 g parsley, chopped
- 15 ml lemon juice

Preparation

1. Blend olives with salt, pepper, 30 mL olive oil, lemon juice, and parsley in a food processor until smooth. Transfer to a bowl.
2. Season the chicken with salt & pepper, massage with the oil and garlic, and cook for 8 minutes at 187 degrees C in a preheated air fryer.
3. Serve the chicken on plates with the olive sauce on top.
4. Enjoy!

Nutritional information: calories 270, fat 12g, fiber 12g, carbs 23g, protein 22g

182. PEPPERONI CHICKEN

Preparation time: 10 minutes
Cooking time: 22 minutes
Servings: 6

Ingredients:
- 397 g tomato paste
- 15 ml olive oil
- 4 medium chicken breasts, skinless and boneless
- Salt and black pepper to the taste
- 5 ml oregano, dried
- 170 g mozzarella, sliced
- 5 ml garlic powder
- 57 g pepperoni, sliced

Preparation
1. Toss chicken in a bowl with salt, pepper, garlic powder, and oregano.
2. Place the chicken in your air fryer and cook at 176°C for 6 minutes before transferring it to a pan that fits your air fryer.
3. Top with mozzarella slices, tomato paste, and pepperoni pieces, then place in your air fryer and cook for 15 minutes at 176 degrees C.
4. Serve on individual plates.
5. Enjoy!

Nutritional information: calories 320, fat 10g, fiber 16g, carbs 23g, protein 27g

183. TURKEY, PEAS, AND

MUSHROOMS CASSEROLE

Preparation time: 10 minutes
Cooking time: 20 minutes
Servings: 4

Ingredients:
- 907 g turkey breasts, skinless, boneless
- Salt and black pepper to the taste
- 1 yellow onion, chopped
- 1 celery stalk, chopped
- 73 g peas
- 237 g chicken stock
- 122 g cream of mushrooms soup
- 35 g bread cubes

Preparation
1. Mix turkey with salt, pepper, onion, celery, peas, and stock in a pan that fits your air fryer, then place it in the air fryer and cook at 182 degrees C for 15 minutes.
2. Cook for 5 mins at 182 degrees C after adding the bread cubes and cream of mushroom soup.
3. Serve immediately on plates.
4. Enjoy!

Nutritional information: calories 271, fat 9g, fiber 9g, carbs 16g, protein 7g

184. GREEK CHICKEN

Preparation time: 10 minutes
Cooking time: 15 minutes
Servings: 4

Ingredients:
- 30 ml olive oil
- Juice from 1 lemon
- 1 g oregano, dried
- 3 garlic cloves, minced
- 454 g chicken thighs
- Salt and black pepper to the taste
- 227 g asparagus, trimmed
- 1 zucchini, roughly chopped
- 1 lemon sliced

Preparation
1. Toss chicken pieces with oil, lemon juice, oregano, garlic, salt, pepper, asparagus, zucchini, and lemon slices on a heat-proof plate that fits your air fryer, then place in a warmed air fryer and cook at 193 degrees C for 15 minutes.
2. Serve everything on individual plates.
3. Enjoy!

Nutritional information: calories 300, fat 8g, fiber 12g, carbs 20g, protein 18g

185. CHICKEN AND PEACHES

Preparation time: 10 minutes
Cooking time: 30 minutes

Servings: 6

Ingredients:
- 1 whole chicken, cut into medium pieces
- 177 ml water
- 79 ml honey
- Salt and black pepper to the taste
- 60 ml olive oil
- 4 peaches, halved

Preparation
1. In a pot, bring the water to a simmer over medium heat, add the honey, mix thoroughly, and set aside.
2. Rub the oil over the chicken pieces, season with salt and pepper, and place in the air fryer basket for 10 minutes at 176 degrees C.
3. Brush chicken with some of the honey mixture, cook for 6 minutes more, turn, brush with honey mixture again, and cook for 7 minutes more.
4. Place the chicken on plates and keep warm.
5. Brush the peaches with the remaining honey marinade, then place them in the air fryer for 3 minutes.
6. Serve alongside the chicken pieces on individual plates.
7. Enjoy!

Nutritional information: calories 430, fat 14g, fiber 3g, carbs 15g, protein 20g

186.   CHICKEN AND RADISH

MIX

Preparation time: 10 minutes
Cooking time: 30 minutes
Servings: 4

Ingredients:
- 4 chicken things, bone-in
- Salt and black pepper to the taste
- 15 ml olive oil
- 237 ml chicken stock
- 6 radishes, halved
- 5 g sugar
- 3 carrots, cut into thin sticks
- 6 g chives, chopped

Preparation
1. Heat a skillet wide enough to fit your air fryer over medium heat, then add stock, carrots, sugar, and radishes, stirring gently. Reduce heat to medium, partially cover the pot, and simmer for 20 minutes.
2. Rub the chicken with olive oil, season with salt and pepper, and cook at 176 degrees C for 4 minutes.
3. Toss the chicken with the radish mixture before placing everything in the air fryer for 4 minutes longer. Divide among plates and serve.
4. Enjoy!

Nutritional information: calories 237, fat 10g, fiber 4g, carbs 19g, protein 29g

187.   TEA GLAZED CHICKEN

Preparation time: 10 minutes
Cooking time: 30 minutes
Servings: 6

Ingredients:
- 169 g apricot preserves
- 105 g pineapple preserves
- 6 chicken legs
- 237 ml hot water
- 6 black tea bags
- 15 ml soy sauce
- 1 onion, chopped
- 2.5 ml red pepper flakes
- 15 ml olive oil
- Salt and black pepper to the taste
- 6 chicken legs

Preparation
1. Put the boiling water in a bowl, add the tea bags, cover and let aside for 10 minutes, then discard the bags and transfer the tea to another bowl.
2. Whisk in the soy sauce, pepper flakes, apricot, and pineapple preserves, and remove from heat.
3. Season your chicken with salt & pepper, rub with oil, and cook at 176 degrees C for 5 minutes.

4. Spread the onion on the bottom of an air fryer-compatible baking dish, add the chicken pieces, drizzle the tea glaze on top, and cook at 160 degrees C for 25 minutes.
5. Serve everything on individual plates.
6. Enjoy!

Nutritional information: calories 298, fat 14g, fiber 1g, carbs 14g, protein 30g

188. CHICKEN BREASTS AND BBQ CHILI SAUCE

Preparation time: 10 minutes
Cooking time: 20 minutes
Servings: 6

Ingredients:
- 473 ml chili sauce
- 470 g ketchup
- 120 g pear jelly
- 60 ml honey
- 2.5 ml liquid smoke
- 5 ml chili powder
- 5 ml mustard powder
- 5 ml sweet paprika
- Salt and black pepper to the taste
- 5 ml garlic powder
- 6 chicken breasts, skinless and boneless

Preparation
1. Season chicken breasts with salt & pepper put in a hot air fryer, and cook for 10 minutes at 176 degrees C.
2. Meanwhile, boil the chilli sauce in a skillet over medium heat, then add the ketchup, pear jelly, honey, liquid smoke, chilli powder, mustard powder, sweet paprika, salt, pepper, and garlic powder, swirl, and cook for 10 minutes.
3. Toss in the air-fried chicken breasts, divide among plates and serve.
4. Enjoy!

Nutritional information: calories 473, fat 13g, fiber 7g, carbs 39g, protein 33g

189. VEGGIE STUFFED CHICKEN BREASTS

Preparation time: 10 minutes
Cooking time: 15 minutes
Servings: 4

Ingredients:
- 4 chicken breasts, skinless and boneless
- 30 ml olive oil
- Salt and black pepper to the taste
- 1 zucchini, chopped
- 5 ml Italian seasoning
- 2 yellow bell peppers, chopped
- 3 tomatoes, chopped
- 1 red onion, chopped
- 225 g mozzarella, shredded

Preparation
1. Make a pocket in each chicken breast, season with salt and pepper, then rub with olive oil.
2. Stir zucchini, Italian seasoning, bell peppers, tomatoes, and onion in a mixing bowl.
3. Stuff chicken breasts with this mixture, top with mozzarella, and cook for 15 minutes at 176° C in an air fryer basket.
4. Serve on individual plates.
5. Enjoy!

Nutritional information: calories 300, fat 12g, fiber 7g, carbs 22g, protein 18g

190. CIDER GLAZED CHICKEN

Preparation time: 10 minutes
Cooking time: 14 minutes
Servings: 4

Ingredients:
- 1 sweet potato, cubed
- 2 apples, cored and sliced
- 15 ml olive oil
- 2 g rosemary, chopped
- Salt and black pepper to the taste
- 6 chicken thighs, bone-in & skin on
- 158 ml apple cider
- 15 g mustard
- 30 ml honey

- 14 g butter

Preparation
1. Heat half of the oil in your pan that fits your air fryer over medium-high heat, then whisk in the cider, honey, butter, and mustard. Bring to a simmer, remove from heat, and toss in the chicken.
2. Toss potato cubes with rosemary, apples, salt, pepper, and the remaining oil in a basin, then add to the chicken mixture.
3. Cook for 14 minutes at 198 degrees Celsius in an air fryer.
4. Serve everything on individual plates.
5. Enjoy!

Nutritional information: calories 241, fat 7, fiber 12, carbs 28, protein 22

191. CHICKEN AND CHESTNUTS MIX

Preparation time: 10 minutes
Cooking time: 12 minutes
Servings: 2

Ingredients:
- 227 g chicken pieces
- 1 small yellow onion, chopped
- 6 g garlic, minced
- A pinch of ginger, grated
- A pinch of allspice, ground
- 35 g water chestnuts
- 30 ml soy sauce
- 30 ml chicken stock
- 30 ml balsamic vinegar
- 2 tortillas for serving

Preparation
1. Mix chicken meat with onion, garlic, ginger, allspice, chestnuts, soy sauce, stock, and vinegar in a pan that fits your air fryer stir, and cook at 182 degrees C for 12 minutes.
2. Serve everything on individual plates.

Nutritional information: calories 301, fat 12g, fiber 7g, carbs 24g, protein 12g

192. CHICKEN AND SPINACH SALAD

Preparation time: 10 minutes
Cooking time: 12 minutes
Servings: 2

Ingredients:
- 10 ml parsley, dried
- 2 chicken breasts, skinless and boneless
- 5 ml onion powder
- 10 ml sweet paprika
- 118 ml lemon juice
- Salt and black pepper to the taste
- 150 g baby spinach
- 8 strawberries, sliced
- 1 small red onion, sliced
- 30 ml balsamic vinegar
- 1 avocado, pitted, peeled, and chopped
- 60 ml olive oil
- 2 g tarragon, chopped

Preparation
1. Toss the chicken with lemon juice, parsley, onion powder, and paprika in a mixing dish.
2. Cook the chicken in air fryer for 12 minutes at 182 degrees Celsius.
3. Toss spinach, onion, strawberries, and avocado in a mixing bowl.
4. In a different bowl, whisk together the oil, vinegar, salt, pepper, and tarragon, then add to the salad and toss.
5. Serve the chicken on plates with the spinach salad on the side.
6. Enjoy!

Nutritional information: calories 240, fat 5g, fiber 13g, carbs 25g, protein 22g

193. DUCK AND VEGGIES

Preparation time: 10 minutes
Cooking time: 20 minutes
Servings: 8

Ingredients:
- 1 duck, chopped into medium pieces
- 3 cucumbers, chopped

- 45 ml white wine
- 2 carrots, chopped
- 237 ml chicken stock
- 1 small ginger piece, grated
- Salt and black pepper to the taste

Preparation
1. Toss duck pieces with cucumbers, wine, carrots, ginger, stock, salt, and pepper in a pan that fits your air fryer, then place in your air fryer and cook at 187 degrees C for 20 minutes.
2. Serve everything on individual plates.
3. Enjoy!

Nutritional information: calories 200, fat 10g, fiber 8g, carbs 20g, protein 22g

194. CHICKEN AND GARLIC SAUCE

Preparation time: 10 minutes
Cooking time: 20 minutes
Servings: 4

Ingredients:
- 14 g butter, melted
- 4 chicken breasts, skin on and bone-in
- 15 ml olive oil
- Salt and black pepper to the taste
- 40 garlic cloves, peeled and chopped
- 2 thyme springs
- 60 ml chicken stock
- 8 g parsley, chopped
- 60 ml dry white wine

Preparation
1. Season the chicken breasts with salt & pepper, rub with the oil, place in air fryer, and cook for 4 mins on each side @ 182 degrees C. Transfer to a heat-proof dish that fits your air fryer.
2. Toss in the melted butter, garlic, thyme, stock, wine, and parsley, then place in the air fryer and cook for 15 minutes at 176° C.
3. Serve everything on individual plates.
4. Enjoy!

Nutritional information: calories 227, fat 9g, fiber 13g, carbs 22g, protein 12g

195. CHEESE CRUSTED CHICKEN

Preparation time: 10 minutes
Cooking time: 15 minutes
Servings: 4

Ingredients:
- 4 bacon slices, cooked and crumbled
- 4 chicken breasts, skinless and boneless
- 15 ml water
- 118 ml avocado oil
- 1 egg, whisked
- Salt and black pepper to the taste
- 80 g asiago cheese, shredded
- 1.25 ml garlic powder
- 90 g parmesan cheese, grated

Preparation
1. Stir together the parmesan, garlic, salt, and pepper in a mixing bowl.
2. In a different bowl, whisk together the egg and the water.
3. Season the chicken with salt and pepper before dipping it into the egg mixture and then into the cheese mixture.
4. Cook the chicken in your air fryer for 15 minutes @ 160° C.
5. Serve the chicken on plates with bacon and asiago cheese on top.
6. Enjoy!

Nutritional information: calories 400, fat 22g, fiber 12g, carbs 32g, protein 47g

196. CHICKEN PARMESAN

Preparation time: 10 minutes
Cooking time: 15 minutes
Servings: 4

Ingredients:
- 119 g panko bread crumbs
- 23 g parmesan, grated

- 1 g garlic powder
- 240 g white flour
- 1 egg, whisked
- 680 g chicken cutlets, skinless and boneless
- Salt and black pepper to the taste
- 113 g mozzarella, grated
- 473 ml tomato sauce
- 4 g basil, chopped

Preparation

1. Stir together panko, parmesan, and garlic powder in a mixing basin.
2. In another basin, mix the flour and the egg.
3. Season the chicken with salt and pepper before dipping it in flour, egg mixture, and panko.
4. Cook the chicken pieces in your air fryer for 3 minutes on each side at 182 degrees C.
5. Put the chicken into a baking dish that fits your air fryer, cover with tomato sauce, and top with mozzarella. Place in air fryer and cook at 190 degrees C for 7 minutes.
6. Divide among plates, cover with basil and serve.
7. Enjoy!

Nutritional information: calories 304g, fat 12g, fiber 11g, carbs 22g, protein 15g

197.   AIR FRYER LEMON

PEPPER WINGS

Prep Time: 5 Minutes
Cook Time: 25 Minutes
Total Time: 30 Minutes
Yield: 4 Servings

Ingredients
- 680 g chicken wings, drumettes, and flats separated and tips discarded
- 5 ml lemon pepper seasoning
- 1.25 ml cayenne pepper

For The Lemon Pepper Sauce
- 42 g butter
- 5 ml lemon pepper seasoning
- 5 ml honey

Preparation

1. Preheat your air fryer to 193°C.

2. Season the chicken wings with lemon pepper and cayenne pepper.
3. Fill the air fryer no more than halfway with the lemon pepper wings. Cook the basket for 20-22 minutes, shaking halfway through.
4. Cook for a further 3-5 minutes at 204 degrees C to achieve a lovely crispy skin on the chicken wings.
5. In a bowl, combine the melted butter, extra lemon pepper seasoning, and honey while the chicken wings are cooking.
6. Remove the chicken wings from the air fryer and cover with the lemon honey sauce. Enjoy!

Nutrition Information: Calories: 462 Total Fat: 36.2g Carbohydrates: 2g Fiber: 0g Sugar: 1g Protein: 31.2g

198.   AIR FRYER PINEAPPLE

CHICKEN

Prep Time 5 Minutes
Cook Time 10 Minutes
Total Time 15 Minutes
Servings 2

Ingredients
For The Grilled Chicken
- 2 raw chicken breasts
- 14 g butter
- 1.25 ml salt
- 1.25 ml pepper

For The Pineapple Sauce
- 118 ml pineapple juice
- 50 g brown sugar
- 60 ml low-sodium soy sauce
- 1 clove of garlic, minced
- 3 g ground ginger
- 10 g water
- 5 g cornstarch
- chunks of fresh or canned pineapple (optional)

Preparation

1. Preheat the air fryer to 193 degrees Celsius.
2. In a mixing dish, combine the melted butter, salt, and pepper. Coat both faces of the chicken breasts with butter and set in the air

fryer for 10-15 minutes, flipping halfway through. They are finished when the interior temperature reaches 74 degrees Celsius. Allow the chicken to rest for at least 5 minutes.

3. Meanwhile, make the pineapple sauce by whisking together the pineapple juice, brown sugar, soy sauce, minced garlic, and ginger in a small saucepan over medium heat for 5 minutes.

4. In a separate bowl, combine the cornstarch and water and stir into the sauce. Allow to boil for 1 minute more while stirring, then remove from heat.

5. Rested grilled chicken breasts should be cut into long strips and either completely coated with sauce or poured over the top of the chicken before serving.

6. If preferred, add canned or fresh pineapple chunks.

Nutrition Information: Calories: 503 Total fat: 11g Carbohydrates: 55g fiber: 1g Sugar: 47g Protein: 46g

199. EASY CHILI SPICED AIR FRYER CHICKEN DRUMSTICKS (KETO & PALEO)

Prep Time 10 minutes
Cook Time 17 minutes
Total Time 27 minutes
Servings 8 servings

Ingredients
- 907 g Chicken drumsticks
- 15 ml avocado oil
- 3 g sea salt
- 1.25 ml pepper
- 1.25 ml garlic powder
- 2.5 ml onion powder
- 2.5 ml paprika
- 1 g chili flakes
- 5 ml powder or chili powder
- 1.25 ml cayenne pepper optional- for hotter spice

Preparation
1. Preheat the air fryer to 198°C if necessary.

2. While it's heating up, toss the drumsticks in a bowl with the avocado oil. Mix well to coat evenly.

3. In another bowl, combine and blend the remaining spice ingredients.

4. Sprinkle the spice mixture evenly over all sides of the chicken.

5. When the grill is hot, open the lid and set the drumsticks inside. Close the lid, leaving enough space for the chicken to cook evenly. Set the timer for 17 minutes in total.

6. Cook for 9 minutes before flipping the chicken using a spatula. Cook for another 8 minutes, then check the chicken to ensure it has achieved 74°C. If it is not completely cooked, check it every 3-5 minutes until it reaches an internal temperature of 74°C.

7. Remove from the grill and put aside to cool before serving.

Nutritional information: Calories 198 Fat 12g Carbohydrates 1g Fiber 1g Sugar 1g Protein 20g

200. BROCCOLI CHEDDAR CHICKEN FRITTERS

Prep Time 10 minutes
Cook Time 10 minutes
Servings 8 fritters

Ingredients
- 454 g boneless skinless chicken thighs, cut into small pieces
- 2 large eggs
- 5 ml garlic powder
- 63 g all-purpose flour
- 235 g shredded cheddar cheese
- 142 g broccoli florets, steamed and chopped fine
- salt & pepper to taste
- Olive oil

Preparation
1. Combine the bite-size chicken pieces, garlic powder, eggs, almond flour, shredded cheese, broccoli, salt, and pepper in a large mixing bowl.

2. Combine gently.

3. Scoop the batter into a GREASED basket. In your air fryer, make uniform-sized fritters. The number of fritters you make will be determined by the size of your air fryer. Flatten them with the back of a spoon.
4. Preheat your air fryer to 204 degrees Celsius and cook for 8 minutes.
5. Cook for another 2 mins on the other side.
6. The cook time will need to be increased if you make thicker fritters. Before removing it from the air fryer, always check for doneness.
7. Repeat these processes until your "battery" is depleted.

Nutritional information Calories: 166kcal Carbohydrates: 2g Protein: 17g Fat: 11g Fiber: 1g Sugar: 1g

201. CHICKEN BREAST FILLET WITH BRIE CHEESE AND RAW HAM

Preparation time: 15 mins
cooking time: 15 mins
Servings: 4 people

Ingredients
- 2 large chicken breast fillets
- Freshly ground pepper
- 4 small slices of brie
- 3 g chives, finely chopped
- 4 slices of raw ham
- 15 ml of olive oil

Preparation
1. Preheat the air fryer to 180 ° C.
2. Divide the chicken breast fillets into four equal pieces and cut horizontally with a 1 cm gap to the edge. Unfold the chicken breast fillets and sprinkle them with salt and pepper. Put a slice of brie cheese and some chives on each piece.
3. Push the basket into the air fryer and set the timer to 15 minutes. Fry the chicken breast fillets until they are nice and brown. Delicious with mashed potatoes and fried chicory.

Nutritional information: calories 281 kcal protein 9 g fat14 g carbohydrates 28 g

202. CRISPY CHICKEN NUGGETS WITH CANARIAN POTATOES

Total time 25 min
Servings: 4

Ingredients
- 400g chicken breast
- 15 ml honey
- 7 g Pepper
- 1/2 clove of garlic
- 200g plain yogurt
- 80g cornflakes
- lemon juice
- Chili spice
- 1 kg of potatoes (firm cooking)
- 150 g sea salt
- 1 liter of water

Preparation
1. First, the chicken fillets are washed off and cut into elongated strips. Then plain yogurt, honey, salt, pepper, chilli, and half a pressed clove of garlic are mixed together and seasoned with lemon juice. Then chop the cornflakes in a bowl or freezer bag. Now the chicken breast strips are placed in the yoghurt marinade and covered on all sides. Then they are turned directly into crushed corn flakes. It is best to put the chicken pieces on the basket of your hot air fryer and set the timer to 15 mins at 182ºC.
2. The potatoes are prepared separately in a saucepan with water. Usually, boiled potatoes are cooked with a similar amount of salt as if you were cooking pasta. The special case with Canarian potatoes is that about 150g of sea salt is added to one liter of water. This gives the potatoes a wonderfully salty crust and goes well with our chicken nuggets.
3. First, wash the potatoes thoroughly, and cover with approx. 1 liter of water and add 150g of

salt. Bring to the boil once and cook within the next 20 minutes. After the cooking process, they are poured off and put back in the hot pot, where they get a white crust with constant shaking.

Nutritional information: calories254 kcal protein 8 g fat 4 g carbohydrates 44 g added sugar 0 g

203.   SLICED TURKEY

Total time 25 min
Servings: 4
Ingredients:
- 500 g turkey breast fillet
- 2 carrots
- 1 bell pepper
- 1 zucchini (small)
- 2 cloves of garlic
- 60 ml white wine
- 1 onion
- 60 g creme fraiche
- 30 ml wine vinegar
- 1 bunch of parsley
- 500 g rice
- Salt, pepper, paprika powder

Preparation:
1. Cook the rice according to the package insert.
2. Cut zucchini and carrots into thin slices, core the peppers, wash and cut into cubes.
3. Put a little oil in the air fryer. Add the carrots and cook for 5 minutes at 182 °C. Add remaining vegetables and cook again for 10 minutes.
4. Peel the garlic and onion and cut them into fine cubes.
5. Cut the turkey fillet into strips, and add the onion and garlic to the hot air fryer.
6. Mix the wine and vinegar well and pour over the turkey meat. Let it cook for 10 minutes.
7. Add salt, pepper, and paprika powder and refine with creme fraiche.
8. Chop parsley and pour over the sliced meat. Remove this from the hot air fryer and serve with rice.

Nutritional information Calories 214 kcal protein 8 g fat 8 g carbohydrates 27 g added sugar   0 g

204.   CURRY CHICKEN
SKEWERS

Total time: 20 min.
Servings: 4
Ingredients
- 4 chicken breasts
For marinade:
- 19 g curry powder
- 150 ml yogurt
- 1 bunch of coriander
- 100 ml coconut milk
- salt
- pepper

Preparation:
1. Cut the chicken into fine strips. Wash and finely chop the coriander.
2. Mix all ingredients for the marinade well. Put the chicken breast strips in and let them marinate for several hours.
3. Put the chicken on skewers and grill at 180 degrees C for about 10 minutes.

Nutritional information
Calories 457 kcal protein 19 g fat 9 g carbohydrates 73 g added sugar 0 g

205.   CHICKEN QUESADILLAS

Cooking time: 10 min.
Total time: 20 min.
Servings: 2

Ingredients
- 4 corn tortillas 200 g
- Cheddar cheese
- 1 Mug of creme fraiche
- 1 bunch coriander
- 200 g   Chicken breast
- 1 small avocado
- 1 red chili pepper
- 1 pinch Salt pepper

Preparation

1. Put the tortillas on your work surface and cut to the size of your Airfryer if necessary. Rinse the chicken breast, pat dry, and cut into strips. Halve the avocado, remove the peel, take out the core and cut it into small pieces. Rinse the cilantro and pluck the leaves from the stem, wash the chilli and cut into fine rings.

2. Place the tortilla in the Airfryer, cover half of the ingredients: First sprinkle the cheese, then put the chicken, avocado, and chilli on top, spread the creme fraîche with a spoon, and finally pluck the coriander over it. Salt and pepper to taste. Place a second tortilla on top and bake in the Airfryer for 7 minutes at 180 ° C.

Nutritional information: Calories 450 kcal protein 35 g fat 30 g carbohydrates 8 g added sugar 0 g

206.   CHINESE STUFFED

CHICKEN

Preparation time: 10 minutes
Cooking time: 35 minutes
Servings: 8

Ingredients:
- 1 whole chicken
- 10 wolfberries
- 2 red chilies, chopped
- 4 ginger slices
- 1 yam, cubed
- 5 ml soy sauce
- Salt and white pepper to the taste
- 15 ml sesame oil

Preparation

1. Rub soy sauce and sesame oil over chicken, season with salt and pepper, then fill with wolfberries, yam cubes, chilies, and ginger.

2. Place in your air fryer and cook for 15 minutes at 182 degrees C after 20 minutes at 204 degrees C.

3. Serve chicken by carving it, dividing it among plates.

4. Enjoy!

Nutritional information: calories 320, fat 12g, fiber 17g, carbs 22g, protein 12g

SANDWICHES, PIZZA, AND BURGER RECIPE

207. AMAZING BREAKFAST BURGER

Preparation time: 10 minutes
Cooking time: 45 minutes
Servings: 4

Ingredients:
- 454 g beef, ground
- One yellow onion, chopped
- 5 g tomato puree
- 3 g garlic, minced
- 5 g mustard
- 5 ml basil, dried
- 5 ml parsley, chopped
- 15 g cheddar cheese, grated
- Salt and black pepper to the taste
- 4 bread buns for serving

Preparation
1. Mix together meat, onion, tomato puree, garlic, mustard, basil, parsley, cheese, salt, and pepper in a mixing bowl, and toss well. Form 4 burgers from this mixture.
2. Preheat your air fryer to 204 °C, add the burgers and cook for 25 minutes.
3. Reduce the temperature to 176° C and bake the burgers for another 20 minutes.
4. Serve them with toast buns for a quick breakfast.
5. Enjoy!

Nutritional information: calories 234, fat 5g, fiber 8g, carbs 12g, protein 4g

208. AIR FRIED SANDWICH

Preparation time: 10 minutes
Cooking time: 6 minutes
Servings: 2

Ingredients:

- 2 English muffins, halved
- 2 eggs
- 2 bacon strips
- Salt and black pepper to the taste

Preparation
1. Crack eggs into your air fryer, top with bacon, and cook at 200 degrees C for 6 minutes.
2. Heat your English muffin halves for a few seconds, then split the eggs between two halves, top with bacon, season with salt and pepper, and serve for breakfast.
3. Enjoy!

Nutritional information: calories 261, fat 5g, fiber 8g, carbs 12g, protein 4g

209. TUNA SANDWICHES

Preparation time: 10 minutes
Cooking time: 5 minutes
Servings: 4
Ingredients:
- 454 g canned tuna, drained
- 58 g mayonnaise
- 30 g mustard
- 15 ml lemon juice
- 2 green onions, chopped
- 3 English muffins, halved
- 43 g butter
- 6 provolone cheese

Preparation
1. Stir tuna with mayo, lemon juice, mustard, and green onions in a mixing dish.
2. Butter the muffin halves and place them in a prepared air fryer for 4 minutes at 176 degrees C.
3. Spread tuna mixture over muffin halves, then top with provolone cheese. Return sandwiches to air fryer for 4 minutes, then divide among plates and serve for breakfast immediately.
4. Enjoy!

Nutritional information: calories 182, fat 4g, fiber 7g, carbs 8g, protein 6g

210.   CHICKEN SANDWICHES

Preparation time: 10 minutes
Cooking time: 10 minutes
Servings: 4

Ingredients:
- 2 chicken breasts, skinless, boneless, and cubed
- 1 red onion, chopped
- 1 red bell pepper, sliced
- 29 g Italian seasoning
- 0.75 g thyme, dried
- 113 g butter lettuce, torn
- 4 pita pockets
- 1 cup cherry tomatoes, halved
- 15 ml olive oil

Preparation
1. Toss the chicken with the onion, bell pepper, Italian spice, and oil in an air fryer and cook at 193 degrees C for 10 minutes.
2. Toss the chicken mixture with the thyme, butter lettuce, and cherry tomatoes in a mixing bowl. Stuff pita pockets with this mixture and serves for lunch.
3. Enjoy!

Nutritional information: calories 126, fat 4g, fiber 8g, carbs 14g, protein 4g

211.   ITALIAN EGGPLANT

SANDWICH

Preparation time: 10 minutes
Cooking time: 16 minutes
Servings: 2

Ingredients:
- 1 eggplant, sliced
- 2 g parsley, dried
- Salt and black pepper to the taste
- 60 g breadcrumbs
- 2.5 ml Italian seasoning
- 2.5 ml garlic powder
- 2.5 ml onion powder
- 30 ml milk
- 4 bread slices
- Cooking spray

- 115 g mayonnaise
- 169 g tomato sauce
- 450 g mozzarella cheese, grated

Preparation
1. Season the eggplant slices with salt & pepper, set aside for 10 minutes, and pat dry well.
2. Mix parsley, breadcrumbs, Italian seasoning, onion and garlic powder, salt, and black pepper in a mixing bowl.
3. In another bowl, whisk together the milk & mayonnaise.
4. Brush the eggplant slices with the mayo mixture, then roll them in the breadcrumbs. Put them in your air-fryer basket, spritz with cooking oil, and cook at 204 degrees C for 15 minutes, rotating them after 8 minutes.
5. Scrub each slice of bread with olive oil and place two on a work surface.
6. Add mozzarella and parmesan to each, then top with baked eggplant slices, tomato sauce, and basil, then the other bread pieces, greased side down.
7. Sandwiches should be placed on plates, split in half, and served for lunch.
8. Enjoy!

Nutritional information: calories 324, fat 16g, fiber 4g, carbs 39g, protein 12g

212.   MEATBALLS SANDWICH

Preparation time: 10 minutes
Cooking time: 22 minutes
Servings: 4

Ingredients:
- 3 baguettes, sliced more than halfway through
- 397 g beef, ground
- 199 g tomato sauce
- 1 small onion, chopped
- 1 egg, whisked
- 7 g bread crumbs
- 29 g cheddar cheese, grated
- 3 g oregano, chopped
- 15 ml olive oil
- Salt and black pepper to the taste
- 5 ml thyme, dried
- 5 ml basil, dried

Preparation

1. In a mixing bowl, mix the meat, pepper, salt, onion, breadcrumbs, egg, cheese, oregano, thyme, and basil, and stir. Form medium meatballs and place them in an air fryer greased with oil.
2. Cook for 12 minutes at 193 degrees Celsius, flipping midway.
3. Cook the meatballs for another 10 minutes in the tomato sauce before placing them on sliced baguettes.
4. Serve them immediately.
5. Enjoy!

Nutritional information: calories 380, fat 5g, fiber 6g, carbs 34g, protein 20g

213.   TURKEY BURGERS

Preparation time: 10 minutes
Cooking time: 8 minutes
Servings: 4

Ingredients:

- 454 g turkey meat, ground
- 1 shallot, minced
- A drizzle of olive oil
- 1 small jalapeno pepper, minced
- 30 ml lime juice
- Zest from 1 lime, grated
- Salt and black pepper to the taste
- 5 ml cumin, ground
- 5 ml sweet paprika
- Guacamole for serving

Preparation

1. In a mixing bowl, combine turkey meat, salt, pepper, cumin, paprika, shallot, jalapeño, lime juice, and zest, and toss well. Form burgers from this mixture, coat with oil and cook at 187 degrees C for 8 minutes on each side.
2. Divide among plates and top with guacamole.
3. Enjoy!

Nutritional information: calories 200, fat 12g, fiber 0g, carbs 0g, protein 12g

214.   STUFFED MUSHROOMS

Preparation time: 10 minutes
Cooking time: 20 minutes
Servings: 4

Ingredients:

- 4 big Portobello mushroom caps
- 15 ml olive oil
- 63 g ricotta cheese
- 6 g parmesan, grated
- 30 g spinach, torn
- 33 g bread crumbs
- 140 mg rosemary, chopped

Preparation

1. Rub the mushroom caps with the oil, place them in the air fryer basket and cook for 2 minutes at 176 degrees C.
2. Meanwhile, combine half of the parmesan with the ricotta, spinach, rosemary, and bread crumbs in a mixing dish.
3. Stuff the mushrooms with this mixture, cover with the remaining parmesan, and cook for 10 minutes at 176° C in the air fryer basket.
4. For lunch, divide them among plates and serve them with a side salad.
5. Enjoy!

Nutritional information: calories 152, fat 4g, fiber 7g, carbs 9g, protein 5g

215.   QUICK LUNCH PIZZAS

Preparation time: 10 minutes
Cooking time: 7 minutes
Servings: 4

Ingredients:

- 4 pitas
- 15 ml olive oil
- 169 g pizza sauce
- 113 g jarred mushrooms, sliced
- 360 mg basil, dried
- 2 green onions, chopped
- 450 g mozzarella, grated
- 180 g grape tomatoes, sliced

Preparation
1. Spread pizza sauce over each pita bread, then top with green onions, basil, mushrooms, and cheese.
2. Arrange pita pizzas in your air fryer and cook for 7 minutes at 204 degrees C.
3. Serve each pizza with tomato slices on top, divided among plates.
4. Enjoy!

Nutritional information: calories 200, fat 4, fiber 6, carbs 7, protein 3

216. TUNA AND ZUCCHINI TORTILLAS

Preparation time: 10 minutes
Cooking time: 10 minutes
Servings: 4

Ingredients:
- 4 corn tortillas
- 27 g butter, soft
- 170 g canned tuna, drained
- 124 g zucchini, shredded
- 77 g mayonnaise
- 30 g mustard
- 235 g cheddar cheese, grated

Preparation
1. Spread butter on tortillas and place them in the air fryer basket for 3 minutes at 204 degrees C.
2. Meanwhile, combine tuna, zucchini, mayo, and mustard in a mixing dish.
3. Divide this mixture among the tortillas, cover with cheese, roll tortillas, and place them in the air fryer basket for another 4 minutes at 204 degrees C.
4. Serve.
5. Enjoy!

Nutritional information: calories 162, fat 4, fiber 8, carbs 9, protein 4

217. HOT BACON SANDWICHES

Preparation time: 10 minutes
Cooking time: 7 minutes
Servings: 4

Ingredients:
- 93 g bbq sauce
- 30 ml honey
- 8 bacon slices, cooked and cut into thirds
- 1 red bell pepper, sliced
- 1 yellow bell pepper, sliced
- 3 pita pockets, halved
- 94 g butter lettuce leaves, torn
- 2 tomatoes, sliced

Preparation
1. Whisk together the barbecue sauce and honey in a mixing basin.
2. Brush the bacon and all of the bell peppers with some of this mixture, set them in your air fryer and bake for 4 minutes at 176 degrees C.
3. Shake the fryer and cook for another 2 minutes.
4. Stuff pita pockets with bacon mixture, tomatoes, and lettuce, then top with the remaining barbecue sauce and serve for lunch.
5. Enjoy!

Nutritional information: calories 186, fat 6, fiber 9, carbs 14, protein 4

218. CHICKEN PIE

Preparation time: 10 minutes
Cooking time: 16 minutes
Servings: 4

Ingredients:
- 2 chicken thighs, boneless, skinless, and cubed
- 1 carrot, chopped
- 1 yellow onion, chopped
- 2 potatoes, chopped
- 2 mushrooms, chopped
- 6 g soy sauce
- Salt and black pepper to the taste
- 5 ml Italian seasoning

- 5 ml garlic powder
- 6 g Worcestershire sauce
- 9 g flour
- 15 ml milk
- 2 puff pastry sheets
- 14 g butter, melted

Preparation
1. Heat the saucepan over medium-high heat, add the potatoes, carrots, and onion and cook for 2 minutes, stirring occasionally.
2. Stir in the chicken and mushrooms, salt, soy sauce, pepper, Italian seasoning, garlic powder, Worcestershire sauce, flour, and milk, and remove from the fire.
3. Trim the edge excess of 1 puff pastry sheet and place it on the bottom of your air fryer's pan.
4. Top with the remaining puff pastry sheet cut the excess, and brush the pie with butter.
5. Cook for 6 minutes at 182 degrees Celsius in your air fryer.
6. Allow the pie to cool before slicing and serving for breakfast.
7. Enjoy!

Nutritional information: calories 300, fat 5, fiber 7, carbs 14, protein 7

219. HASH BROWN TOASTS

Preparation time: 10 minutes
Cooking time: 7 minutes
Servings: 4

Ingredients:
- 4 hash brown patties, frozen
- 15 ml olive oil
- 50 g cherry tomatoes, chopped
- 42 g mozzarella, shredded
- 11 g parmesan, grated
- 15 ml balsamic vinegar
- 1 g basil, chopped

Preparation
1. Put the hash brown patties in the air fryer, pour with oil, and cook for 7 minutes at 204 degrees C.

2. Mix tomatoes, mozzarella, parmesan, vinegar, and basil in a mixing basin.
3. Divide the hash brown patties among the dishes, top with the tomato mixture, and serve for lunch.
4. Enjoy!

Nutritional information: calories 199, fat 3, fiber 8, carbs 12, protein 4

220. TASTY CHEESEBURGERS

Preparation time: 10 minutes
Cooking time: 20 minutes
Servings: 2

Ingredients:
- 340 g lean beef, ground
- 20 g ketchup
- 10 g yellow onion, chopped
- 10 g mustard
- Salt and black pepper to the taste
- 4 cheddar cheese slices
- 2 burger buns, halved

Preparation
1. Mix the beef, onion, ketchup, mustard, salt, and pepper in a mixing bowl, and toss well. Form 4 patties from this mixture.
2. Divide the cheese between two patties and top with the other two patties.
3. Put them in a preheated air fryer set to 187°C for 20 minutes.
4. Divide the cheeseburger between two bun halves, top with the remaining two, and serve for lunch.
5. Enjoy!

Nutritional information: calories 261, fat 6g, fiber 10g, carbs 20g, protein 6g

221. EASY HOT DOGS

Preparation time: 10 minutes
Cooking time: 7 minutes
Servings: 2

Ingredients:
- 2 hot dog buns

- 2 hot dogs
- 15 g Dijon mustard
- 29 g cheddar cheese, grated

Preparation

1. Place hot dogs in a prepared air fryer and cook for 5 minutes at 198 degrees C.
2. Divide hot dogs among hot dog buns, top with mustard and cheese, then return to air fryer for 2 minutes at 198 degrees C.
3. Serve at lunchtime.
4. Enjoy!

Nutritional information: calories 211, fat 3g, fiber 8g, carbs 12g, protein 4g

222. AIR FRYER GRILLED CHEESE SANDWICH

Prep Time 5 Mins
Cook Time 10 Mins
Servings 2

Ingredients

- 4 slices of white bread
- 14 g butter
- 2 slices of cheddar cheese

Preparation

1. Each slice of bread should have a thin coating of butter on one side.
2. In the air fryer basket, place the greased side down.
3. A cheese slice should be placed on top of the bread slice.
4. The final piece of bread, butter side up, is placed on top of the cheese.
5. Cook for approximately 5 minutes at 187 degrees C. Turn the sandwich over after the bread has turned golden and continue cooking for an additional 4 to 5 minutes, or until the bottom side is golden.

Nutritional information: Calories: 210kcal Carbs: 25g Protein: 9g Fat: 8g Fiber: 1g Sugar: 3g

223. AIR FRYER HAM AND CHEESE SANDWICH

Prep Time 5 Mins
Cook Time 10 Mins
Total Time 15 Mins

Ingredients

- 1 (312 g) Package Carved Slow Roasted Seasoned Ham (Hillshire Farm® Premium)
- Colby Jack Cheese 2 slices per sandwich
- Butter
- Multi-Grain or Deli Style Bread of Choice

Preparation

1. Each piece of bread should have a thin layer of butter on one side.
2. To assemble the sandwich, place the buttered side down in the air fryer and top with a piece of cheese, ham, then another slice of cheese.
3. Add the final slice of bread, butter side up.
4. 5 minutes at 182 °C in an air fryer.
5. Flip the sandwich carefully and give it another five minutes in the air fryer.
6. Serve hot.

Nutritional information: Calories: 680 Carbohydrates: 29g Protein: 38g Fat: 45g

224. AIR FRYER MONTE CRISTO SANDWICH

Prep Time 15 mins
Cook Time 9 mins
Servings: 4

Ingredients

- 8 slices bread
- 165 g pancake mix
- 1 egg
- 60 ml water
- 375 ml milk whole
- 16 slices ham
- 16 slices cheese Swiss, Gouda, or Gruyer

Preparation

1. Your air fryer will be ready after 7 minutes at 193 C. In the meantime, combine the pancake mix with the egg, milk, and water in a large mixing dish.
2. The water and milk should be progressively incorporated until you get a thick pancake mixture; you want it to be thicker than your typical batter, not runny. Place aside.
3. Put the sandwiches together as follows: Place two pieces of cheese, four slices of ham, two more slices of cheese, and then the second piece of bread on one piece of bread.
4. Gently push down on the sandwich with your palm. Four toothpicks should be carefully inserted at an angle along each side of the bread to hold the sandwich together. The air fryer ought to have finished preheating by this point, so put a paper liner inside the basket and shut the lid without turning it back on.
5. The sandwich should be thoroughly coated in the pancake batter on one side before being carefully flipped over and coated on the opposite side. Do not omit the lifting up and letting the extra batter run off the step. Then add to the air fryer basket on top of the liner paper.
6. A timer for 7 minutes at 193 degrees C should be set. To complete browning and frying the second side, flip the food over and adjust the temperature and timer to 182°C and 1 minute, respectively. (Due to the modest variations in time due to batter thickness)
7. After removing the sandwiches from the air fryer, remove the toothpicks, keep them warm by covering them in an aluminium foil container, and let the sandwiches cool completely.
8. To serve, slice each sandwich in half, sprinkle with as much powdered sugar as desired, then serve with a little amount of raspberry preserves for dipping. Enjoy!

Nutritional information: Calories 980kcal Carbs 40g Protein 63g Fat 62g Fiber 3g Sugar 6g

225.   AIR FRYER PEANUT BUTTER AND JELLY SANDWICH

Prep Time 5 minutes
Cook Time 5 minutes
Total Time 10 minutes
Servings 1

Ingredients
- 2 slices bread
- 32 g peanut butter
- 39 g strawberry jelly
- 2 fresh strawberries sliced
- 14 g butter softened

Preparation
1. Set the air fryer's temperature to 204°C and the timer for 5 minutes.
2. A slice of bread spread a layer of peanut butter, and on the other, a layer of jelly.
3. Sandwich the two pieces of bread together by placing the strawberry slices on the slice of bread with the jelly in a uniform layer.
4. Put some butter on the sandwich's two sides using a butter knife.
5. The sandwich will cook in the air fryer for 5 minutes. Halfway through, flip.
6. Remove the finished sandwich from the air fryer. Let cool before enjoying!

Nutritional information: Calories: 564 Carbs: 63g Protein: 14g Fat: 30g Fiber: 5g Sugar: 27g

226.   AIR FRYER CLUB SANDWICH

Prep Time 5 mins
Cook Time 5 mins
Servings: 1 sandwich

Ingredients
- 43 g Mayonnaise
- 2 slices of Sandwich bread
- 3 slices of Turkey deli meat
- 3 slices of Ham deli meat
- 2 slices Cheese
- 2 slices Roma tomato

- Salt and pepper to taste

Preparation
1. On one side of each slice of bread, spread mayo.
2. Place the bread in the air fryer mayo side up. Get a small trivet to put on top of the bread if necessary to prevent it from flying about.
3. Toast for three minutes at 182 C.
4. Take the bread out of your air fryer, then apply mayo on the other side (the non-toasted sides).
5. A slice of bread should be topped with cheese.
6. On the other slice of bread, arrange your meat slices.
7. Toast for 2 minutes at 182 degrees C.
8. Add your chilled lettuce and tomatoes after taking the food out of the air fryer. Add salt and pepper to taste on top of the tomatoes.
9. Combine the two halves, then devour your sandwich.

Nutritional information: Calories: 677kcal Carbs 30g Protein 20g Fat 53g Fiber 3g Sugar: 5g

227. **AIR FRYER PANINI**

Prep Time: 5 minutes
Cook Time: 8 minutes
Total Time: 13 minutes
Yield: 1 sandwich

Ingredients
- 1 ciabatta roll
- 1 grilled chicken breast
- 1 small tomato, sliced
- 28 g fresh mozzarella, sliced
- 16 g pesto
- 14 g mayonnaise
- Cooking Spray
- Cast iron panini press or small weight

Preparation
1. You should set your air fryer to 176°C.
2. Cut the roll in half crosswise. The chicken should be put on the bottom half. Tomato slices on top of the chicken. Lay the cheese on top of the tomatoes.

3. Combine the pesto and mayonnaise in a small bowl.
4. On the sliced side of the top roll half, spread the pesto mayonnaise. Wrap the top of the roll around the sandwich.
5. Put the sandwich in the basket of your air fryer. Use cooking spray to spritz.
6. To weigh down the sandwich, use a panini press or a small weight on top of it.
7. For five minutes, cook.
8. Remove the weight with care, then cook the sandwich for an additional 3 to 4 minutes, or until it is crispy and the fillings are hot.

Nutritional information: Calories 755 Fat 30.9g Carbs 43.4g Sugars 5.1g Protein 77.4g

228. **AIR FRYER GRILLED CHEESE AND TOMATO**

Prep Time: 5 Minutes
Cook Time: 10 Minutes
Total Time: 15 Minutes
Yield: 2 Servings

Ingredients
- 4 pieces of sandwich bread
- 28 g butter, softened
- 4 slices of cheese
- 6-8 tomato slices

Preparation
1. Each piece of bread should have butter on one side.
2. Place the butter side down on the bread slices. Two slices of bread should have one piece of cheese on them.
3. On the same two pieces, arrange 3–4 tomato slices.
4. Top each sandwich with the other buttered slices of bread.
5. Put the air fryer basket with the sandwiches inside.
6. 8–10 minutes at 187 °C, flipping halfway through. When the tops start to turn brown, they are finished.

229. AIR FRYER VEGGIE SANDWICH

Prep Time: 5 Mins
Cook Time: 10 Mins
Total Time: 15 Mins
1 sandwich

Ingredients
- A handful of grated cheese
- A few red bell pepper slices
- A few mushroom slices
- 1 cherry tomato, quartered
- A large spoonful of pesto
- 2 slices of bread
- little olive oil (for spritzing the bread)

Preparation
1. First, spray a little oil on the peppers and mushrooms, and air fry for five minutes at 200°C.
2. Put your sandwich together. Spread pesto on both sides of the bread before stuffing it with cheese, pepper, tomato, and mushrooms.
3. Olive oil should be brushed or sprayed on the bread's outside. Add a little additional cheese to the sandwich's top.
4. In an air fryer at 200°C for 5 minutes, air fried the bread until it is suitably brown and crispy.

Nutritional information: Calories: 491 Carbs 35g Protein 16g Fat 32g Fiber 2g Sugar 5g

230. AIR FRYER PITA PIZZA

Prep Time 4 mins
Cook Time 5 mins
Total Time 9 mins
Servings: 1

Ingredients
- 1 pita bread
- 5 ml olive oil
- 22 ml tomato sauce
- 56 g shredded mozzarella cheese

Preparation
1. Spray nonstick cooking spray inside the air fryer basket.
2. In the air fryer basket, place the pita.
3. Apply olive oil on the pita.
4. The pita should be covered in tomato sauce.
5. Shredded cheese should be added to the pita.
6. Pita pizza should be cooked in the air fryer for five minutes at 204 °C.

Nutritional information: Calories: 283 Carbs: 33g Protein: 12g Fat: 11g Fiber: 2g Sugar: 1g

231. AIR FRYER FROZEN TOTINO'S PIZZA

Cook Time 8 mins
Total Time 8 mins
Servings: 1 pizza

Ingredients
- 1 Totino's Frozen Party Pizza, any flavor

Preparation
1. Put a frozen pizza in the air fryer basket's middle.
2. For 6 to 8 minutes at 204 °C, air-fried frozen pizza until the cheese is melted and the dough is crispy.
3. Serve right away and delight in it!

Nutritional information: Calories 700kcal Carbs 37g Protein 10g Fat 18g Fiber 2g Sugar: 3g

232. AIR FRYER FRENCH BREAD PIZZA

Prep Time: 5 minutes
Cook Time: 9 minutes
Total Time: 14 minutes
Servings: 4

Ingredients
- 340 g loaf of French bread
- 15 ml olive oil
- 1.5 g oregano
- 1 g garlic powder
- 118 ml pizza sauce
- 12 slices of mozzarella or provolone cheese or 166 g of shredded cheese

- 12 slices of pepperoni cut into fourths (optional)

Preparation
1. If necessary, preheat the air fryer to 187 degrees C.
2. To make two long pieces, equally cut the french bread loaf in half along its length. Make four pieces by halving each component.
3. Combine the olive oil, oregano, and garlic powder in a small mixing basin. Apply a thin layer of pastry cream equally across the cut side of the french bread slices.
4. Working in batches, if necessary, place the seasoned french bread in the basket or on the tray of your air fryer. Simply toast the bread for 3 minutes at 187 degrees Celsius.
5. Take the air-fried French bread out of the fryer. Pizza sauce should be properly distributed over each piece before adding cheese slices. Slices of pepperoni and other preferred toppings should be equally distributed on the pizzas.
6. Working in batches, if necessary, put the pizzas back in the air fryer and cook for an additional 5 to 6 minutes at 187 degrees C or until the cheese is melted.
7. Before serving, let the pizzas cool for a few minutes.

Nutritional information: Calories 433kcal Carbs 47g Protein 20g Fat 19g Fiber 2g Sugar 5g

233.   AIR FRYER PIZZA BAGELS

Prep Time 5 mins
Cook Time 3 mins
Total Time 8 mins
Servings: 4

Ingredients
- 2 bagels cut in half
- 118 ml pizza sauce
- 113 g shredded mozzarella cheese
- 138 g mini pepperoni

Preparation
1. Set the air fryer's thermostat to 190 degrees C.

2. Each bagel half should be covered in pizza sauce, followed by cheese and pepperoni.
3. Put the pizzas in the basket of the air fryer once it has heated up, and cook for 2-3 mins, or until the cheese has melted.
4. Take the pizza bagels out of the air fryer and let them cool. Enjoy!

Nutritional information: Calories 282kcal Carbs 30g Protein 14g Fat 11g Fiber 2g Sugar 2g

234.   AIR FRYER NAAN PIZZA

Prep Time: 2 minutes
Cook Time: 7 minutes
Total Time: 9 minutes
Servings: 4 servings

Ingredients
- 4 pieces of mini naan
- 56 g pizza sauce
- 170 g mozzarella cheese shredded
- toppings (veggies, pepperoni, sausage.)

Preparation
1. In the air fryer's basket, arrange the naan in a single layer. Work in groups if required. (4 tiny naan pieces)
2. For two minutes or until the edges are just beginning to crisp up, air fried at 187°C. Carefully remove from the air fryer.
3. Pizza sauce, cheese, and any additional toppings of your choosing should be spread onto the naan pieces back at the air fryer.
4. For another 5 mins in the air fryer at 187°C, or until the cheese is melted and the naan is golden and crispy.

Nutritional information: Calories 388 kcal Carbs 42 g Protein 16 g Fat 16 g Fibe 2 g Sugar 4 g

235. EASY AIR FRYER PIZZA ROLL-UPS

Prep Time 4 minutes
Cook Time 5 minutes
Total Time 9 minutes
Servings 4

Ingredients
- 4 (8-inch) flour tortillas
- 56 g pizza sauce
- 20 slices pepperoni
- 2 mozzarella string cheese
- 5 ml olive oil

Preparation
1. To reheat the tortillas, stack them on a plate that can be heated in the microwave and cover the platter with a wet paper towel. The tortillas should be heated for 20 seconds in the microwave. If you have a tortilla warmer, you may also use it.
2. Set the air fryer's temperature to 190 degrees Celsius and its timer for 5 minutes.
3. The string cheese should be split lengthwise.
4. Place 14 g of pizza sauce in the bottom of a tortilla that has been laid flat. Pizza sauce should be topped with 5 pepperoni slices, followed by a layer of string cheese, before everything is rolled up. Continue until you have 4 roll-ups for each tortilla.
5. Olive oil should be equally applied to the top of each roll-up to give them a little more crispiness.
6. Pizza roll-ups should be added to the air fryer seam-side down and cooked for 5 minutes, or until golden brown.
7. Pizza roll-ups should be carefully taken out of the air fryer, cooled, and then eaten. When dipped in some pizza sauce, they are delicious.

Nutritional information: Calories 255 Carbs 27g Protein 10g Fat: 12g Fiber 1g Sugar 3g

236. AIR FRYER TORTILLA PIZZA

Prep Time: 1 minute
Cook Time: 4 minutes
Total Time: 5 minutes
Yield: 1 pizza

Ingredients
- 3 ml olive oil
- 8-inch flour tortilla
- 65g low-calorie pizza sauce
- 56g shredded mozzarella cheese

Preparation
1. Brush some olive oil on the flour tortilla before placing it in the air fryer basket.
2. The tortilla should be covered with pizza sauce before being topped with mozzarella cheese and your preferred toppings.
3. Cook for 4 minutes at 190°C in the air fryer, or until the cheese is bubbling and brown. To ensure the pizza doesn't overcook, inspect it after just one minute.
4. Pizza should be taken out of the air fryer, let to cool, and then cut into triangles.

Nutritional information: Calories: 250 Fat: 10 Carbs: 35Fiber: 26Protein: 20

237. AIR FRYER PIZZA

Prep Time 10 minutes
Cook Time 12 minutes
Total Time 22 minutes
Servings 4 personal pizzas

Ingredients
- 454 g homemade pizza dough or store-bought
- Semolina or Cornmeal cornflour in the UK, to stretch the dough
- 225 g pizza sauce homemade or store-bought
- 2 balls buffalo mozzarella sliced, or 336 g shredded mozzarella
- Olive oil
- Fresh basil leaves

Preparation

1. Set the air fryer to 180 ºC and line the basket with parchment Air Fryer Liners or spray it with air fryer-safe nonstick spray.
2. With the aid of semolina or cornmeal, roll out the dough into 4 personal-size pizzas that can fit your air fryer basket (it should be about 12 inches thick), or 2 larger ones, depending on the size of your air fryer basket. Divide the dough into 4 balls (or 2 if making larger pizzas, but this depends on the size of your air fryer basket).
3. After placing the dough in the air fryer, cover it with pizza sauce, cheese, and a drizzle of olive oil (prefer brushing the edges for nice browning). Additionally, you may add any preferred toppings, like as parmesan, pepperoni, chicken, etc., as well as fresh black pepper.
4. Reposition the basket into the air fryer, and cook for 10 to 12 minutes. Since every Air Fryer is unique, check after 8 minutes.
5. Slice and serve after carefully removing from the Air Fryer basket and adding chopped basil leaves on top.

Nutritional information: Calories 519 Carbs 59g Protein 26g Fat 20g Fiber 3g Sugar 10g

238.   AIR FRYER BACON WRAPPED HOT DOGS

Prep Time 5 mins
Cook Time 10 mins
Total Time 15 mins
Servings: 4 Servings

Ingredients
- 4 hot dogs
- 4 hot dog buns
- 4 slices bacon
-
- For serving: ketchup, BBQ sauce, mustard, pickles, jalapeños, onions, etc.

Preparation
1. Wrap the hot dogs tightly with pieces of bacon. To hold the bacon to the hot dog, if desired, use a toothpick. Make sure the hot dogs' tips are covered in bacon. Put in the air fryer's tray or basket.
2. Depending on your chosen texture, the size of the hot dogs, and how done you like your bacon, air fry at 193°C for 8–10 minutes. During the second half of cooking, flip the hot dogs. If you're using toothpicks, take them out before serving!
3. Cook your hot dogs and bacon a little hotter if you want them extra crispy. Follow these guidelines instead: 204°C air fry for 6 to 8 minutes. During the second half of cooking, flip the hot dogs. If you're using toothpicks, take them out before serving!
4. Place bacon-wrapped hot dogs in the buns and air fry for a further minute, or until the bread is warm, for crispy warm hot dog buns. Serve with your preferred garnishes.

Nutritional information: Calories 321kcal Carbohydrates 30g Protein 12g Fat 17g Fiber 1g Sugar 3g

239.   AIR FRYER TURKEY MELT

Prep Time 5 mins
Cook Time 10 mins
Total Time 15 mins
Servings: 1 Sandwich

Ingredients
- 2 slices bread
- Slices leftover turkey slices or deli meat
- 14 g butter
- good melting cheese (Swiss, cheddar, Gruyere, etc.)

Preparation
1. Slices of turkey and cheese are arranged between the bread. Butter the outside of the bread. Through the sandwich, insert toothpicks to hold the top slice of bread. In your air fryer basket, place the sandwich.
2. To melt the cheese, air fry at 182°C for around 3 to 5 minutes.
3. To complete and crisp the bread, flip the sandwich over and raise the temperature to 193°C. For about 5 minutes, air fry the

sandwich at 193°C, or until the texture is to your liking. Make frequent checks on the sandwich to prevent burning (different breads will toast quicker or slower than others). Before cutting into the delicious grilled cheese sandwich, give it some time to cool.

Nutritional information: Calories: 592kcal Carbohydrates: 30g Protein: 47g Fat: 31g Fiber: 2g Sugar: 4g

240.   AIR FRYER FROZEN

TURKEY BURGERS

Prep Time 5 mins
Cook Time 18 mins
Total Time 23 mins
Servings: 4 Burgers

Ingredients
- 4 frozen raw turkey patties , usually sold as either 113g or 150g
- salt , to taste if needed
- Lots of black pepper
- oil spray , for coating

Burger Assembly:
- 4 Buns , plus optional cheese, pickles, lettuce, onion, tomato, avocado, cooked bacon etc.

Preparation
1. Spray oil on both sides of frozen turkey patties. Add optional salt and pepper to taste. Spray oil on the air fryer basket. Put all of the patties in one layer in the basket. If necessary, cook in batches.
2. Fry 113 g of frozen turkey patties in the air for 12 to 17 minutes at 193 °C. Air fry the patties for a further 2–7 minutes at 193°C, or until they are cooked to your chosen level of doneness, after flipping them after the first 10 minutes. The temperature inside should be 74 °C.
3. Fry 150 g of frozen turkey patties in the air for a total of 13 to 18 minutes at 193 °C. After the first ten minutes, flip the patties over, and continue air frying at 193°C for an additional three to eight minutes, depending

on how done you want your food. The temperature inside should be 74 °C.
4. Put the Slices of cheese on top of fried patties for cheeseburgers. For roughly 30 to 1 minute, air fried at 193°C to melt the cheese.
5. Allow the patties to rest for three minutes under cover. While the patties are resting, warm the buns in the air fryer at 193°C for around 3 minutes. Serve with your preferred burger toppings on buns.

Nutritional information: Calories: 316kcal Carbohydrates: 22g Protein: 26g Fat: 12g Fiber: 1g Sugar: 3g

241.   AIR FRYER SLIDERS

Prep Time 15 mins
Cook Time 10 mins
Total Time 25 mins
Servings: 6 -8 Servings

Ingredients
- 454 g ground beef (chicken, pork, turkey,lamb)
- 2.5 ml garlic powder
- 30 ml Worcestershire sauce
- black pepper , to taste
- salt , to taste
- 6-8 slider buns or rolls

Burger Toppings:
- lettuce, tomato, onion slices,pickles, blue cheese, avocado, bacon, fried onions, etc.
- ketchup, gochujang, mustard, mayo, hot sauce, bbq sauce, etc.

Preparation
1. For five minutes, preheat the air fryer to 193 °C.
2. Beef, Worcestershire sauce, and garlic powder should be mixed barely. Form ingredients into 6–8 evenly sized balls. Each ball should be lightly pressed into a tiny patty. Try not to overwork the patties for the greatest texture. Just enough shaping is required so that the patties maintain their form.
3. Spray oil on patties sparingly. Top the patties with a generous quantity of salt and pepper.

4. Sliders should be placed in the oil-sprayed air fryer basket or tray.

5. 5 minutes at 193 °C of air frying. When the centre of the patties is cooked to your chosen level of doneness or the internal temperature reaches 71°C, flip them over and cook for an additional 1–3 minutes.

6. Put the slices of cheese on top of the fried patties for Cheeseburger Sliders. For roughly 30 to 1 minute, air fried at 193°C to melt the cheese.

7. Cover the patties and allow them rest for a few minutes for maximum juiciness. Warm the buns in your air fryer at 193°C for about a minute while the patties are resting. Serve with your preferred toppings on buns.

Nutritional information: Calories: 211kcal Carbohydrates: 17g Protein: 13g Fat: 10g Fiber: 1g Sugar: 3g

242.   AIR FRYER TURKEY AVOCADO BURGERS

Prep Time 15 mins
Cook Time 15 mins
Total Time 30 mins
Servings: 4 Burgers

Ingredients
- 454 g ground turkey
- 2 cloves garlic , minced
- 15 ml Worcestershire ,soy sauce or fish sauce, (fish sauce is our favorite)
- 5 ml dried herbs (oregano, thyme, basil, dill, marjoram)
- 80 g minced fresh onion
- 2.5 ml salt , or to taste
- Lots of black pepper
- oil spray , for coating

Burger Assembly:
- 4 Buns
- 1 avocado , sliced
- Optional: cheese, radish sprouts, lettuce, tomato, etc.

Preparation

1. For five minutes, preheat the air fryer to 193 °C.

2. Turkey, garlic, Worcestershire sauce (fish sauce or soy sauce), dried herbs, onion, salt, and pepper should all be combined in a bowl. Just mix everything after blending.

3. Divide into four 4" broad patties and flatten. Apply oil evenly on both sides. You'll have to cook in two batches if your air fryer is smaller.

4. Flip after 6 minutes and air fry for 10 to 12 minutes at 193 °C. Cook to taste or until internal temperature reaches 74°C. You might need to cook the patties for a few more minutes if it is thicker.

5. Slices of cheese should be added on top of the cooked patties for turkey cheeseburgers. For roughly 30 sec to 1 minute, air fried at 193°C to melt the cheese.

6. Cover the patties and let them rest for three minutes for the juiciest results. While the patties are resting, warm the buns for roughly a minute in the air fryer at 193°C. Serve on buns with your preferred burger toppings and 1/4 avocado on top.

Nutritional information: Calories: 356kcal Carbohydrates: 30g Protein: 32g Fat: 13g Fiber: 5g Sugar: 4g

243.   AIR FRYER BURGERS FROM FROZEN PATTIES

Prep Time 5 mins
Cook Time 15 mins
Total Time 20 mins
Servings: 4 Burgers

Ingredients
- 4 frozen raw beef patties , commonly sold as either 113g or 150g
- salt , to taste if needed
- Lots of black pepper
- oil spray , for coating

Burger Assembly:
- 4 Buns , plus optional cheese, pickles, lettuce, onion, tomato, avocado, cooked bacon etc.

Preparation

1. Burger patties that are frozen should be oiled on all sides. If necessary, season with salt and pepper. Oil the air fryer basket with a spray bottle, then arrange the patties in it in a single layer. If necessary, cook in batches.

2. For 113g frozen hamburger patties, air fry for 8 to 12 minutes at 180°C. Air fry the patties for a further 2–6 minutes at 180°C, or until they are cooked to your chosen level of doneness, after flipping them after the first 6 minutes. 71°C should be the temperature inside.

3. Air fry 150g. frozen hamburger patties for a total of 12–16 minutes at 180°C. The burgers should be cooked to your chosen degree of doneness after additional 2–6 minutes of Air Frying at 180°C after the initial 10 minutes of cooking. 71°C should be the temperature inside.

4. Slices of cheese can be added on top of fried patties to make cheeseburgers. For roughly 30 sec to 1 minute, air fried at 180°C to melt the cheese.

5. Allow the patties to rest for three minutes under cover. While the patties are resting, warm the buns in the air fryer at 193°C for around 3 minutes. Serve with your preferred burger toppings on buns.

Nutritional information: Calories: 366kcal Carbohydrates: 22g Protein: 21g Fat: 21g Fiber: 1g Sugar: 3g

244. AIR FRYER HAM AND CHEESE MELT

Prep Time 5 mins
Cook Time 10 mins
Total Time 15 mins
Servings: 1 Sandwich

Ingredients
- 2 slices bread
- 2-4 slices good melting cheese (American, Swiss, cheddar, Gruyere, etc.)
- 1-2 slices ham , about 1/4-inch thick
- 14 g butter

Preparation

1. Put the top slice of bread on top of the layers of bread, cheese, ham, and cheese (you want the ham in-between the cheese so when it melts, the cheese will hold everything together).

2. Bread's outside should be buttered. Butter the top and bottom slices equally.

3. Through the sandwich, insert toothpicks to hold the top slice of bread. In your air fryer basket, place the sandwich.

4. To melt the cheese, air fry at 182°C for around 3 to 5 minutes.

5. To complete and crisp the bread, flip the sandwich over and raise the temperature to 193°C. For about 5 minutes, air fry the sandwich at 193°C, or until the texture is to your liking. Make frequent checks on the sandwich to prevent burning (different breads will toast quicker or slower than others). Before cutting into the delicious grilled cheese sandwich, give it some time to cool.

Nutritional information: Calories: 455kcal Carbohydrates: 27g Protein: 21g Fat: 29g Fiber: 2g Sugar: 3g

245. AIR FRYER AMAZING BURGERS

Prep Time 10 mins
Cook Time 12 mins
Total Time 22 mins
Servings: 4 Burgers

Ingredients
- 567 g ground beef
- 5 ml garlic powder
- 15 ml Worcestershire , or soy sauce or fish sauce (fish sauce is our favorite)
- 2.5 ml salt , or to taste
- Lots of black pepper
- oil spray , for coating

Burger Assembly:
- 4 Buns , plus optional cheese, pickles, lettuce, onion, tomato, avocado, cooked bacon etc.

Preparation
1. The Air Fryer should be preheated for around 4-5 minutes at 193°C.
2. Beef, garlic, garlic powder, Worcestershire sauce (or other sauce of choice), salt, and pepper should all be combined in a bowl. Just mix everything after blending.
3. Divide the mixture into four equal-sized patties, each approximately 4 inches across. Don't pack the patties too tightly or you'll end up with a dense burger; instead, give them just enough shape to hold. Spray the air fryer basket on all sides with oil. Cooking in two batches could be necessary if your air fryer is smaller.
4. Flip after 6 minutes and air fry for roughly 8 to 12 minutes at 193 °C. Cook to taste or until internal temperature reaches 71°C. Timing will change based on the air fryer model and the thickness of the patties.
5. Slices of cheese can be added on top of fried patties to make cheeseburgers. For roughly 30 sec to 1 minute, air fried at 193°C to melt the cheese.
6. Cover the patties and let them rest for around 3 minutes for the juiciest results. Warm the buns in your air fryer at 193°C for about a minute while the patties are resting. Serve with your preferred burger toppings on buns.

Nutritional information: Calories: 500kcal
Carbohydrates: 23g Protein: 29g Fat: 31g Fiber: 1g
Sugar: 3g

246.   AIR FRYER BREAKFAST

SANDWICHES

Cook Time 10 mins
Total Time 10 mins
Servings: 1 Serving

Ingredients
* 1 Frozen Breakfast Sandwich

Preparation
1. The breakfast sandwich should be split in two. Turn the filling over so that the cheese is next to the bread (because the cheese will blow off if it is on top). Consider the pictures in the recipe description above.
2. Place the two halves, bread side down and meat and egg side up, in the air fryer basket. Air fry for 6-8 mins at 170 °C.
3. Put the breakfast sandwich back together. Air fry the bread for a further two minutes at 170°C, or until golden.

Nutritional information: Calories: 400kcal
Carbohydrates: 29g Protein: 13g Fat: 26g Fiber: 2g
Sugar: 5g

BEEF, PORK, AND LAMB RECIPE

247. GARLIC AND BELL PEPPER BEEF

Preparation time: 30 minutes
Cooking time: 30 minutes
Servings: 4

Ingredients:

- 312 g steak fillets, sliced
- 4 garlic cloves, minced
- 30 ml olive oil
- 1 red bell pepper, cut into strips
- Black pepper to the taste
- 12 g sugar
- 30 ml fish sauce
- 10 ml corn flour
- 240 ml beef stock
- 4 green onions, sliced

Preparation

1. In an air fryer-safe pan, combine beef, oil, garlic, black pepper, and bell pepper; stir, cover, and chill for 30 minutes.
2. Place the pan in your prepared air fryer and cook for 14 minutes at 182 degrees C.
3. Mix sugar and fish sauce in a bowl, then pour over beef and simmer for 7 minutes more at 182 degrees C.
4. Toss in the stock, corn flour, and green onions, and simmer for 7 minutes more at 187 degrees C.
5. Serve everything on individual plates.
6. Enjoy!

Nutritional information: calories 343, fat 3, fiber 12, carbs 26, protein 38

248. CHINESE STEAK AND BROCCOLI

Preparation time: 45 minutes
Cooking time: 12 minutes
Servings: 4

Ingredients:

- 340 ground steak, cut into strips
- 454 g broccoli florets
- 79 ml oyster sauce
- 10 ml sesame oil
- 5 ml soy sauce
- 5 g sugar
- 79 ml sherry
- 15 ml olive oil
- 1 garlic clove, minced

Preparation

1. In a mixing bowl, combine sesame oil, oyster sauce, soy sauce, sherry, and sugar. Stir well, add meat, toss, and set aside for 30 minutes.
2. Transfer the beef to an air fryer-compatible pan, along with the broccoli, garlic, and oil. Toss everything together and cook at 193 degrees Celsius for 12 minutes.
3. Serve on individual plates.
4. Enjoy!

Nutritional information: calories 330, fat 12, fiber 7, carbs 23, protein 23

249. FLAVORED RIB EYE STEAK

Preparation time: 10 minutes
Cooking time: 20 minutes
Servings: 4

Ingredients:

- 907 g rib eye steak
- Salt and black pepper to the taste
- 15 ml olive oil

For the rub:

- 45 ml sweet paprika
- 30 ml onion powder
- 30 ml garlic powder

- 12 g brown sugar
- 30 ml oregano, dried
- 15 ml cumin, ground
- 15 ml rosemary, dried

Preparation

1. In a mixing bowl, combine paprika, onion and garlic powder, sugar, oregano, rosemary, salt, pepper, and cumin; whisk and rub this mixture over the steak.
2. Season the steak with salt and pepper, massage with oil again, and cook at 204 degrees C for 20 minutes, flipping halfway.
3. Carry the steak to a cutting board, cut it into slices, and serve with a side salad.
4. Enjoy!

Nutritional information: calories 320, fat 8, fiber 7, carbs 22, protein 21

250. BEEF STRIPS WITH SNOW PEAS AND MUSHROOMS

Preparation time: 10 minutes
Cooking time: 22 minutes
Servings: 2

Ingredients:

- 2 beef steaks, cut into strips
- Salt and black pepper to the taste
- 199 g snow peas
- 227 g white mushrooms, halved
- 1 yellow onion, cut into rings
- 30 ml soy sauce
- 5 ml olive oil

Preparation

1. Whisk together the olive oil and soy sauce in a mixing dish before adding the beef strips and tossing.
2. Toss snow peas, onion, and mushrooms with salt, pepper, and oil in a separate dish, then place in a pan that fits your air fryer and cook at 176 degrees C for 16 minutes.
3. Cook for 6 minutes further at 204 degrees C after adding the beef strips.
4. Serve everything on individual plates.
5. Enjoy!

Nutritional information: calories 235, fat 8, fiber 2, carbs 22, protein 24

251. MEDITERRANEAN STEAKS AND SCALLOPS

Preparation time: 10 minutes
Cooking time: 14 minutes Servings: 2

Ingredients:

- 10 sea scallops
- 2 beef steaks
- 4 garlic cloves, minced
- 1 shallot, chopped
- 30 ml lemon juice
- 8 g parsley, chopped
- 3 g basil, chopped
- 2 g lemon zest
- 57 g butter
- 59 g veggie stock
- Salt and black pepper to the taste

Preparation

1. Season the steaks with salt & pepper, place them in the air fryer, and cook at 182 degrees C for 10 minutes before transferring them to a fryer-compatible pan.
2. Toss in the shallot, garlic, butter, stock, basil, lemon juice, parsley, lemon zest, and scallops, and simmer for 4 minutes more at 182 degrees C.
3. Serve the steaks and scallops on separate platters.
4. Enjoy!

Nutritional information: calories 150, fat 2, fiber 2, carbs 14, protein 17

252. AIR FRYER LAMB SHANKS

Preparation time: 10 minutes
Cooking time: 45 minutes
Servings: 4

Ingredients:

- 4 lamb shanks

- 1 yellow onion, chopped
- 15 ml olive oil
- 7 g coriander seeds, crushed
- 8 g white flour
- 4 bay leaves
- 10 ml honey
- 142 g dry sherry
- 600 ml chicken stock
- Salt and pepper to the taste

Preparation
1. Season the lamb shanks with salt & pepper, rub with half of the oil, and cook for 10 minutes at 182 degrees Celsius in an air fryer.
2. Heat the remaining oil in a pan that fits your air fryer over medium-high heat, add the onion and coriander, mix, and cook for 5 minutes.
3. Stir in the flour, sherry, stock, honey, bay leaves, salt, and pepper, and bring to a simmer. Add the lamb and cook at 182 degrees C for 30 minutes.
4. Serve everything on individual plates.
5. Enjoy!

Nutritional information: calories 283, fat 4, fiber 2, carbs 17, protein 26

253. INDIAN PORK

Preparation time: 35 minutes
Cooking time: 10 minutes
Servings: 4
Ingredients:
- 5 ml ginger powder
- 10 ml chili paste
- 2 garlic cloves, minced
- 397 g pork chops, cubed
- 1 shallot, chopped
- 5 ml coriander, ground
- 207 ml coconut milk
- 30 ml olive oil
- 85 g peanuts, ground
- 45 ml soy sauce
- Salt and black pepper to the taste

Preparation
1. In a mixing bowl, whisk together ginger, 5 ml chilli paste, half of the garlic, half of the soy sauce, and half of the oil. Add meat, toss, and set aside for 10 minutes.
2. Place the meat in the basket of your air fryer and cook at 204 °C for 12 minutes, flipping halfway.
3. Meanwhile, heat the remaining oil in a skillet over medium-high heat, then add the shallot, garlic, coriander, coconut milk, peanuts, chilli paste, and soy sauce, stirring and cooking for 5 minutes.
4. Serve the pork on plates with the coconut mixture on top.
5. Enjoy!

Nutritional information: calories 423, fat 11, fiber 4, carbs 42, protein 18

254. LAMB SHANKS AND CARROTS

Preparation time: 10 minutes
Cooking time: 45 minutes
Servings: 4

Ingredients:
- 4 lamb shanks
- 30 ml olive oil
- 1 yellow onion, finely chopped
- 6 carrots, roughly chopped
- 2 garlic cloves, minced
- 30 ml tomato paste
- 5 ml oregano, dried
- 1 tomato, roughly chopped
- 30 ml water
- 360 ml red wine
- Salt and black pepper to the taste

Preparation
1. Season the lamb with salt & pepper, massage with oil, and cook for 10 minutes at 360 degrees F in an air fryer.
2. Toss onion, carrots, garlic, tomato paste, oregano, wine, and water in a pan that fits your air fryer.
3. Toss the lamb, then place it in the air fryer for 35 minutes at 187° C.
4. Serve everything on individual plates.
5. Enjoy!

Nutritional information: calories 432, fat 17, fiber 8, carbs 17, protein 43

255. LAMB AND CREAMY BRUSSELS SPROUTS

Preparation time: 10 minutes
Cooking time: 1 hour and 10 minutes
Servings:4

Ingredients:
- 907 g leg of lamb, scored
- 30 ml olive oil
- 2 g rosemary, chopped
- 15 ml lemon thyme, chopped
- 1 garlic clove, minced
- 680 g Brussels sprouts, trimmed
- 14 g butter, melted
- 118 ml sour cream
- Salt and black pepper to the taste

Preparation
1. Season the leg of lamb with salt, pepper, thyme, and rosemary, brush with oil and set it in the basket of your air fryer. Cook at 149 degrees C for 1 hour, then transfer to a platter and keep warm.
2. Toss Brussels sprouts with salt, pepper, garlic, butter, and sour cream in a pan that fits your air fryer, then place in the air fryer and cook at 204 degrees C for 10 minutes.
3. Serve the lamb on plates with Brussels sprouts on the side.
4. Enjoy!

Nutritional information: calories 440, fat 23, fiber 0, carbs 2, protein 49

256. BEEF FILLETS WITH GARLIC MAYO

Preparation time: 10 minutes
\Cooking time: 40 minutes
Servings: 8

Ingredients:
- 230 g mayonnaise
- 79 ml sour cream
- 2 garlic cloves, minced
- 1360 g beef fillet
- 6 g chives, chopped
- 30 g mustard
- 14 g tarragon, chopped
- Salt and black pepper to the taste

Preparation
1. Season the beef to taste with salt & pepper, then place it in the air fryer and cook at 187 degrees C for 20 minutes before transferring it to a plate and setting it aside for a few minutes.
2. In a mixing bowl, stir together garlic, sour cream, chives, mayo, salt, and pepper, and set aside.
3. Whisk together the mustard, Dijon mustard, and tarragon in another bowl. Add the beef, toss, and return to the air fryer for another 20 minutes at 176 degrees C.
4. Serve beef on plates with garlic mayonnaise on top.
5. Enjoy!

Nutritional information: calories 400, fat 12, fiber 2, carbs 27, protein 19

257. TASTY LAMB RIBS

Preparation time: 15 minutes
Cooking time: 40 minutes
Servings: 8

Ingredients:
- 8 lamb ribs
- 4 garlic cloves, minced
- 2 carrots, chopped
- 2 cups veggie stock
- 15 ml rosemary, chopped
- 30 ml extra virgin olive oil
- Salt and black pepper to the taste
- 23 g white flour

Preparation
1. Season lamb ribs with salt and pepper, massage with oil and garlic and cook for 10

minutes at 182 degrees C in a prepared air fryer.

2. Whisk together stock and flour in a heatproof dish that fits your fryer.
3. Place the rosemary, carrots, and lamb ribs in the air fryer and cook for 30 minutes at 176 degrees C.
4. Serve the lamb mixture on hot plates.
5. Enjoy!

Nutritional information: calories 302, fat 7, fiber 2, carbs 22, protein 27

258.   MARINATED PORK CHOPS

AND ONIONS

Preparation time: 24 hours
Cooking time: 25 minutes
Servings: 6

Ingredients:
- 2 pork chops
- 60 ml olive oil
- 2 yellow onions, sliced
- 2 garlic cloves, minced
- 10 g mustard
- 5 ml sweet paprika
- Salt and black pepper to the taste
- 2.5 ml oregano, dried
- 2.5 ml thyme, dried
- A pinch of cayenne pepper

Preparation
1. Mix the oil, garlic, mustard, paprika, black pepper, oregano, thyme, and cayenne in a mixing bowl.
2. Toss onions with meat and mustard mixture to coat, cover, and refrigerate for 1 day.
3. Transfer the beef & onion mixture to an air fryer pan and cook for 25 minutes at 182 degrees C.
4. Serve everything on individual plates.
5. Enjoy!

Nutritional information: calories 384, fat 4, fiber 4, carbs 17, protein 25

259.   PORK WITH COUSCOUS

Preparation time: 10 minutes
Cooking time: 35 minutes
Servings: 6

Ingredients:
- 1134 g pork loin, boneless and trimmed
- 177 ml chicken stock
- 30 ml olive oil
- 2.5 ml sweet paprika
- 3.5 g sage, dried
- 5 g garlic powder
- 1.25 ml rosemary, dried
- 1.25 ml marjoram, dried
- 5 ml basil, dried
- 5 ml oregano, dried
- Salt and black pepper to the taste
- 360 g couscous, cooked

Preparation
1. Mix the oil, stock, paprika, garlic powder, sage, rosemary, thyme, marjoram, oregano, salt, and pepper to taste in a medium bowl, and set aside for 1 hour.
2. Transfer everything to an air fryer-compatible pan and cook for 35 minutes at 187° C.
3. Serve on individual dishes with couscous on the side.
4. Enjoy!

Nutritional information: calories 310, fat 4, fiber 6, carbs 37, protein 34

260.   FENNEL FLAVORED PORK

ROAST

Preparation time: 10 minutes
Cooking time: 1 hour
Servings: 10

Ingredients:
- 2495 g pork loin roast, trimmed
- Salt and black pepper to the taste
- 3 garlic cloves, minced
- 7 g rosemary, chopped
- 5 ml fennel, ground
- 2 g fennel seeds

- 10 ml red pepper, crushed
- 60 ml olive oil

Preparation

1. In a food processor, combine garlic, fennel seeds, rosemary, red pepper, black pepper, and olive oil to make a paste.
2. Spread 2 tablespoons garlic paste on pork loin, massage well, season with salt and pepper, and place in a preheated air fryer for 30 minutes at 176 degrees C.
3. Reduce the heat to 149 degrees C and cook for another 15 minutes.
4. Pork should be sliced, divided among plates, and served.
5. Enjoy!

Nutritional information: calories 300, fat 14, fiber 9, carbs 26, protein 22

261.   BEEF ROAST AND WINE

SAUCE

Preparation time: 10 minutes
Cooking time: 45 minutes
Servings: 6

Ingredients:
- 1360 g beef roast
- Salt and black pepper to the taste
- 502 ml beef stock
- 87 ml red wine
- 2.5 ml chicken salt
- 2.5 ml smoked paprika
- 1 yellow onion, chopped
- 4 garlic cloves, minced
- 3 carrots, chopped
- 5 potatoes, chopped

Preparation

1. Mix salt, pepper, chicken salt, and paprika in a bowl, then rub this mixture over the beef in a large pan that fits your air fryer.
2. Add the onion, garlic, stock, wine, potatoes, and carrots to your air fryer and cook for 45 minutes at 182 degrees C.
3. Serve everything on individual plates.
4. Enjoy!

Nutritional information: calories 304, fat 20, fiber 7, carbs 20, protein 32

262.   BEEF MEDALLIONS MIX

Preparation time: 2 hours
Cooking time: 10 minutes
Servings: 4

Ingredients:
- 2 teaspoons chili powder
- 200 g tomatoes, crushed
- 4 beef medallions
- 5 g onion powder
- 30 ml soy sauce
- Salt and black pepper to the taste
- 15 ml hot pepper
- 30 ml lime juice

Preparation

1. Whisk together tomatoes, hot pepper, soy sauce, chilli powder, onion powder, a bit of salt, black pepper, and lime juice in a mixing bowl.
2. Place the beef medallions in a dish, pour the sauce over them, stir, and set aside for 2 hours.
3. Remove the steak from the marinade and place it in your preheated air fryer for 10 minutes at 182 degrees C.
4. Serve the steaks on plates with a side of salad.
5. Enjoy!

Nutritional information: calories 230, fat 4, fiber 1, carbs 13, protein 14

263.   LEMONY LAMB LEG

Preparation time: 10 minutes
Cooking time: 1 hour
Servings: 6
Ingredients:
- 1814 g lamb leg
- 30 ml olive oil
- 2 springs rosemary, chopped
- 7 g parsley, chopped
- 6 g oregano, chopped
- Salt and black pepper to the taste

- 6 g lemon rind, grated
- 3 garlic cloves, minced
- 30 ml lemon juice
- 907 g baby potatoes
- 200 ml beef stock

Preparation
1. Make small cuts over the lamb, insert rosemary springs, and season with salt and pepper.
2. Mix 15 ml oil with oregano, parsley, garlic, lemon juice, and rind; stir and rub the lamb with this mix.
3. Heat a pan that fits your air fryer with the rest of the oil over medium-high heat, add potatoes, stir and cook for 3 minutes.
4. Add lamb and stock, stir, introduce in your air fryer and cook at 182 degrees C for 1 hour.
5. Divide everything into plates and serve.
6. Enjoy!

Nutritional information: calories 264, fat 4, fiber 12, carbs 27, protein 32

264. ROASTED PORK BELLY

AND APPLE SAUCE

Preparation time: 10 minutes
Cooking time: 40 minutes
Servings: 6

Ingredients:
- 25 g sugar
- 15 ml lemon juice
- 946 ml water
- 482 g apples, cored and cut into wedges
- 907 g pork belly, scored
- Salt and black pepper to the taste
- A drizzle of olive oil

Preparation
1. Blend water, apples, lemon juice, and sugar in a blender until smooth. Transfer to a bowl, add pork, combine well, drain, and cook at 204 degrees C for 40 minutes.
2. Pour the sauce into a pot and heat over medium heat for 15 minutes.

3. Slice the pork belly, divide it among plates, and sprinkle with the sauce.
4. Enjoy!

Nutritional information: calories 456, fat 34, fiber 4, carbs 10, protein 25

265. PORK CHOPS AND

ROASTED PEPPERS

Preparation time: 10 minutes
Cooking time: 16 minutes
Servings: 4

Ingredients:
- 45 ml olive oil
- 45 ml lemon juice
- 7 g smoked paprika
- 5 g thyme, chopped
- 3 garlic cloves, minced
- 4 pork chops, bone-in
- Salta and black pepper to the taste
- 2 roasted bell peppers, chopped

Preparation
1. Mix pork chops with oil, lemon juice, smoked paprika, thyme, garlic, bell peppers, salt, and pepper in a pan that fits your air fryer, toss well and cook at 204 degrees C for 16 minutes.
2. Serve the pork chops and pepper mixture immediately on plates.
3. Enjoy!

Nutritional information: calories 321, fat 6, fiber 8, carbs 14, protein 17

266. PORK CHOPS AND

MUSHROOMS MIX

Preparation time: 10 minutes
Cooking time: 40 minutes
Servings: 3

Ingredients:
- 226 g mushrooms, sliced

- 5 ml garlic powder
- 1 yellow onion, chopped
- 230 g mayonnaise
- 3 pork chops, boneless
- 5 ml nutmeg
- 15 ml balsamic vinegar
- 118 ml olive oil

Preparation

1. Heat the oil in a skillet that fits your air fryer over medium heat, then add the mushrooms and onions, mix, and cook for 4 minutes.
2. Brown the pork chops on each side with the nutmeg and garlic spice.
3. Preheat your air fryer to 165 degrees Celsius and cook for 30 minutes.
4. Stir in the vinegar and mayonnaise before plating everything.
5. Enjoy!

Nutritional information: calories 600, fat 10, fiber 1, carbs 8, protein 30

267.   LAMB AND SPINACH MIX

Preparation time: 10 minutes
Cooking time: 35 minutes
Servings: 6
Ingredients:

- 12 g ginger, grated
- 2 garlic cloves, minced
- 4 g cardamom, ground
- 1 red onion, chopped
- 454 g lamb meat, cubed
- 10 ml cumin powder
- 5 ml garam masala
- 2.5 ml chili powder
- 2.5 ml turmeric
- 10 ml coriander, ground
- 454 g spinach
- 397 g canned tomatoes, chopped

Preparation

1. Mix lamb with spinach, tomatoes, ginger, garlic, onion, cardamom, cloves, cumin, garam masala, chile, turmeric, and coriander in a heatproof dish that fits your air fryer, swirl, and cook at 182 degrees C for 35 minutes.
2. Serve in individual bowls.

3. Enjoy!

Nutritional information: calories 160, fat 6, fiber 3, carbs 17, protein 20

268.   AIR FRIED SAUSAGE AND

MUSHROOMS

Preparation time: 10 minutes
Cooking time: 40 minutes
Servings: 6

Ingredients:

- 3 red bell peppers, chopped
- 907 g pork sausage, sliced
- Salt and black pepper to the taste
- 907 g Portobello mushrooms, sliced
- 2 sweet onions, chopped
- 12 g brown sugar
- 5 ml olive oil

Preparation

1. Toss sausage slices with oil, salt, pepper, bell pepper, mushrooms, onion, and sugar in a baking dish that fits your air fryer, then place in your air fryer and cook at 149 degrees C for 40 minutes.
2. Serve immediately on individual plates.
3. Enjoy!

Nutritional information: calories 130, fat 12, fiber 1, carbs 13, protein 18

269.   SAUSAGE AND KALE

Preparation time: 10 minutes
Cooking time: 20 minutes
Servings: 4

Ingredients:

- 222 g yellow onion, chopped
- 680 g Italian pork sausage, sliced
- 79 g red bell pepper, chopped
- Salt and black pepper to the taste
- 2268 g kale, chopped
- 5 ml garlic, minced
- 40 g red hot chili pepper, chopped

- 237 ml water

Preparation
1. Toss sausage with onion, bell pepper, salt, pepper, kale, garlic, water, and chilli pepper in a pan that fits your air fryer, then place in a warmed air fryer and cook at 149 degrees C for 20 minutes.
2. Serve everything on individual plates.
3. Enjoy!

Nutritional information: calories 150, fat 4, fiber 1, carbs 12, protein 14

270.   BEEF STUFFED SQUASH

Preparation time: 10 minutes
Cooking time: 40 minutes
Servings: 2

Ingredients:
- 1 spaghetti squash, pricked
- 454 g beef, ground
- Salt and black pepper to the taste
- 3 garlic cloves, minced
- 1 yellow onion, chopped
- 1 Portobello mushroom, sliced
- 794 g canned tomatoes, chopped
- 5 ml oregano, dried
- 1.25 ml cayenne pepper
- 2.5 ml thyme, dried
- 1 green bell pepper, chopped

Preparation
1. Place spaghetti squash in an air fryer and cook at 176°C for 20 minutes. Transfer to a cutting board and cut into halves, discarding seeds.
2. Heat a pan over medium-high heat, then add the meat, garlic, onion, and mushroom, constantly stirring until the meat is browned.
3. Cook for 10 minutes after adding salt, pepper, thyme, oregano, cayenne pepper, tomatoes, and green pepper.
4. Stuff squash with this meat mixture, place in the fryer and cook for 10 minutes at 182 degrees Celsius.
5. Serve on individual plates.
6. Enjoy!

Nutritional information: calories 260, fat 7, fiber 2, carbs 14, protein 10

271.   BEEF CASSEROLE

Preparation time: 30 minutes
Cooking time: 35 minutes
Servings: 12

Ingredients:
- 15 ml olive oil
- 907 g beef, ground
- 174 g eggplant, chopped
- Salt and black pepper to the taste
- 10 g mustard
- 10 ml gluten-free Worcestershire sauce
- 794 g canned tomatoes, chopped
- 450 g mozzarella, grated
- 450 g tomato sauce
- 8 g parsley, chopped
- 5 ml oregano, dried

Preparation
1. To coat, toss eggplant in a bowl with salt, pepper, and oil.
2. In a separate bowl, combine the meat, salt, pepper, mustard, and Worcestershire sauce; toss well and put on the bottom of an air fryer pan.
3. In the end, combine the eggplant mixture, tomatoes, tomato sauce, parsley, oregano, and mozzarella.
4. Cook for 35 minutes at 182 degrees Celsius in your air fryer.
5. Serve immediately on plates.
6. Enjoy!

Nutritional information: calories 200, fat 12, fiber 2, carbs 16, protein 15

272.   LAMB AND LEMON SAUCE

Preparation time: 10 minutes
Cooking time: 30 minutes
Servings: 4

Ingredients:
- 2 lamb shanks
- Salt and black pepper to the taste

- 2 garlic cloves, minced
- 60 ml olive oil
- Juice from ½ lemon
- Zest from ½ lemon
- 2.5 ml oregano, dried

Preparation

1. Season the lamb with salt and pepper, rub it with garlic, and cook for 30 minutes at 176 degrees Celsius in an air fryer.
2. Meanwhile, mix the lemon juice, zest, salt & pepper, olive oil, and oregano in a mixing bowl.
3. Discard bone, shred lamb, divide among plates, sprinkle with lemon dressing, and serve.
4. Enjoy!

Nutritional information: calories 260, fat 7, fiber 3, carbs 15, protein 12

273.   LAMB AND GREEN PESTO

Preparation time: 1 hour
Cooking time: 45 minutes
Servings: 4

Ingredients:

- 61 g parsley
- 30 g mint
- 1 small yellow onion, roughly chopped
- 42 g pistachios, chopped
- 5 ml lemon zest, grated
- 75 ml olive oil
- Salt and black pepper to the taste
- 907 g lamb riblets
- ½ onion, chopped
- 5 garlic cloves, minced
- Juice from 1 orange

Preparation

1. Blend parsley, mint, onion, pistachios, lemon zest, salt, pepper, and oil in a food processor until smooth.
2. Rub this mixture over the lamb, place in a basin, cover, and chill for 1 hour.
3. Transfer the lamb to a baking dish that fits your air fryer, add the garlic, pour with orange

juice, and cook for 45 minutes at 149 degrees C.

4. Serve the lamb on individual plates.
5. Enjoy!

Nutritional information: calories 200, fat 4, fiber 6, carbs 15, protein 7

274.   BURGUNDY BEEF MIX

Preparation time: 10 minutes
Cooking time: 1 hour
Servings: 7

Ingredients:

- 907 g beef chuck roast, cubed
- 425 g canned tomatoes, chopped
- 4 carrots, chopped
- Salt and black pepper to the taste
- 227 g mushrooms, sliced
- 2 celery ribs, chopped
- 2 yellow onions, chopped
- 200 ml beef stock
- 3 g thyme, chopped
- 2.5 ml mustard powder
- 6 g almond flour
- 237 ml water

Preparation

1. Heat a heatproof saucepan that fits your air fryer over medium-high heat, then add the beef, stir, and brown for a few minutes.
2. Stir in the tomatoes, mushrooms, onions, carrots, celery, salt, pepper, mustard, stock, and thyme.
3. Mix water and flour in a basin, stir well, add to saucepan, toss, place in the air fryer, and cook at 149 degrees C for 1 hour.
4. Serve in individual bowls.
5. Enjoy!

Nutritional information: calories 275, fat 13, fiber 4, carbs 17, protein 28

275. PORK CHOPS AND SAGE SAUCE

Preparation time: 10 minutes
Cooking time: 15 minutes
Servings: 2

Ingredients:
- 2 pork chops
- Salt and black pepper to the taste
- 15 ml olive oil
- 28 g butter
- 1 shallot, sliced
- 1 handful sage, chopped
- 5 ml lemon juice

Preparation
1. Season the pork chops with salt and pepper, massage with the oil, and cook at 187 degrees C for 10 minutes, flipping halfway.
2. Meanwhile, melt the butter in a pan over medium heat, add the shallot, swirl, and cook for 2 minutes.
3. Stir in the sage and lemon juice, simmer for a few minutes more, then remove from heat.
4. Serve pork chops on plates with sage sauce drizzled all over.
5. Enjoy!

Nutritional information: calories 265, fat 6, fiber 8, carbs 19, protein 12

276. CREAMY HAM AND CAULIFLOWER MIX

Preparation time: 10 minutes
Cooking time: 4 hours
Servings: 6

Ingredients:
- 227 g cheddar cheese, grated
- 4 cups ham, cubed
- 396 g chicken stock
- 2.5 ml garlic powder
- 2.5 ml onion powder
- Salt and black pepper to the taste
- 4 garlic cloves, minced
- 60 ml heavy cream
- 213 g cauliflower florets

Preparation
1. Mix ham with stock, cheese, cauliflower, garlic powder, onion powder, salt, pepper, garlic, and heavy cream in a saucepan that fits your air fryer. Stir and cook at 149 degrees C for 1 hour.
2. Serve in individual bowls.
3. Enjoy!

Nutritional information: calories 320, fat 20, fiber 3, carbs 16, protein 23

277. BEEF KABOBS

Preparation time: 10 minutes
Cooking time: 10 minutes
Servings: 4

Ingredients:
- 2 red bell peppers, chopped
- 907 g sirloin steak, cut into medium pieces
- 1 red onion, chopped
- 1 zucchini, sliced
- Juice from 1 lime
- 12 g chili powder
- 30 ml hot sauce
- 7.5 ml cumin, ground
- 60 ml olive oil
- 69 g salsa
- Salt and black pepper to the taste

Preparation
1. In a mixing bowl, combine salsa, lime juice, oil, hot sauce, chilli powder, cumin, salt, and black pepper.
2. Divide the pork, bell peppers, zucchini, and onion onto skewers, spray with the salsa mixture you produced previously, and cook for 10 minutes at 187 degrees C, flipping kabobs midway.
3. Serve with a side salad on individual plates.
4. Enjoy!

Nutritional information: calories 170, fat 5, fiber 2, carbs 13, protein 16

278.   BALSAMIC BEEF

Preparation time: 10 minutes
Cooking time: 1 hour
Servings: 6
Ingredients:

- 1 medium beef roast
- 15 ml Worcestershire sauce
- 120 ml balsamic vinegar
- 200 ml beef stock
- 15 ml honey
- 15 ml soy sauce
- 4 garlic cloves, minced

Preparation

1. Mix roast with Worcestershire sauce, vinegar, stock, honey, soy sauce, and garlic in a heatproof dish that fits your air fryer, toss well, and place in your air fryer for 1 hour at 187 degrees C.
2. Slice the roast, divide it among plates, and drizzle it with the sauce.
3. Enjoy!

Nutritional information: calories 311, fat 7, fiber 12, carbs 20, protein 16

279.   PORK CHOPS AND GREEN

BEANS

Preparation time: 10 minutes
Cooking time: 15 minutes
Servings: 4

Ingredients:

- 4 pork chops, bone-in
- 30 ml olive oil
- 4 g sage, chopped
- Salt and black pepper to the taste
- 251 g green beans
- 3 garlic cloves, minced
- 7 g parsley, chopped

Preparation

1. Mix pork chops with olive oil, sage, salt, pepper, green beans, garlic, and parsley in a pan that fits your air fryer, toss and cook at 182 degrees C for 15 minutes.

2. Serve everything on individual plates.
3. Enjoy!

Nutritional information: calories 261, fat 7, fiber 9, carbs 14, protein 20

280.   HAM AND VEGGIE AIR

FRIED MIX

Preparation time: 10 minutes
Cooking time: 20 minutes
Servings: 6

Ingredients:

- 57 g butter
- 34 g flour
- 710 ml milk
- 2.25 ml thyme, dried
- 295 g ham, chopped
- 200 g sweet peas
- 44 g mushrooms, halved
- 4 g baby carrots

Preparation

1. Melt the butter in a big pan large enough to fit your air fryer over medium heat, then stir in the flour.
2. Remove from heat and add milk again.
3. Toss in the thyme, ham, peas, mushrooms, and young carrots, then place in the air fryer for 20 minutes at 182 degrees C.
4. Serve everything on individual plates.
5. Enjoy!

Nutritional information: calories 311, fat 6, fiber 8, carbs 12, protein 7

281.   GREEK BEEF MEATBALLS

SALAD

Preparation time: 10 minutes
Cooking time: 10 minutes
Servings: 6

Ingredients:

- 60 ml milk

- 482 g beef, ground
- 1 yellow onion, grated
- 5 bread slices, cubed
- 1 egg, whisked
- 15 g parsley, chopped
- Salt and black pepper to the taste
- 2 garlic cloves, minced
- 7.5 g mint, chopped
- 12 ml oregano, dried
- 15 ml olive oil
- Cooking spray
- 198 g cherry tomatoes, halved
- 30 g baby spinach
- 22 ml lemon juice
- 207 ml Greek yogurt

Preparation

1. Place torn bread in a bowl, cover with milk, and soak for a few minutes before squeezing and transferring to another basin.
2. Stir in the beef, egg, salt, pepper, oregano, mint, parsley, garlic, and onion, and form medium meatballs from the mixture.
3. Spray them with frying spray, place them in your air fryer, and cook for 10 minutes at 187 degrees C.
4. Combine spinach, cucumber, and tomato in a salad bowl.
5. Toss in the meatballs, oil, salt, pepper, lemon juice, and yoghurt, and serve.
6. Enjoy!

Nutritional information: calories 200, fat 4, fiber 8, carbs 13, protein 27

282.   SHORT RIBS AND SPECIAL

SAUCE

Preparation time: 10 minutes
Cooking time: 36 minutes
Servings: 4

Ingredients:
- 2 green onions, chopped
- 5 ml vegetable oil
- 3 garlic cloves, minced
- 3 ginger slices
- 1 .8 kg short ribs

- 118 ml water
- 118 ml soy sauce
- 60 ml rice wine
- 60 ml pear juice
- 10 ml sesame oil

Preparation

1. Heat the oil in a skillet that fits your air fryer over medium heat, then add the green onions, ginger, and garlic, mix, and cook for 1 minute.
2. Stir in the ribs, water, wine, soy sauce, sesame oil, and pear juice before placing them in the air fryer and cooking at 176° C for 35 minutes.
3. Serve the ribs and sauce on separate plates.
4. Enjoy!

Nutritional information: calories 321, fat 12, fiber 4, carbs 20, protein 14

283.   ORIENTAL AIR FRIED

LAMB

Preparation time: 10 minutes
Cooking time: 42 minutes
Servings: 8

Ingredients:
- 1134 g lamb shoulder, chopped
- 45 ml honey
- 85 g almonds, peeled and chopped
- 255 g plumps, pitted
- 230 ml veggie stock
- 2 yellow onions, chopped
- 2 garlic cloves, minced
- Salt and black pepper to the tastes
- 5 ml cumin powder
- 5 ml turmeric powder
- 5 ml ginger powder
- 5 ml cinnamon powder
- 45 ml olive oil

Preparation

1. Combine cinnamon powder, ginger, cumin, turmeric, garlic, olive oil, and lamb in a mixing bowl, stir to coat, and cook at 176 degrees C for 8 minutes.

2. Transfer the beef to an air fryer-safe dish, add the onions, stock, honey, and plums, stir, and cook at 176 degrees C for 35 minutes.
3. Divide everything amongst plates and top with almonds.
4. Enjoy!

Nutritional information: calories 432, fat 23, fiber 6, carbs 30, protein 20

284.   BEEF CURRY

Preparation time: 10 minutes
Cooking time: 45 minutes
Servings: 4

Ingredients:
- 907 g beef steak, cubed
- 30 ml olive oil
- 3 potatoes, cubed
- 15 ml wine mustard
- 18 g curry powder
- 2 yellow onions, chopped
- 2 garlic cloves, minced
- 296 ml canned coconut milk
- 30 ml tomato sauce
- Salt and black pepper to the taste

Preparation
1. Heat the oil in a pan that fits your air fryer over medium-high heat, add the onions and garlic, swirl, and cook for 4 minutes.
2. Cook for 1 minute after adding the potatoes and mustard.
3. Stir in the beef, curry powder, salt, pepper, coconut milk, and tomato sauce before placing it in the air fryer and cooking for 40 minutes at 182 degrees C.
4. Serve in individual bowls.
5. Enjoy!

Nutritional information: calories 432, fat 16, fiber 4, carbs 20, protein 27

285.   LAMB ROAST AND POTATOES

Preparation time: 10 minutes
Cooking time: 45 minutes
Servings: 6

Ingredients:
- 1.8 kg lamb roast
- 1 spring rosemary
- 3 garlic cloves, minced
- 6 potatoes, halved
- 118 ml lamb stock
- 4 bay leaves
- Salt and black pepper to the taste

Preparation
1. Put potatoes in a dish that fits your air fryer, add lamb, garlic, rosemary spring, salt, pepper, bay leaves, and stock, toss, introduce in your air fryer and cook at 182 degrees C for 45 minutes.
2. Slice lamb, divide among plates, and serve with potatoes and cooking.
3. Juices.
4. Enjoy!

Nutritional information: calories 273, fat 4, fiber 12, carbs 25, protein 29

286.   BEEF AND GREEN ONIONS MARINADE

Preparation time: 10 minutes
Cooking time: 20 minutes
Servings: 4

Ingredients:
- 98 g green onion, chopped
- 237 ml soy sauce
- 118 ml water
- 50 g brown sugar
- 60 ml sesame seeds
- 5 garlic cloves, minced
- 5 ml black pepper
- 454 g lean beef

Preparation

1. Whisk together the onion, soy sauce, water, sugar, garlic, sesame seeds, and pepper in a mixing bowl. Add the meat, toss, and set aside for 10 minutes.
2. Drain the steak and place it in your prepared air fryer for 20 minutes at 198 degrees C.
3. Slice, divide among plates, and serve with a salad on the side.
4. Enjoy!

Nutritional information: calories 329, fat 8, fiber 12, carbs 26, protein 22

SIDE DISHES RECIPE

287.   CAULIFLOWER CAKES

Preparation time: 10 minutes
Cooking time: 10 minutes
Servings: 6

Ingredients:
- 200 g cauliflower rice
- 2 eggs
- 31 g white flour
- 45 g parmesan, grated
- Salt and black pepper to the taste
- Cooking spray

Preparation
1. In a mixing dish, combine cauliflower rice with salt and pepper, whisk, and wring out any extra water.
2. Transfer cauliflower to a separate bowl, add eggs, salt, pepper, flour, and parmesan, and combine thoroughly before shaping your cakes.
3. Cooking spray your air fryer, heat it to 204 degrees C, add cauliflower cakes, and cook for 10 minutes, flipping halfway.
4. Serve the cakes on plates as a side dish.
5. Enjoy!

Nutritional information: calories 125, fat 2, fiber 6, carbs 8, protein 3

288.   CHEDDAR BISCUITS

Preparation time: 10 minutes
Cooking time: 20 minutes
Servings: 8

Ingredients:
- 260 g self-rising flour
- 113 g butter+ 14 g, melted
- 25 g sugar
- 60 g cheddar cheese, grated
- 315 ml cup buttermilk
- 120 g flour

Preparation
1. In a mixing bowl, combine self-rising flour, 113 g butter, sugar, cheddar cheese, buttermilk, and whisk until a dough forms.
2. Spread 120 g flour on a work surface, spread out the dough, flatten it, and cut 8 circles with a cookie cutter, coating them in flour.
3. Line the basket of your air fryer with tin foil, add the biscuits, brush with melted butter, and cook at 193 degrees C for 20 minutes.
4. Serve as a side on individual plates.
5. Enjoy!

Nutritional information: calories 221, fat 3, fiber 8, carbs 12, protein 4

289.   GREEN BEANS SIDE DISH

Preparation time: 10 minutes
Cooking time: 25 minutes
Servings: 4

Ingredients:
- 680 g green beans, trimmed and steamed for 2 minutes
- Salt and black pepper to the taste
- 227 g shallots, chopped
- 32 g almonds, toasted
- 30 ml olive oil

Preparation
1. Toss green beans with salt, pepper, shallots, almonds, and oil in an air fryer basket and cook at 204 degrees C for 25 minutes.
2. Serve as a side dish on individual plates.
3. Enjoy!

Nutritional information: calories 152, fat 3, fiber 6, carbs 7, protein 4

290.   CORN WITH LIME AND CHEESE

Preparation time: 10 minutes
Cooking time: 15 minutes
Servings: 2

Ingredients:

- 2 corns on the cob, husks removed
- A drizzle of olive oil
- 83 g feta cheese, grated
- 5 g sweet paprika
- Juice from 2 limes

Preparation

1. Cook at 204 degrees C for 15 minutes, flipping once, after rubbing corn with oil and paprika.
2. Divide corn among plates, cover with cheese, drizzle with lime juice, and serve as a side dish.
3. Enjoy!

Nutritional information: calories 200, fat 5, fiber 2, carbs 6, protein 6

291.   POTATO WEDGES

Preparation time: 10 minutes
Cooking time: 25 minutes
Servings: 4

Ingredients:

- 2 potatoes, cut into wedges
- 15 ml olive oil
- Salt and black pepper to the taste
- 45 ml sour cream
- 30 ml sweet chili sauce

Preparation

1. Toss potato wedges with oil, salt, and pepper in a bowl, add to the air fryer basket, and cook at 182 degrees C for 25 minutes, flipping once.
2. Serve potato wedges with sour cream and chilli sauce drizzled as a side dish.
3. Enjoy!

Nutritional information: calories 171, fat 8, fiber 9, carbs 18, protein 7

292.   AVOCADO FRIES

Preparation time: 10 minutes
Cooking time: 10 minutes
Servings: 4

Ingredients:

- 1 avocado, pitted, peeled, sliced, and cut into medium fries
- Salt and black pepper to the taste
- 50 g panko bread crumbs
- 15 ml lemon juice
- 1 egg, whisked
- 15 ml olive oil

Preparation

1. Stir panko with salt and pepper in a mixing bowl.
2. In another bowl, whisk together the egg and a touch of salt.
3. Toss avocado fries with lemon juice and oil in a third bowl.
4. Dip fries in egg, then in panko, then place in air fryer basket and cook for 10 minutes at 198 °C, shaking midway.
5. Serve as a side dish on individual plates.
6. Enjoy!

Nutritional information: calories 130, fat 11, fiber 3, carbs 16, protein 4

293.   SWEET POTATO FRIES

Preparation time: 10 minutes
Cooking time: 20 minutes
Servings: 2

Ingredients:

- 2 sweet potatoes, peeled and cut into medium fries
- Salt and black pepper to the taste
- 30 ml olive oil
- 2.5 ml curry powder
- 1.25 ml coriander, ground
- 59 ml ketchup
- 29 g mayonnaise
- 2.5 ml cumin, ground
- A pinch of ginger powder
- A pinch of cinnamon powder

Preparation

1. Stir sweet potato fries with salt, pepper, coriander, curry powder, and oil in the basket

of your air fryer, toss well, and cook at 187 degrees C for 20 minutes, flipping once.

2. Meanwhile, stir together ketchup, mayonnaise, cumin, ginger, and cinnamon in a mixing dish.

3. Serve the fries on plates with the ketchup mixture as a side dish.

4. Enjoy!

Nutritional information: calories 200, fat 5, fiber 8, carbs 9, protein 7

294. MUSHROOM CAKES

Preparation time: 10 minutes
Cooking time: 8 minutes
Servings: 8

Ingredients:
- 113 g mushrooms, chopped
- 1 yellow onion, chopped
- Salt and black pepper to the taste
- 2.5 ml nutmeg, ground
- 30 ml olive oil
- 14 g butter
- 10 g flour
- 7 g bread crumbs
- 414 ml milk

Preparation
1. Heat the butter in a pan over medium-high heat, add the onion and mushrooms, mix, and cook for 3 minutes, then add the flour, stir well, and remove from heat.

2. Stir in the milk, salt, pepper, and nutmeg gradually, and set aside to cool fully.

3. Whisk together the oil and bread crumbs in a mixing bowl.

4. Take spoonfuls of the mushroom filling, add to the breadcrumbs mixture, coat well, create patties out of this mixture, set them in the basket of your air fryer, and cook at 204° C for 8 minutes.

5. Divide among plates and serve with a steak.

6. Enjoy!

Nutritional information: calories 192, fat 2, fiber 1, carbs 16, protein 6

295. HASSELBACK POTATOES

Preparation time: 10 minutes
Cooking time: 20 minutes
Servings: 2

Ingredients:
- 2 potatoes, peeled and thinly sliced almost all the way horizontally
- 30 ml olive oil
- 3 g garlic, minced
- Salt and black pepper to the taste
- 2.5 ml oregano, dried
- 2.5 ml basil, dried
- 2.5 ml sweet paprika

Preparation
1. Mix the oil, garlic, salt, pepper, oregano, basil, and paprika in a mixing bowl.

2. Rub the potatoes with this mixture, place them in your air fryer's basket and cook for 20 minutes at 182 degrees C.

3. Serve as a side dish, divided into plates.

4. Enjoy!

Nutritional information: calories 172, fat 6, fiber 6, carbs 9, protein 6

296. CREAMY ROASTED PEPPERS SIDE DISH

Preparation time: 10 minutes
Cooking time: 10 minutes
Servings: 4

Ingredients:
- 15 ml lemon juice
- 1 red bell pepper
- 1 green bell pepper
- 1 yellow bell pepper
- 1 lettuce head, cut into strips
- 28 g rocket leaves
- Salt and black pepper to the taste
- 45 ml Greek yogurt
- 30 ml olive oil

Preparation

1. Place bell peppers in the basket of your air fryer, cook at 204 degrees C for 10 minutes, transfer to a bowl, set aside for 10 minutes, peel, discard seeds, cut into strips, transfer to a bigger dish, toss with rocket leaves and lettuce strips.
2. Mix the oil, lemon juice, yoghurt, salt, and pepper in a mixing dish.
3. Toss this over the bell pepper mixture, divide among plates, and serve as a side salad.
4. Enjoy!

Nutritional information: calories 170, fat 1, fiber 1, carbs 2, protein 6

297.   PARMESAN MUSHROOMS

Preparation time: 10 minutes
Cooking time: 15 minutes
Servings: 3

Ingredients:
- 9 button mushroom caps
- 3 cream cracker slices, crumbled
- 1 egg white
- 11 g parmesan, grated
- 5 ml Italian seasoning
- A pinch of salt and black pepper
- 14 g butter, melted

Preparation

1. Mix crackers with egg white, parmesan, Italian seasoning, butter, salt, and pepper in a mixing dish, then fill mushrooms with this mixture.
2. Place the mushrooms in the basket of your air fryer and cook for 15 minutes at 182 degrees Celsius.
3. Serve as a side dish on individual plates.
4. Enjoy!

Nutritional information: calories 124, fat 4, fiber 4, carbs 7, protein 3

298.   EGGPLANT SIDE DISH

Preparation time: 10 minutes
Cooking time: 10 minutes
Servings: 4

Ingredients:
- 8 baby eggplants, scooped in the center and pulp reserved
- Salt and black pepper to the taste
- A pinch of oregano, dried
- 1 green bell pepper, chopped
- 15 ml tomato paste
- 1 bunch coriander, chopped
- 2.5 ml garlic powder
- 15 ml olive oil
- 1 yellow onion, chopped
- 1 tomato chopped

Preparation

1. Heat the oil in a pan over medium heat, add the onion, stir, and cook for 1 minute.
2. Stir in salt, pepper, eggplant pulp, oregano, green bell pepper, tomato paste, garlic powder, coriander, and tomato, simmer for another 1-2 minutes, then remove from heat and set aside to cool.
3. Stuff eggplants with this mixture, place in an air fryer basket and cook for 8 minutes at 182 degrees C.
4. Divide the eggplants among plates and serve as a side dish.
5. Enjoy!

Nutritional information: calories 200, fat 3, fiber 7, carbs 12, protein 4

299.   FRIED TOMATOES

Preparation time: 10 minutes
Cooking time: 5 minutes
Servings: 4

Ingredients:
- 2 green tomatoes, sliced
- Salt and black pepper to the taste
- 63 g flour
- 237 g buttermilk
- 119 g panko bread crumbs
- 6 g Creole seasoning
- Cooking spray

Preparation

1. Season the tomato slices with salt and pepper to taste.
2. Put the flour in one bowl, the buttermilk in another, and the panko crumbs and Creole spice in the third.
3. Dredge tomato slices in flour, buttermilk, and panko bread crumbs, set them in an air fryer basket sprayed with cooking spray, and cook for 5 minutes at 204 degrees C.
4. Serve as a side dish on individual plates.
5. Enjoy!

Nutritional information: calories 124, fat 5, fiber 7, carbs 9, protein 4

300. CREAMY BRUSSELS SPROUTS

Preparation time: 10 minutes
Cooking time: 25 minutes
Servings: 8

Ingredients:

- 1.3 kg Brussels sprouts, halved
- A drizzle of olive oil
- 454 g bacon, chopped
- Salt and black pepper to the taste
- 57 g butter
- 3 shallots, chopped
- 27 ml milk
- 473 ml heavy cream
- 1.25 g nutmeg, ground
- 45 g prepared horseradish

Preparation

1. Heat your air fryer to 187 degrees Celsius, then add the oil, bacon, salt, pepper, and Brussels sprouts and stir.
2. Cook for 25 minutes after adding the butter, shallots, heavy cream, milk, nutmeg, and horseradish.
3. Serve as a side dish on individual plates.
4. Enjoy!

Nutritional information: calories 214, fat 5, fiber 8, carbs 12, protein 5

301. SIMPLE POTATO CHIPS

Preparation time: 30 minutes
Cooking time: 30 minutes
Servings: 4

Ingredients:

- 4 potatoes, scrubbed, peeled into thin chips, soaked in water for 30 minutes, drained, and pat dried
- Salt the taste
- 15 ml olive oil
- 2 g rosemary, chopped

Preparation

1. Toss potato chips in a bowl with salt and oil to coat, then set them in the basket of your air fryer and cook at 165 degrees C for 30 minutes.
2. Divide among dishes, top with rosemary, and serve as a side dish.
3. Enjoy!

Nutritional information: calories 200, fat 4, fiber 4, carbs 14, protein 5

302. ZUCCHINI FRIES

Preparation time: 10 minutes
Cooking time: 12 minutes
Servings: 4

Ingredients:

- 1 zucchini, cut into medium sticks
- A drizzle of olive oil
- Salt and black pepper to the taste
- 2 eggs, whisked
- 150 g bread crumbs (dry)
- 63 g flour

Preparation

1. Mix the flour, salt, and pepper in a mixing basin, and stir.
2. In a separate bowl, combine the breadcrumbs.
3. In a third bowl, whisk together the eggs with a touch of salt and pepper.
4. Dredge zucchini fries in flour, then in eggs, and finally in bread crumbs.

5. Grease your air fryer with olive oil, set it to 204 degrees Celsius, and cook the zucchini fries for 12 minutes.
6. As a side dish, serve them.
7. Enjoy!

Nutritional information: calories 172, fat 3, fiber 3, carbs 7, protein 3

303.   ROASTED PEPPERS

Preparation time: 10 minutes
Cooking time: 20 minutes
Servings: 4

Ingredients:
- 7 g sweet paprika
- 15 ml olive oil
- 4 red bell peppers, cut into medium strips
- 4 green bell peppers, cut into medium strips
- 4 yellow bell peppers, cut into medium strips
- 1 yellow onion, chopped
- Salt and black pepper to the taste

Preparation
1. Combine red, green, and yellow bell peppers in your air fryer.
2. Toss in the paprika, oil, onion, salt, and pepper, and cook for 20 minutes at 176° C.
3. Serve as a side dish on individual plates.
4. Enjoy!

Nutritional information: calories 142, fat 4, fiber 4, carbs 7, protein 4

304.   RICE AND SAUSAGE SIDE
·   DISH

Preparation time: 10 minutes
Cooking time: 20 minutes
Servings: 4

Ingredients:
- 350 g white rice, already boiled
- 14 g butter
- Salt and black pepper to the taste
- 4 garlic cloves, minced

- 1 pork sausage, chopped
- 16 g carrot, chopped
- 16 g cheddar cheese, grated
- 28 g mozzarella cheese, shredded

Preparation
1. Preheat your air fryer to 176°C, add the butter, melt it, add the garlic, stir, and brown for 2 minutes.
2. Stir in the sausage, salt, pepper, carrots, and rice and cook for 10 minutes at 176° C.
3. Toss in the cheddar and mozzarella, divide among plates and serve as a side dish.
4. Enjoy!

Nutritional information: calories 240, fat 12, fiber 5, carbs 20, protein 13

305.   DELICIOUS ROASTED
CARROTS

Preparation time: 10 minutes
Cooking time: 20 minutes
Servings: 4

Ingredients:
- 454 g baby carrots
- 10 ml olive oil
- 5 ml herbs de Provence
- 60 ml orange juice

Preparation
1. Toss carrots with herbs de Provence, oil, and orange juice in an air fryer basket and cook at 160° C for 20 minutes.
2. Serve as a side dish on individual plates.
3. Enjoy!

Nutritional information: calories 112, fat 2, fiber 3, carbs 4, protein 3

306.   BEER RISOTTO

Preparation time: 10 minutes
Cooking time: 30 minutes
Servings: 4

Ingredients:

- 30 ml olive oil
- 2 yellow onions, chopped
- 28 g mushrooms, sliced
- 5 ml basil, dried
- 5 ml oregano, dried
- 300 g rice
- 473 ml beer
- 475 ml chicken stock
- 14 g butter
- 45 g parmesan, grated

Preparation

1. Stir the oil, onions, mushrooms, basil, and oregano in a dish that fits your air fryer.
2. Stir in the rice, beer, butter, stock, and butter, then place in the air fryer basket and cook at 176° C for 30 minutes.
3. As a side dish, divide among plates and sprinkle with grated parmesan.
4. Enjoy!

Nutritional information: calories 142, fat 4, fiber 4, carbs 6, protein 4

307. DELICIOUS AIR FRIED BROCCOLI

Preparation time: 10 minutes
Cooking time: 20 minutes
Servings: 4

Ingredients:

- 13 g duck fat
- 1 broccoli head, florets separated
- 3 garlic cloves, minced
- Juice from ½ lemon
- 9 g sesame seeds

Preparation

1. Preheat your air fryer to 176 degrees Celsius, add the duck fat, and cook it.
2. Toss in the broccoli, garlic, lemon juice, and sesame seeds and cook for 20 minutes.
3. Serve as a side dish on individual plates.
4. Enjoy!

Nutritional information: calories 132, fat 3, fiber 3, carbs 6, protein 4

308. ONION RINGS SIDE DISH

Preparation time: 10 minutes
Cooking time: 10 minutes
Servings: 3

Ingredients:

- 1 onion cut into medium slices and rings separated
- 125 g cups white flour
- A pinch of salt
- 1 egg
- 237 ml milk
- 5 ml baking powder
- 89 g bread crumbs

Preparation

1. Mix flour, salt, and baking powder in a basin dredge onion rings in this mixture, and lay them on a separate dish.
2. Whisk together the flour, milk, and egg.
3. Dip onion rings in this mixture, then in breadcrumbs, and cook for 10 minutes at 182 degrees C in an air fryer basket.
4. Divide among plates and serve with a steak as a side dish.
5. Enjoy!

Nutritional information: calories 140, fat 8, fiber 20, carbs 12, protein 3

309. TORTILLA CHIPS

Preparation time: 10 minutes
Cooking time: 6 minutes
Servings: 4

Ingredients:

- 8 corn tortillas, cut into triangles
- Salt and black pepper to the taste
- 15 ml olive oil
- A pinch of garlic powder
- A pinch of sweet paprika

Preparation
1. Toss tortilla chips with oil, season with salt, pepper, garlic powder, and paprika, and set in your air fryer basket for 6 minutes at 204 degrees C.
2. Serve them alongside a seafood meal.
3. Enjoy!

Nutritional information: calories 53, fat 1, fiber 1, carbs 6, protein 4

310.   AIR FRIED CREAMY CABBAGE

Preparation time: 10 minutes
Cooking time: 20 minute
Servings: 4

Ingredients:
- 1 green cabbage head, chopped
- 1 yellow onion, chopped
- Salt and black pepper to the taste
- 4 bacon slices, chopped
- 60 g whipped cream
- 15 g cornstarch

Preparation
1. In your air fryer, put cabbage, bacon, and onion.
2. In a mixing basin, combine cornstarch, cream, salt, and pepper; stir and pour over cabbage.
3. Toss, cook for 20 minutes at 204° C, divide among plates, and serve as a side dish.
4. Enjoy!

Nutritional information: calories 208, fat 10, fiber 3, carbs 16, protein 5

311.   CREAMY POTATOES

Preparation time: 10 minutes
Cooking time: 20 minutes
Servings: 4

Ingredients:
- 680 g potatoes, peeled and cubed
- 30 ml olive oil

- Salt and black pepper to the taste
- 7 g hot paprika
- 237 ml Greek yogurt

Preparation
1. Put the potatoes in a bowl, cover with water, and set aside for 10 minutes. Drain, pat dry, transfer to another bowl, and combine with salt, pepper, paprika, and half of the oil.
2. Put potatoes in the basket of your air fryer and cook for 20 minutes at 182 degrees Celsius.
3. Whisk the yoghurt, salt, pepper, and the remaining oil in a mixing bowl.
4. Divide potatoes among plates, sprinkle with yoghurt dressing, stir, and serve as a side dish.
5. Enjoy!

Nutritional information: calories 170, fat 3, fiber 5, carbs 20, protein 5

312.   BRUSSELS SPROUTS AND POMEGRANATE SEEDS SIDE DISH

Preparation time: 5 minutes
Cooking time: 10 minutes
Servings: 4

Ingredients:
- 454 g Brussels sprouts, trimmed and halved
- Salt and black pepper to the taste
- 140 g pomegranate seeds
- 35 g pine nuts, toasted
- 15 ml olive oil
- 30 ml veggie stock

Preparation
1. Mix Brussels sprouts with salt, pepper, pomegranate seeds, pine nuts, oil, and stock in a heatproof bowl that fits your air fryer. Swirl and cook at 198 degrees C for 10 minutes.
2. Serve as a side dish on individual plates.
3. Enjoy!

Nutritional information: calories 152, fat 4, fiber 7, carbs 12, protein 3

313.   COCONUT CREAM

POTATOES

Preparation time: 10 minutes
Cooking time: 20 minutes
Servings: 4

Ingredients:
- 2 eggs, whisked
- Salt and black pepper to the taste
- 7.5 g cheddar cheese, grated
- 8 g flour
- 2 potatoes, sliced
- 118 ml coconut cream

Preparation
1. Place potato slices in the basket of your air fryer and cook for 10 minutes at 182 degrees C.
2. Meanwhile, whisk together the eggs, coconut cream, salt, pepper, and flour in a mixing dish.
3. Arrange potatoes in an air fryer pan, top with coconut cream mixture, sprinkle with cheese, return to the air fryer basket, and cook at 204° C for 10 minutes.
4. Serve as a side dish on individual plates.
5. Enjoy!

Nutritional information: calories 170, fat 4, fiber 1, carbs 15, protein 17

314.   FRIED RED CABBAGE

Preparation time: 10 minutes
Cooking time: 15 minutes
Servings: 4

Ingredients:
- 4 garlic cloves, minced
- 26 g yellow onion, chopped
- 15 ml olive oil
- 6 cups red cabbage, chopped
- 237 ml veggie stock
- 15 ml apple cider vinegar
- 237 ml applesauce
- Salt and black pepper to the taste

Preparation
1. Combine cabbage, onion, garlic, oil, stock, vinegar, applesauce, salt, and pepper in a heatproof dish that fits your air fryer basket, toss well, and cook at 193 degrees C for 15 minutes.
2. Serve as a side dish on individual plates.
3. Enjoy!

Nutritional information: calories 172, fat 7, fiber 7, carbs 14, protein 5

315.   FLAVORED CAULIFLOWER

SIDE DISH

Preparation time: 10 minutes
Cooking time: 10 minutes
Servings: 4

Ingredients:
- 12 cauliflower florets, steamed
- Salt and black pepper to the taste
- 1.25 ml turmeric powder
- 7.5 ml red chili powder
- 6 g ginger, grated
- 30 ml lemon juice
- 23 g white flour
- 30 ml water
- Cooking spray
- 2.5 ml corn flour

Preparation
1. Mix chilli powder, turmeric powder, ginger paste, salt, pepper, lemon juice, white flour, corn flour, and water in a mixing bowl. Add cauliflower, toss well, and place in the basket of your air fryer.
2. Coat with cooking spray, cook for 10 minutes at 204° C, divide among plates, and serve as a side dish.
3. Enjoy!

Nutritional information: calories 70, fat 1, fiber 2, carbs 12, protein 3

316. CAULIFLOWER AND BROCCOLI DELIGHT

Preparation time: 10 minutes
Cooking time: 7 minutes
Servings: 4

Ingredients:
- 2 cauliflower heads, florets separated and steamed
- 1 broccoli head, florets separated and steamed
- Zest from 1 orange, grated
- Juice from 1 orange
- A pinch of hot pepper flakes
- 4 anchovies
- 7.5 g capers, chopped
- Salt and black pepper to the taste
- 60 ml olive oil

Preparation
1. Whisk together orange zest, orange juice, pepper flakes, anchovies, capers, salt, pepper, and olive oil in a mixing bowl.
2. Toss in the broccoli and cauliflower, then put in the basket of your air fryer and cook for 7 minutes at 204 degrees C.
3. Divide among plates and serve as a side dish with a sprinkle of the orange vinaigrette.
4. Enjoy!

Nutritional information: calories 300, fat 4, fiber 7, carbs 28, protein 4

317. CAJUN ONION WEDGES

Preparation time: 10 minutes
Cooking time: 15 minutes
Servings: 4

Ingredients:
- 2 big white onions, cut into wedges
- Salt and black pepper to the taste
- 2 eggs
- 60 ml milk
- 28 g panko
- A drizzle of olive oil
- 1 and ½ teaspoon paprika
- 5 ml garlic powder
- 2.5 ml Cajun seasoning

Preparation
1. Stir together panko, Cajun spice, and oil in a mixing basin.
2. Whisk together the egg, milk, salt, and pepper in another separate bowl.
3. Sprinkle paprika and garlic powder on onion wedges, dip them in egg mixture, bread crumbs mixture, and place in air fryer basket. Cook at 182 degrees C for 10 minutes, then flip and cook for 5 minutes more.
4. Serve as a side dish on individual plates.
5. Enjoy!

Nutritional information: calories 200, fat 2, fiber 2, carbs 14, protein 7

318. WILD RICE PILAF

Preparation time: 10 minutes
Cooking time: 25 minutes
Servings: 12

Ingredients:
- 1 shallot, chopped
- 5 ml garlic, minced
- A drizzle of olive oil
- 152 g farro
- 148 g wild rice
- 4 cups chicken stock
- Salt and black pepper to the taste
- 4 g parsley, chopped
- 65 g hazelnuts, toasted and chopped
- 120 g cherries, dried
- Chopped chives for serving

Preparation
1. Mix shallot with garlic, oil, faro, wild rice, stock, salt, pepper, parsley, hazelnuts, and cherries in a bowl that fits your air fryer, whisk and cook at 176 degrees C for 25 minutes.
2. Serve as a side dish on individual plates.
3. Enjoy!

Nutritional information: calories 142, fat 4, fiber 4, carbs 16, protein 4

319.   LEMONY ARTICHOKES

Preparation time: 10 minutes
Cooking time: 15 minutes
Servings: 4

Ingredients:
- 2 medium artichokes, trimmed and halved
- Cooking spray
- 30 ml lemon juice
- Salt and black pepper to the taste

Preparation
1. Grease your air fryer with frying spray, add the artichokes, drizzle with lemon juice, and season with salt and black pepper. Cook for 15 minutes at 193 degrees Celsius.
2. Serve as a side dish, divided into plates.
3. Enjoy!

Nutritional information: calories 121, fat 3, fiber 6, carbs 9, protein 4

320.   GARLIC BEET WEDGES

Preparation time: 10 minutes
Cooking time: 15 minutes
Servings: 4

Ingredients:
- 4 beets, washed, peeled, and cut into large wedges
- 15 ml olive oil
- Salt and black to the taste
- 2 garlic cloves, minced
- 5 ml lemon juice

Preparation
1. Toss beets with oil, salt, pepper, garlic, and lemon juice in a mixing bowl, then move to your air fryer basket and cook for 15 minutes at 204 degrees C.
2. Serve the beet wedges on plates as a side dish.
3. Enjoy!

Nutritional information: calories 182, fat 6, fiber 3, carbs 8, protein 2

321.   ARTICHOKES AND TARRAGON SAUCE

Preparation time: 10 minutes
Cooking time: 18 minutes
Servings: 4

Ingredients:
- 4 artichokes, trimmed
- 4 g tarragon, chopped
- 30 ml chicken stock
- Lemon zest from 2 lemons, grated
- 30 ml lemon juice
- 1 celery stalk, chopped
- 118 ml olive oil
- Salt to the taste

Preparation
1. Combine tarragon, chicken stock, lemon zest, lemon juice, celery, salt, and olive oil in a food processor and pulse until thoroughly combined.
2. Toss artichokes with tarragon and lemon sauce in a bowl, then place in an air fryer basket and cook at 193 degrees C for 18 minutes.
3. Divide the artichokes among dishes, sprinkle with the remaining sauce, and serve as a side dish.
4. Enjoy!

Nutritional information: calories 215, fat 3, fiber 8, carbs 28, protein 6

322.   VEGGIE FRIES

Preparation time: 10 minutes
Cooking time: 30 minutes
Servings: 4

Ingredients:
- 4 parsnips, cut into medium sticks
- 2 sweet potatoes cut into medium sticks
- 4 mixed carrots cut into medium sticks
- Salt and black pepper to the taste
- 7 g rosemary, chopped
- 30 ml olive oil
- 8 g flour

- 2.5 ml garlic powder

Preparation
1. Toss the veggie fries in a bowl with the oil, garlic powder, salt, pepper, flour, and rosemary to coat.
2. Place sweet potatoes in a preheated air fryer and cook for 10 minutes at 176 degrees C before transferring them to a platter.
3. Cook the parsnip fries in the air fryer for 5 minutes before adding the potato fries.
4. Cook for 15 minutes at 176 degrees C in your air fryer, then transfer to a platter with the other fries.
5. Divide the veggie fries among the plates and serve as a side dish.
6. Enjoy!

Nutritional information: calories 100, fat 0, fiber 4, carbs 7, protein 4

323.   ROASTED EGGPLANT

Preparation time: 10 minutes
Cooking time: 20 minutes
Servings: 6

Ingredients:
- 640 g eggplant, cubed
- 15 ml olive oil
- 5 ml garlic powder
- 5 ml onion powder
- 5 ml sumac
- 10 ml za'atar
- Juice from ½ lemon
- 2 bay leaves

Preparation
1. Toss eggplant cubes with oil, garlic powder, onion powder, sumac, za'atar, lemon juice, and bay leave in your air fryer for 20 mins at 187 degrees C.
2. Serve as a side dish on individual plates.
3. Enjoy!

Nutritional information: calories 172, fat 4, fiber 7, carbs 12, protein 3

324.   VERMOUTH MUSHROOMS

Preparation time: 10 minutes
Cooking time: 25 minutes
Servings: 4

Ingredients:
- 15 ml olive oil
- 907 g white mushrooms
- 30 ml white vermouth
- 10 ml herbs de Provence
- 2 garlic cloves, minced

Preparation
1. Toss the mushrooms, herbs de Provence, and garlic in the oil in the air fryer and cook at 176 degrees C for 20 minutes.
2. Cook for 5 minutes more after adding the vermouth.
3. Serve as a side dish on individual plates.
4. Enjoy!

Nutritional information: calories 121, fat 2, fiber 5, carbs 7, protein 4

325.   CREAMY ENDIVES

Preparation time: 10 minutes
Cooking time: 10 minutes
Servings: 6

Ingredients:
- 6 endives, trimmed and halved
- 5 ml garlic powder
- 118 ml Greek yogurt
- 2.5 ml curry powder
- Salt and black pepper to the taste
- 45 ml lemon juice

Preparation
1. Toss endives with garlic powder, yoghurt, curry powder, salt, pepper, and lemon juice in a mixing bowl for 10 minutes before placing them in a hot air fryer at 176 degrees C.
2. Cook for 10 minutes, divide among plates and serve as a side dish.
3. Enjoy!

Nutritional information: calories 100, fat 2, fiber 2, carbs 7, protein 4

326. HERBED TOMATOES

Preparation time: 10 minutes
Cooking time: 15 minutes
Servings: 4

Ingredients:
- 4 big tomatoes, halved and insides scooped out
- Salt and black pepper to the taste
- 15 ml olive oil
- 2 garlic cloves, minced
- 2.5 ml thyme, chopped

Preparation
1. Toss endives with garlic powder, yoghurt, curry powder, salt, pepper, and lemon juice in a mixing bowl for 10 minutes before placing them in a hot air fryer at 176 degrees C.
2. Cook for 10 minutes, divide among plates and serve as a side dish.
3. Enjoy!

Nutritional information: calories 112, fat 1, fiber 3, carbs 4, protein 4

DESSERTS RECIPE

327. TASTY ORANGE CAKE

Preparation time: 10 minutes
Cooking time: 32 minutes
Servings: 12

Ingredients:
- 6 eggs
- 1 orange, peeled and cut into quarters
- 5 ml vanilla extract
- 5 ml baking powder
- 255 g flour
- 57 g sugar + 25 g tablespoons
- 30 ml orange zest
- 112 g cream cheese
- 118 ml yogurt

Preparation
1. Orange should be thoroughly pulsed in a food processor.
2. Pulse in the flour, 25 g sugar, eggs, baking powder, and vanilla extract.
3. Place this in two springform pans, one in each fryer, and cook at 165° C for 16 minutes.
4. Meanwhile, in a mixing dish, combine the cream cheese, orange zest, yoghurt, and the remaining sugar.
5. Place one cake layer on a plate, half of the cream cheese mixture, the other cake layer, and the remaining cream cheese mixture.
6. Spread it evenly, then slice and serve.
7. Enjoy!

Nutritional information: calories 200, fat 13, fiber 2, carbs 9, protein 8

328. CRISPY APPLE

Preparation time: 10 minutes
Cooking time: 10 minutes
Servings: 4
Ingredients:
- 10 ml cinnamon powder
- 5 apples, cored and cut into chunks
- 2.5 ml nutmeg powder
- 15 ml maple syrup
- 118 ml water
- 57 g butter
- 34 g flour
- 67 g old-fashioned rolled oats
- 50 g brown sugar

Preparation
1. Place the apples in an air fryer-safe pan, along with the cinnamon, nutmeg, maple syrup, and water.
2. Mix butter, oats, sugar, salt, and flour; whisk. Drop spoonfuls of this mixture on top of apples; place in the air fryer, and cook at 176° C for 10 minutes.
3. Serve hot.
4. Enjoy!

Nutritional information: calories 200, fat 6, fiber 8, carbs 29, protein 12

329. SPECIAL BROWNIES

Preparation time: 10 minutes
Cooking time: 17 minutes
Servings: 4

Ingredients:
- 1 egg
- 35 g cocoa powder
- 67 g sugar
- 100 g butter
- 2.5 ml vanilla extract
- 31 g white flour
- 37 g walnuts, chopped
- 2.5 ml baking powder
- 16 g peanut butter

Preparation
1. Heat a skillet with 85 g butter and the sugar over medium heat, mix, and cook for 5 minutes. Transfer to a bowl, add salt, vanilla extract, cocoa powder, egg, baking powder, walnuts, and flour, and whisk thoroughly. Pour into an air fryer-compatible pan.
2. In a mixing dish, combine 14 g of butter and peanut butter. Microwave for a few seconds, whisk well and sprinkle over brownie mix.

3. Place in your air fryer and bake for 17 minutes at 160 degrees Celsius.
4. Allow the brownies to cool before cutting and serving.
5. Enjoy!

Nutritional information: calories 223, fat 32, fiber 1, carbs 3, protein 6

330.   COFFEE CHEESECAKES

Preparation time: 10 minutes
Cooking time: 20 minutes
Servings: 6

Ingredients:
For the cheesecakes:
- 28 g butter
- 227 g cream cheese
- 16 g coffee
- 3 eggs
- 67 g sugar
- 15 ml caramel syrup

For the frosting:
- 45 ml caramel syrup
- 42 g butter
- 227 g mascarpone cheese, soft
- 25 g sugar

Preparation
1. In a blender, combine cream cheese, eggs, 28 g butter, coffee, 15 ml caramel syrup, and 67 g sugar, and pulse until smooth. Spoon into a cupcake pan that fits your air fryer, place in the fryer, and bake at 160 degrees C for 20 minutes.
2. Allow cooling before placing in the freezer for 3 hours.
3. Meanwhile, in a mixing bowl, combine 42g butter, 45ml caramel syrup, 25g sugar, and mascarpone; whisk well. Spoon over cheesecakes and serve.
4. Enjoy!

Nutritional information: calories 254, fat 23, fiber 0, carbs 21, protein 5

331.   CHOCOLATE COOKIES

Preparation time: 10 minutes
Cooking time: 25 minutes
Servings: 12

Ingredients:
- 5 ml vanilla extract
- 113 g butter
- 1 egg
- 50 g sugar
- 250 g flour
- 85 g unsweetened chocolate chips

Preparation
1. Melt the butter in a skillet over medium heat, swirl, and cook for 1 minute.
2. Mix the egg, vanilla essence, and sugar in a mixing dish and stir thoroughly.
3. Stir in the melted butter, flour, and half of the chocolate chips.
4. Transfer to a pan that fits your air fryer, sprinkle with the remaining chocolate chips and bake for 25 minutes at 165 degrees C.
5. When it's cool enough to slice, serve.
6. Enjoy!

Nutritional information: calories 230, fat 12, fiber 2, carbs 4, protein 5

332.   SIMPLE CHEESECAKE

Preparation time: 10 minutes
Cooking time: 15 minutes
Servings: 15

Ingredients:
- 454 g cream cheese
- 2.5 g vanilla extract
- 2 eggs
- 50 g sugar
- 100 g graham crackers, crumbled
- 28 g butter

Preparation
1. Combine crackers and butter in a mixing basin.

2. Press the cracker mixture onto the bottom of a lined cake pan, place it in your air fryer, and cook for 4 minutes at 176 degrees C.
3. Meanwhile, mix the sugar, cream cheese, eggs, and vanilla in a mixing dish.
4. Spread the filling over the cracker shell and cook the cheesecake in the air fryer for 15 minutes at 154 degrees C.
5. Refrigerate the cake for 3 hours before slicing and serving.
6. Enjoy!

Nutritional information: calories 245, fat 12, fiber 1, carbs 20, protein 3

333.   BREAD DOUGH AND

AMARETTO DESSERT

Preparation time: 10 minutes
Cooking time: 12 minutes
Servings: 12

Ingredients:
- 454 g bread dough
- 200 g sugar
- 113 g butter, melted
- 237 ml heavy cream
- 340 g chocolate chips
- 30 ml amaretto liqueur

Preparation
1. Roll out the dough and cut it into 20 slices, then cut each slice in half.
2. Brush dough pieces with butter, sprinkle with sugar, set them in your air fryer basket after brushing them with butter, cook for 5 minutes at 176 degrees C, turn them, cook for 3 minutes more, and transfer to a platter.
3. Heat the heavy cream in a saucepan over medium heat, then add the chocolate chips and stir until they melt.
4. Stir in the liquor, then transfer to a bowl and serve with bread dippers.
5. Enjoy!

Nutritional information: calories 200, fat 1, fiber 0, carbs 6, protein 6

334.   AIR FRIED APPLES

Preparation time: 10 minutes
Cooking time: 17 minutes
Servings: 4

Ingredients:
- 4 big apples, cored
- A handful raisins
- 8 g cinnamon, ground
- Raw honey to the taste

Preparation
1. Fill each apple with raisins, sprinkle with cinnamon, drizzle with honey, and cook at 186 degrees C for 17 minutes.
2. Allow to cool before serving.
3. Enjoy!

Nutritional information: calories 220, fat 3, fiber 4, carbs 6, protein 10

335.   MINI LAVA CAKES

Preparation time: 10 minutes
Cooking time: 20 minutes
Servings: 3

Ingredients:
- 1 egg
- 50 g sugar
- 30 ml olive oil
- 60 ml milk
- 31 g flour
- 7 g cocoa powder
- 2.5 ml baking powder
- 2.5 ml orange zest

Preparation
1. In a mixing bowl, combine the egg, sugar, oil, milk, flour, salt, cocoa powder, baking powder, and orange zest; stir well and pour into prepared ramekins.
2. Cook the ramekins in the air fryer for 20 minutes at 160° C.
3. Warm lava cakes should be served.
4. Enjoy!

Nutritional information: calories 201, fat 7, fiber 8, carbs 23, protein 4

336. WRAPPED PEARS

Preparation time: 10 minutes
Cooking time: 15 minutes
Servings: 4

Ingredients:
- 4 puff pastry sheets
- 396 g vanilla custard
- 2 pears, halved
- 1 egg, whisked
- 2.5 ml cinnamon powder
- 25 g sugar

Preparation
1. Place puff pastry pieces on a work surface, fill with spoonfuls of vanilla custard, top with pear halves, and wrap.
2. Brush pears with egg, sprinkle with sugar and cinnamon and cook for 15 minutes at 160° C in an air fryer basket.
3. Place the parcels on plates and serve.
4. Enjoy!

Nutritional information: calories 200, fat 2, fiber 1, carbs 14, protein 3

337. AIR FRIED BANANAS

Preparation time: 10 minutes
Cooking time: 15 minutes
Servings: 4

Ingredients:
- 42 g butter
- 2 eggs
- 8 bananas, peeled and halved
- 80 g corn flour
- 24 g cinnamon sugar
- 84 g panko

Preparation
1. Heat the butter in a pan over medium-high heat, add the panko, mix, and cook for 4 minutes before transferring it to a bowl.

2. Roll each in the flour, egg, and panko mixture, place in the air fryer basket and cook for 10 minutes at 138 degrees Celsius.
3. Serve immediately.
4. Enjoy!

Nutritional information: calories 164, fat 1, fiber 4, carbs 32, protein 4

338. COCOA CAKE

Preparation time: 10 minutes
Cooking time: 17 minutes
Servings: 6

Ingredients:
- 99 g butter, melted
- 3 eggs
- 85 g sugar
- 5 ml cocoa powder
- 85 g flour
- 2.5 ml lemon juice

Preparation
1. Whisk together 14 g of butter and cocoa powder in a mixing dish.
2. Whisk together the remaining butter, sugar, eggs, flour, and lemon juice in a separate bowl, then pour half into a cake pan that fits your air fryer.
3. Spread half of the cocoa mixture on top, add the remaining butter layer and top with the remaining cocoa.
4. Cook for 17 minutes at 182 degrees Celsius in your air fryer.
5. Allow the cake to cool before slicing and serving.
6. Enjoy!

Nutritional information: calories 340, fat 11, fiber 3, carbs 25, protein 5

339. STRAWBERRY COBBLER

Preparation time: 10 minutes
Cooking time: 25 minutes
Servings: 6

Ingredients:
- 150 g sugar
- 1200 g strawberries, halved
- 1 g baking powder
- 15 ml lemon juice
- 63 g flour
- A pinch of baking soda
- 118 ml water
- 52 ml olive oil
- Cooking spray

Preparation
1. In a mixing bowl, combine strawberries and half of the sugar, sprinkle with flour, add lemon juice, whisk, and pour into a baking dish greased with cooking spray that fits your air fryer.
2. Whisk together the flour, remaining sugar, baking powder, and soda in a separate dish.
3. Mix in the olive oil with your hands until evenly distributed.
4. Spread strawberries with 118 ml water.
5. Bake for 25 minutes at 124 degrees Celsius in the fryer.
6. Allow the cobbler to cool before slicing and serving.
7. Enjoy

Nutritional information: calories 221, fat 3, fiber 3, carbs 6, protein 9

340. STRAWBERRY PIE

Preparation time: 10 minutes
Cooking time: 20 minutes
Servings: 12
Ingredients:
For the crust:
- 95 g coconut, shredded
- 133 g sunflower seeds
- 57 g butter
For the filling:
- 5 ml gelatin

- 227 g cream cheese
- 113 g strawberries
- 30 ml water
- 7.5 ml lemon juice
- 1.25 ml stevia
- 120 ml heavy cream
- 200 g strawberries, chopped for serving

Preparation
1. In a food processor, combine sunflower seeds, coconut, a bit of salt, and butter, pulse, and press into the bottom of an air fryer cake pan.
2. Heat the water in a saucepan over medium heat, then add the gelatin and whisk until it dissolves. Set aside to cool before combining with the 113 g of strawberries, cream cheese, lemon juice, and stevia in a food processor.
3. Stir in the heavy cream and distribute it over the crust.
4. Top with 200 g strawberries, place in the air fryer, and cook at 165° C for 15 minutes.
5. Refrigerate until ready to serve.
6. Enjoy!

Nutritional information: calories 234, fat 23, fiber 2, carbs 6, protein 7

341. COCOA COOKIES

Preparation time: 10 minutes
Cooking time: 14 minutes
Servings: 12

Ingredients:
- 177 ml coconut oil, melted
- 6 eggs
- 85 g cocoa powder
- 10 ml vanilla
- 2.5 ml baking powder
- 113 g cream cheese
- 63 g sugar

Preparation
1. Add eggs, coconut oil, cocoa powder, baking powder, vanilla, and cream cheese, and swerve in a blender.

2. Pour this into a prepared baking dish that fits your air fryer, and bake for 14 minutes at 160 degrees C.
3. Serve by cutting the cookie sheet into rectangles.
4. Enjoy!

Nutritional information: calories 178, fat 14, fiber 2, carbs 3, protein 5

342.   CASHEW BARS

Preparation time: 10 minutes
Cooking time: 15 minutes
Servings: 6

Ingredients:
- 113 g honey
- 24 g almond meal
- 16 g almond butter
- 225 g cashews, chopped
- 4 dates, chopped
- 53 g shredded
- 10 g chia seeds

Preparation
1. In a mixing dish, combine honey, almond meal, and almond butter.
2. Stir in the cashews, coconut, dates, and chia seeds.
3. Spread this on a baking sheet coated with parchment paper that fits your air fryer and press firmly.
4. Place in the fryer and cook for 15 minutes at 149° C.
5. Allow the mixture to cool before cutting it into medium bars and serving.
6. Enjoy!

Nutritional information: calories 121, fat 4, fiber 7, carbs 5, protein 6

343.   BLUEBERRY SCONES

Preparation time: 10 minutes
Cooking time: 10 minutes
Servings: 10

Ingredients:
- 120 g white flour

- 148 g blueberries
- 2 eggs
- 118 ml heavy cream
- 113 g butter
- 63 g sugar
- 10 ml vanilla extract
- 10 ml baking powder

Preparation
1. Mix the flour, salt, baking powder, and blueberries in a mixing dish.
2. In a separate bowl, thoroughly combine heavy cream, butter, vanilla extract, sugar, and eggs.
3. Combine the two mixtures, knead until you have a dough, shape 10 triangles from this mixture, set them on a lined baking sheet that fits your air fryer, and cook for 10 minutes at 160 degrees C.
4. Serve them chilled.
5. Enjoy!

Nutritional information: calories 130, fat 2, fiber 2, carbs 4, protein 3

344.   PLUM BARS

Preparation time: 10 minutes
Cooking time: 16 minutes
Servings: 8

Ingredients:
- 2 cups dried plums
- 90 ml water
- 180 g rolled oats
- 213 g brown sugar
- 2.5 g baking soda
- 5 g cinnamon powder
- 28 g butter, melted
- 1 egg, whisked
- Cooking spray

Preparation
1. Blend plums with water in a food processor until you have a sticky spread.
2. Whisk together the oats, cinnamon, baking soda, sugar, egg, and butter in a large mixing basin.
3. In a baking pan that has been sprayed with cooking oil, press half of the oats mix, then

distribute the plums mix and top with the other half of the oats mix.

4. Cook for 16 minutes at 176 degrees Celsius in your air fryer.
5. Allow the mixture to cool before cutting it into medium bars and serving.
6. Enjoy!

Nutritional information: calories 111, fat 5, fiber 6, carbs 12, protein 6

345. MACAROONS

Preparation time: 10 minutes
Cooking time: 8 minutes
Servings: 20

Ingredients:
- 25 g sugar
- 4 egg whites
- 142 g shredded
- 5 ml vanilla extract

Preparation
1. In a mixing bowl, combine egg whites and stevia and beat with an electric mixer.
2. Add the coconut and vanilla extract and whisk again. Form small balls out of this mixture and place them in your air fryer for 8 minutes at 171 degrees C.
3. Macaroons should be served cold.
4. Enjoy!

Nutritional information: calories 55, fat 6, fiber 1, carbs 2, protein 1

346. PEARS AND ESPRESSO CREAM

Preparation time: 10 minutes
Cooking time: 30 minutes
Servings: 4
Ingredients:
- 4 pears, halved and cored
- 30 ml lemon juice
- 12 g sugar
- 30 ml water

- 28 g butter
- For the cream:
- 237 ml whipping cream
- 240 g mascarpone
- 67 g sugar
- 30 ml espresso, cold

Preparation
1. Toss pears halves with lemon juice, 12 g sugar, butter, and water in a bowl, then put in an air fryer and cook at 182 degrees g for 30 minutes.
2. Meanwhile, in a mixing bowl, combine whipped cream, mascarpone, 43 g sugar, and espresso; whisk thoroughly and chill until the pears are done.
3. Serve the pears on plates with espresso cream on top.
4. Enjoy!

Nutritional information: calories 211, fat 5, fiber 7, carbs 8, protein 7

347. EASY GRANOLA

Preparation time: 10 minutes
Cooking time: 35 minutes
Servings: 4

Ingredients:
- 95 g coconut, shredded
- 71 g almonds
- 75 g pecans, chopped
- 25 g sugar
- 59 g pumpkin seeds
- 66 g sunflower seeds
- 30 ml sunflower oil
- 5 ml nutmeg, ground
- 5 ml apple pie spice mix

Preparation
1. In a mixing bowl, combine almonds and pecans with pumpkin seeds, sunflower seeds, coconut, nutmeg, and apple pie spice mix.
2. Heat the oil in a pan over medium heat, then add the sugar and stir well.
3. Stir this into the nut and coconut mixture.

4. Spread mixture on a lined baking sheet that fits your air fryer, place in your air fryer, and bakes for 25 minutes at 149 degrees C.
5. Allow your granola to cool before cutting and serving.
6. Enjoy!

Nutritional information: calories 322, fat 7, fiber 8, carbs 12, protein 7

348. LEMON BARS

Preparation time: 10 minutes
Cooking time: 25 minutes
Servings: 6

Ingredients:
- 4 eggs
- 281 g cups flour
- Juice from 2 lemons
- 250 g butter, soft
- 400 g sugar

Preparation
1. In a mixing bowl, combine the butter, 100 g sugar, and 240 g flour, whisk well, press on the bottom of a pan that fits your air fryer, place in the fryer, and cook at 176° C for 10 minutes.
2. In a separate bowl, whisk together the remaining sugar, flour, eggs, and lemon juice. Spread over crust.
3. Place in the fryer at 176° C for 15 minutes more, then set aside to cool before cutting into bars and serving.
4. Enjoy!

Nutritional information: calories 125, fat 4, fiber 4, carbs 16, protein 2

349. LENTILS AND DATES BROWNIES

Preparation time: 10 minutes
Cooking time: 15 minutes
Servings: 8

Ingredients:
- 795 g canned lentils, rinsed and drained
- 12 dates
- 15 ml honey
- 1 banana, peeled and chopped
- 2.5 ml baking soda
- 60 ml almond butter
- 30 ml cocoa powder

Preparation
1. Blend lentils, butter, banana, cocoa, baking soda, and honey in a food processor until smooth.
2. Add dates, pulse a couple more times, then pour into an oiled pan that fits your air fryer, spread evenly, and bake for 15 minutes at 182 degrees C.
3. Remove the brownies from the air fryer, cut them, put them on a dish, and serve.
4. Enjoy!

Nutritional information: calories 162, fat 4, fiber 2, carbs 3, protein 4

350. BLUEBERRY PUDDING

Preparation time: 10 minutes
Cooking time: 25 minutes
Servings: 6

Ingredients:
- 120 g flour
- 67 g rolled oats
- 1520 g blueberries
- 1 stick butter, melted
- 124 g walnuts, chopped
- 45 ml maple syrup
- 7 g rosemary, chopped

Preparation
1. Place blueberries in a greased baking dish and set aside.
2. In a food processor, combine rolled oats, flour, walnuts, butter, maple syrup, and rosemary; blend thoroughly. Layer this over blueberries; place in an air fryer, and cook at 176° C for 25 minutes.
3. Allow the dessert to cool before cutting and serving.

4. Enjoy!

Nutritional information: calories 150, fat 3, fiber 2, carbs 7, protein 4

351.   SPONGE CAKE

Preparation time: 10 minutes
Cooking time: 20 minutes
Servings: 12
Ingredients:

- 384 g flour
- 15 ml baking powder
- 80 g cornstarch
- 5 ml baking soda
- 237 ml olive oil
- 355 ml cup milk
- 134 g sugar
- 473 ml water
- 60 ml lemon juice
- 10 ml vanilla extract

Preparation
1. In a mixing bowl, whisk together the flour, cornstarch, baking powder, baking soda, and sugar.
2. In a separate bowl, whisk together the oil, milk, water, vanilla, and lemon juice.
3. Combine the two liquids, stir, and place in a greased baking dish that fits your air fryer. Cook at 176 degrees C for 20 minutes.
4. Allow the cake to cool before cutting and serving.
5. Enjoy!

Nutritional information: calories 246, fat 3, fiber 1, carbs 6, protein 2

352.   FIGS AND COCONUT

BUTTER MIX

Preparation time: 6 minutes
Cooking time: 4 minutes
Servings: 3

Ingredients:

- 27 g coconut butter

- 12 figs, halved
- 50 g sugar
- 130 g almonds, toasted and chopped

Preparation
1. Melt the butter in a pan that fits your air fryer over medium-high heat.
2. Toss in the figs, sugar, and almonds, then place in the air fryer for 4 minutes at 149° C.
3. Serve chilled in individual bowls.
4. Enjoy!

Nutritional information: calories 170, fat 4, fiber 5, carbs 7, protein 9

353.   TASTY ORANGE COOKIES

Preparation time: 10 minutes
Cooking time: 12 minutes
Servings: 8

Ingredients:

- 240 g flour
- 5 ml baking powder
- 113 g butter, soft
- 150 g sugar
- 1 egg, whisked
- 5 ml vanilla extract
- 15 ml orange zest, grated

For the filling:

- 112 g cream cheese, soft
- 113 g butter
- 260 g powdered sugar

Preparation
1. In a mixing dish, combine cream cheese, 113 g butter, and 260 g powdered sugar; stir thoroughly with a mixer and set aside for now.
2. In a separate basin, combine the flour and baking powder.
3. In a third bowl, whisk together 113 g butter, 150 g sugar, egg, vanilla essence, and orange zest.
4. Combine the flour with the orange mixture, stir well, and place 15 mL of the mixture on a lined baking sheet that fits your air fryer.

5. Repeat with the remaining orange batter, then place in the fryer and cook at 171° C for 12 minutes.
6. Allow cookies to cool before spreading cream filling on half of them, topping with the remaining cookies, and serving.
7. Enjoy!

Nutritional information: calories 124, fat 5, fiber 6, carbs 8, protein 4

354.   TANGERINE CAKE

Preparation time: 10 minutes
Cooking time: 20 minutes
Servings: 8

Ingredients:
- 150 g sugar
- 120 g flour
- 60 ml olive oil
- 118 ml milk
- 5 ml cider vinegar
- 2.5 ml vanilla extract
- Juice and zest from 2 lemons
- Juice and zest from 1 tangerine
- Tangerine segments for serving

Preparation
1. Mix flour and sugar in a mixing bowl.
2. In a separate bowl, whisk together the oil, milk, vinegar, vanilla essence, lemon juice and zest, and tangerine zest.
3. Pour mixture into a cake pan that fits your air fryer, place in the fryer, and cook at 182 degrees C for 20 minutes.
4. Serve immediately, garnished with tangerine segments.
5. Enjoy!

Nutritional information: calories 190, fat 1, fiber 1, carbs 4, protein 4

355.   COCOA AND ALMOND

BARS

Preparation time: 30 minutes

Cooking time: 4 minutes
Servings: 6

Ingredients:
- 30 g cocoa nibs
- 143 g almonds, soaked and drained
- 30 ml cocoa powder
- 30 g hemp seeds
- 30 g goji berries
- 18 g coconut, shredded
- 8 dates, pitted and soaked

Preparation
1. Blend almonds in a food processor, then add hemp seeds, cocoa nibs, cocoa powder, goji, and coconut.
2. Blend in the dates again, then put on a lined baking sheet that fits your air fryer and cook for 4 minutes at 160 degrees C.
3. Refrigerate for 30 minutes before serving, and cut into equal halves.
4. Enjoy!

Nutritional information: calories 140, fat 6, fiber 3, carbs 7, protein 19

356.   BERRIES MIX

Preparation time: 5 minutes
Cooking time: 6 minutes
Servings: 4

Ingredients:
- 30 ml lemon juice
- 22 ml maple syrup
- 22 ml champagne vinegar
- 15 ml olive oil
- 454 g strawberries, halved
- 249 g blueberries
- 5 g basil leaves, torn

Preparation
1. Mix lemon juice, maple syrup, and vinegar in a pan that fits your air fryer bring to a boil over medium-high heat add oil, blueberries, and strawberries, stir and cook at 154 degrees C for 6 minutes.
2. Serve with a sprinkle of basil on top!
3. Enjoy!

Nutritional information: calories 163, fat 4, fiber 4, carbs 10, protein 2.1

357.   PUMPKIN COOKIES

Preparation time: 10 minutes
Cooking time: 15 minutes
Servings: 24

Ingredients:
- 313 g flour
- 2.5 ml baking soda
- 7 g flax seed, ground
- 45 ml water
- 122 g pumpkin flesh, mashed
- 60 ml honey
- 28 g butter
- 5 ml vanilla extract
- 80 g chocolate chips

Preparation
1. In a mixing dish, combine flax seed and water, stir, and set aside for a few minutes.
2. In a separate basin, combine the flour, salt, and baking soda.
3. Combine honey, pumpkin puree, butter, vanilla essence, and flaxseed in a third bowl.
4. Stir together the flour, honey mixture, and chocolate chips.
5. Scoop 15 mL of cookie dough onto a lined baking sheet that fits your air fryer, repeat with the remaining dough, place in your air fryer, and cook at 176° C for 15 minutes.
6. Allow cookies to cool before serving.
7. Enjoy!

Nutritional information: calories 140, fat 2, fiber 2, carbs 7, protein 10

358.   BROWN BUTTER COOKIES

Preparation time: 10 minutes
Cooking time: 10 minutes
Servings: 6

Ingredients:
- 340 g butter
- 400 g brown sugar
- 2 eggs, whisked
- 384 g flour
- 85 g pecans, chopped
- 10 ml vanilla extract
- 5 ml baking soda
- 2.5 ml baking powder

Preparation
1. Melt the butter in a pan over medium heat, then add the brown sugar and whisk until it dissolves.
2. In a mixing basin, combine flour, pecans, vanilla extract, baking soda, baking powder, and eggs.
3. Stir in the brown butter and place spoonfuls of this mixture on a lined baking sheet that fits your air fryer.
4. Cook for 10 minutes at 171 degrees Celsius in the fryer.
5. Allow cookies to cool before serving.
6. Enjoy!

Nutritional information: calories 144, fat 5, fiber 6, carbs 19, protein 2

359.   PEACH PIE

Preparation time: 10 minutes
Cooking time: 35 minutes
Servings: 4

Ingredients:
- 1 pie dough
- 1020 g peaches, pitted and chopped
- 15 g cornstarch
- 100 g sugar
- 15 g flour
- A pinch of nutmeg, ground
- 15 ml dark rum
- 15 ml lemon juice
- 28 g butter, melted

Preparation
1. Roll out the pie dough and push it firmly into a pie pan that fits your air fryer.
2. In a mixing bowl, combine peaches, cornstarch, sugar, flour, nutmeg, rum, lemon juice, and butter.

3.   Pour and distribute the mixture into a pie pan, place in an air fryer, and cook at 176° C for 35 minutes.
4.   Serve hot or cold.
5.   Enjoy!

Nutritional information: calories 231, fat 6, fiber 7, carbs 9, protein 5

360.   SWEET POTATO

CHEESECAKE

Preparation time: 10 minutes
Cooking time: 5 minutes
Servings: 4

Ingredients:
- 57 g butter, melted
- 170 g mascarpone, soft
- 227 g cream cheese, soft
- 75 g graham crackers, crumbled
- 177 ml milk
- 5 ml vanilla extract
- 187 g sweet potato puree
- 1.25 cinnamon powder

Preparation
1.   In a mixing bowl, combine the butter and crushed crackers, whisk well, and press into the bottom of a cake pan that fits your air fryer. Refrigerate for now.
2.   In a separate bowl, whisk together the cream cheese, mascarpone, sweet potato puree, milk, cinnamon, and vanilla.
3.   Spread this over the crust, place in the air fryer, cook at 149 degrees C for 4 minutes and chill for a few hours before serving.
4.   Enjoy!

Nutritional information: calories 172, fat 4, fiber 6, carbs 8, protein 3

361.   SWEET SQUARES

Preparation time: 10 minutes
Cooking time: 30 minutes
Servings: 6

Ingredients:
- 120 g flour
- 113 g butter, soft
- 200 g sugar
- 25 g powdered sugar
- 10 ml lemon peel, grated
- 30 ml lemon juice
- 2 eggs, whisked
- 2.5 ml baking powder

Preparation
1.   In a mixing bowl, combine flour, powdered sugar, and butter; stir well. Press on the bottom of a pan that fits your air fryer; place in the fryer and bake at 176°C for 14 minutes.
2.   In a separate dish, whisk together the sugar, lemon juice, lemon peel, eggs, and baking powder. Spread over the baked crust.
3.   Bake for another 15 minutes, then set aside to cool before cutting into medium squares and serving cold.
4.   Enjoy!

Nutritional information: calories 100, fat 4, fiber 1, carbs 12, protein 1

362.   PASSION FRUIT PUDDING

Preparation time: 10 minutes
Cooking time: 40 minutes
Servings: 6

Ingredients:
- 237 ml Paleo passion fruit curd
- 4 passion fruits, pulp, and seeds
- 103 ml maple syrup
- 3 eggs
- 59 ml ghee, melted
- 103 ml almond milk
- 48 g almond flour
- 2.5 ml baking powder

Preparation
1.   In a mixing bowl, combine half of the fruit curd with the passion fruit seeds and pulp, whisk, and divide evenly among 6 heatproof ramekins.

2. Whisk eggs with maple syrup, ghee, the rest of the curd, baking powder, milk, and flour in a mixing dish.
3. Divide this into the ramekins as well, place in the fryer, and cook for 40 minutes at 93 degrees C.
4. Allow the puddings to cool before serving!
5. Enjoy!

Nutritional information: calories 430, fat 22, fiber 3, carbs 7, protein 8

363.   CHOCOLATE AND POMEGRANATE BARS

Preparation time: 2 hours
Cooking time: 10 minutes
Servings: 6

Ingredients:
- 118 ml milk
- 5 ml vanilla extract
- 240 g dark chocolate, chopped
- 46 g almonds, chopped
- 87 g pomegranate seeds

Preparation
1. Heat the milk in a saucepan over medium-low heat, then add the chocolate and whisk for 5 minutes. Remove from the heat and stir in the vanilla extract, half of the pomegranate seeds, and half of the nuts.
2. Pour into a lined baking tray, spread, sprinkle with a bit of salt, the remaining pomegranate arils, and nuts, and place in your air fryer for 4 minutes at 149 degrees C.
3. Refrigerate for 2 hours before serving.
4. Enjoy!

Nutritional information: calories 68, fat 1, fiber 4, carbs 6, protein 1

364.   BLACK TEA CAKE

Preparation time: 10 minutes
Cooking time: 35 minutes
Servings: 12

Ingredients:
- 90 ml black tea powder
- 473 ml milk
- 113 g butter
- 400 g sugar
- 4 eggs
- 10 ml vanilla extract
- 118 ml olive oil
- 438 g cups flour
- 5 ml baking soda
- 15 ml baking powder
- For the cream:
- 88 ml honey
- 804 g sugar
- 250 g butter, soft

Preparation
1. Put the milk in a pot, heat over medium heat, add the tea, stir well, remove from heat, and set aside to cool.
2. In a mixing dish, combine 113 g butter, 400 g sugar, eggs, vegetable oil, vanilla extract, baking powder, baking soda, and 438 g flour.
3. Pour this into two greased round baking pans and bake for 25 minutes at 165 degrees C.
4. In a mixing dish, combine 226 g butter, honey, and 804 g sugar and well combine.
5. Place one cake on a dish, put the cream on top, and place in the refrigerator until ready to serve.
6. Enjoy!

Nutritional information: calories 200, fat 4, fiber 4, carbs 6, protein 2

365.   LIME CHEESECAKE

Preparation time: 4 hours and 10 minutes
Cooking time: 4 minutes
Servings:10

Ingredients:
- 28 g butter, melted
- 8.4 g sugar
- 113 g flour
- 24 g coconut, shredded
- For the filling:
- 454 g cream cheese
- Zest from 1 lime, grated
- Juice from 1 lime
- 473 ml hot water
- 2 sachets of lime jelly

Preparation
1. In a mixing bowl, combine coconut, flour, butter, and sugar; blend well and press into the bottom of an air fryer pan.
2. Meanwhile, in a separate bowl, dissolve the jelly sachets in boiling water.
3. In a mixing bowl, combine cream cheese, jelly, lime juice, and zest, and stir thoroughly.
4. Spread this over the crust, then place it in the air fryer for 4 minutes at 149° C.
5. Refrigerate for 4 hours before serving.
6. Enjoy!

Nutritional information: calories 260, fat 23, fiber 2, carbs 5, protein 7

366.   GINGER CHEESECAKE

Preparation time: 2 hours and 10 minutes
Cooking time: 20 minutes
Servings:6

Ingredients:
- 9 g butter, melted
- 120 g ginger cookies, crumbled
- 454 g cream cheese, soft
- 2 eggs
- 100 g sugar
- 5 ml rum
- 2.5 ml vanilla extract
- 2.5 ml nutmeg, ground

Preparation
1. Grease a baking dish with butter and sprinkle with cookie crumbs.
2. In a mixing bowl, combine cream cheese, nutmeg, vanilla, rum, and eggs; stir well and spread over cookie crumbs.
3. Cook for 20 minutes at 171 degrees Celsius in your air fryer.
4. Allow the cheesecake to cool and chill for 2 hours before slicing and serving.
5. Enjoy!

Nutritional information: calories 412, fat 12, fiber 6, carbs 20, protein 6

COOKING TIMES

OVEN	AIR FRYER
1O MINUTES	8 MINUTES
15 MINUTES	12 MINUTES
20 MINUTES	16 MINUTES
25 MINUTES	20 MINUTES
30 MINUTES	24 MINUTES
35 MINUTES	28 MINUTES
40 MINUTES	32 MINUTES
45 MINUTES	36 MINUTES
50 MINUTES	40 MINUTES
55 MINUTES	44 MINUTES
1 HOUR	48 MINUTES

AIR FRYER CONVERSION CHART

OVEN	OVEN FAN	AIR FRYER
190 ℃	170 ℃	150 ℃
200 ℃	180 ℃	160 ℃
210 ℃	190 ℃	170 ℃
220 ℃	200 ℃	180 ℃
230 ℃	210 ℃	190 ℃

COST OF COOKING CHART

APPLIANCE	COST PER DAY	COST PER WEEK	COST PER MONTH	COST PER YEAR
ELECTRIC COOKER	87P	£6.09	£26.38	£316.54
DUAL FUEL COOKER (GAS AND ELECTRIC)	72P	£5.08	£22.00	£264.03
GAS COOKER	33P	£2.23	£10.07	£120.83
SLOW COOKER	16P	£1.15	£4.98	£59.76
AIR FRYER	**14P**	**£1.01**	**£4.40**	**£52.74**
MICROWAVE	8P	58 P	£2.50	£30.02

<u>CONCLUSION</u>

These days, air fryers are one of the most inventive kitchen gadgets and a common cooking method.

Using an air fryer, you can rapidly cook delicious, healthy meals! You don't have to be a great cook to prepare delicious meals for you and your family!

Just an air fryer and this outstanding air fryer cookbook are required.

Your handmade meals will impress everyone around you, and you'll whip up the finest dishes ever in no time!

Put your trust in us! Get an air fryer and these useful air fryer recipes to start your new culinary endeavour.

excellent experience

Printed in Great Britain
by Amazon

12760511R00086